MN

BLINKING RED

Blinking Red

Crisis and Compromise
in American Intelligence after 9/11

MICHAEL ALLEN

POTOMAC BOOKS
WASHINGTON, D.C.

Potomac Books is an imprint
of the University of Nebraska Press.

Library of Congress
Cataloging-in-Publication Data
Allen, Michael, 1972–
Blinking red: crisis and compromise
in American intelligence after
9/11 / Michael Allen.
pages cm
Includes bibliographical
references and index.
ISBN 978-1-61234-615-1 (hardcover: alk. paper)
ISBN 978-1-61234-616-8 (electronic)
1. Intelligence service—United States.
2. National security—United States.
3. Terrorism—Prevention. I. Title.
JK468.16A826 2013
327.1273—dc23   2013013299

Printed in the United States of
America on acid-free paper that meets
the American National Standards
Institute z39-48 Standard.

Potomac Books
22841 Quicksilver Drive
Dulles, Virginia 20166

First Edition

10 9 8 7 6 5 4 3 2 1

FOR MY WIFE, DIANA, AND
MY SONS, JOE AND HENRY

The system was blinking red.
GEORGE TENET on the summer of 2001

Contents

Preface

On September 11, 2001, in a daring surprise attack, nineteen al Qa'ida terrorists penetrated the nation's security and hijacked four airplanes, causing the deaths of nearly three thousand individuals. And during the investigation of the 9/11 attacks, another massive intelligence failure came into the open: the assessment that weapons of mass destruction were present in Iraq. The primary justification for the 2003 invasion was repudiated. In the aftermath of these failures, a commission created by Congress to study the 9/11 attacks recommended a sweeping reorganization to create a new position to lead the nation's intelligence enterprise and remove these responsibilities from the director of the CIA (DCI).

The 9/11 Commission (the Commission) ignited a frenzy to reform and a battle for control of U.S. intelligence within the executive branch and Congress. Things had changed since the post–World War II era when U.S. intelligence was preoccupied with the Soviet Union.[1] The post–Pearl Harbor system made sense against a "lumbering brute" that offered embassies to bug, diplomats to recruit, and conspicuous tanks and armament for satellites to monitor with relative ease.[2] But this new age marked by terrorists and weapons proliferators demanded "quick, imaginative, and agile responses."[3]

The Commission attributed the failures of 9/11 to a fractured intelligence system: the CIA had not communicated critical information to its historic rival, the Federal Bureau of Investigation (FBI), and had not sufficiently conveyed to policymakers the strategic threat posed by international terrorism. The U.S. intelligence system needed a powerful leader to merge its scattered bureaucracies into a more unified enterprise to counter America's new enemies: stateless international terrorists. This intelligence czar would be charged with "connecting the dots," a shorthand term for "combining reams of fragmentary or individually inconclusive tidbits into a useful overall picture."[4] The czar would infuse analytical rigor into intelligence assessments of the kind that had led us astray in Iraq. To anticipate new threats, U.S. intelligence required someone to pioneer methods to recruit spies within terrorist cells and steal the most sensitive information from dangerous nations, someone to bridge the gap between foreign intelligence, traditionally the province of the CIA, and information collected domestically, usually by the FBI. In short, the United States needed a spymaster, a director of national intelligence (DNI), who could unify American intelligence to fight a new war against enemies who might employ weapons of mass destruction against the United States.

The Commission argued that the new DNI should be liberated from the day-to-day task of running the CIA. The DNI and the CIA must be separate, and the CIA should focus on analysis and the collection of human intelligence. The agency should no longer be the *center* of the constellation of U.S. intelligence agencies.

To make the Intelligence Community (IC) less a collection of specialized, departmental intelligence offices, the new DNI would need more clout than the DCI. The Commission recommended that the position have increased budgetary and personnel authority over the far-flung intelligence agencies, especially the agencies in the Department of Defense (DoD), which constituted most of the Intelligence Community in terms of both people and funding. Without significantly more influence, the Commission warned, the DNI risked becoming a paper tiger that would leave the system worse off than it already was.[5] To bolster its case, the Commission cited the 1998 al Qa'ida attacks on the U.S. embassies in Tanzania and Kenya. In their wake, the DCI had issued a "declaration of war" against al Qa'ida. To the Commission, the declaration was a call to arms for all the intelligence agencies—especially those in the DoD—to devote more time, money, and effort to the fight against this terrorist network. But instead, the agencies had not noticed or had ignored the pronouncement, later leading investigators to conclude that it was a mere fax from a figurehead who could not back up his orders with any redirection of funds or people. To be a true leader of the IC, the new DNI would have to have substantially greater powers. The DNI would need real weight over other departments' intelligence fiefdoms to make good on future "declarations of war" and to ensure greater responsiveness to new priorities.

Fueled by antipathy toward the CIA after the intelligence failures around

9/11 and Iraq, the media hailed the Commission's recommendations as the work of statesmen who had triumphed over partisanship. Dissenters argued that creating a DNI with greater authorities did not fit the problems identified on 9/11, mainly the failure of the Intelligence Community to provide specific warning of an attack. They argued that the failures on 9/11 were being seized to justify what others had recommended in the past (i.e., greater centralized authority in the Intelligence Community). But quick embraces from the Democratic nominee for president and from many in Congress, followed by President George W. Bush's endorsement, launched the Commission's recommendations onto the agenda. However, behind the scenes, the Commission's recommendations touched off a wrenching bureaucratic struggle. Over a seven-week period, the president's National Security Council debated how much authority should be centralized in a new director of national intelligence. Meanwhile, the military's congressional allies marshaled their forces in support of the DoD to guarantee that the top priority mission of DoD intelligence elements would be to support the war-fighters, including those engaged in Afghanistan and Iraq. The issue pitted Senate and House Democrats against House Republicans—and eventually the House Republican leadership against itself. The tug-of-war intensified as the chairman of the House Armed Services Committee rallied his colleagues against the Speaker of the House's efforts to compromise with the Senate and the White House. In the face of a revolt, the Speaker postponed consideration of the intelligence reform bill.

The collapse was portrayed as a slap to the newly reelected president. The media and the congressional Democrats blasted the failure to pass intelligence reform. Frenzied efforts ensued to resurrect the intelligence reform bill brokered by the Senate, the White House, and the Speaker. The controversy blazed for another seventeen days before the parties reached a classic legislative compromise.

The origins of the DNI help to explain how our national-security enterprise fully operates today and illuminate whether the intelligence failures on 9/11 and in Iraq have been addressed. Whether the new intelligence structure will succeed in remaking intelligence into an integrated enterprise and whether integration will lead to more effective national security and prevent other intelligence breakdowns are open questions.[6] The battle for the intelligence system is a case study in American power politics and institutional reform born out of crisis and delivered under compromise.

Acknowledgments

I am grateful to President Bush and his staff, particularly Steve Hadley and Fran Townsend, for giving me the opportunity to work on the Intelligence Reform and Terrorism Prevention Act (IRTPA) as a legislative affairs officer at the White House in 2004. I am also grateful to many friends and colleagues who helped along the way. My wife, Diana; Brian Bennett; and Matt Dallek provided key early encouragement to start the project.

After leaving the White House in 2009, the Bipartisan Policy Center, especially Jason Grumet and Julie Anderson, were very generous to allow me to work on this book while managing Governor Tom Kean and Congressman Lee Hamilton's successor to the 9/11 Commission. I am also grateful to Congressman Mike Rogers, chairman of the House Permanent Select Committee on Intelligence, who allowed me to continue working on this project (in my spare time) when I became his staff director in 2011.

I was lucky to have a variety of friends and colleagues who spent enormous amounts of time helping me get the story right. Gordon Lederman and Jon Rosenwasser suffered through early drafts and provided critically important commentary throughout its evolution. My NSC former colleagues who played large roles in the passage of IRTPA, David Shedd and Steve Slick, were among the most supportive of the project, submitting to numerous interviews and toiling through multiple drafts. Chris Walker and Brett Shogren, who served as Republican leadership staff during the passage of IRTPA, were also early supporters of the project and spent hours with me in reconstructing its legislative history.

The National Archives of the United States is a national treasure and I appreciate the diligence of its Center for Legislative Archives, the custodians of the 9/11 Commission's papers, for their help. I want to thank the archivists at the Bush Presidential Library in Dallas for their work and their critical assistance in reconstructing the White House's consideration of the 9/11 Commission's recommendations. Special thanks to Tobi Young in President Bush's office for her support. I am also grateful to Kate Cruikshank of Indiana University at Bloomington for her assistance in locating numerous key sources among Congressman Lee Hamilton's papers. Secretary Robert Gates was especially helpful in locating a treasure trove of documents among his papers that enriched this story.

I conducted over eighty interviews for the book and I am deeply appreciative of the time and patience of these individuals, especially President Bush, James Clapper, Mike Hayden, Steve Cambone, Condoleezza Rice, John McLaughlin, Senators Susan Collins and Joe Lieberman, Congressman Peter Hoekstra, and Congresswoman Jane Harman. David Hobbs, Scott Palmer, Robert Rangel, David Addington, John Bellinger, and Philip Zelikow also devoted a considerable amount of time to interviews and to reviewing early drafts. I am also indebted to expert reviewers Mark Lowenthal and Michael Warner, whose keen eyes were very helpful. I really appreciate the time many of the key players spent with me, especially Speaker Hastert, Congressman Tom DeLay, Congressman Jim Sensenbrenner, Congressman Duncan Hunter, Congressman Lee Hamilton, Governor Tom Kean, Andy Card, Jamie Gorelick, Tim Roemer, and John Lehman. I also appreciate the counsel of George Tenet. Special thanks to my former boss Steve Hadley for his time and attention to the manuscript. My research assistant, Khizer Syed, was indispensable.

Finally, I want to thank my Dad, who has always been a tough editor from his study in Mobile, Alabama. He and my Mom have always provided unconditional love and support. Most of all, I want to thank my wife, Diana. She is a wonderful wife in every way and not only because she encouraged this project, reviewed manuscripts, and tolerated my pre-dawn writing habits.

Author's Note

As the legislative affairs officer for the Homeland Security Council in the White House in 2004, I became the legislative affairs representative for the working-level team that devised the White House response to the 9/11 Commission's recommendations. Fellow colleagues John Bellinger, David Shedd, Steve Slick, Ben Powell, and Tom Monheim were also on the team, and we all took direction from the White House senior staff. Many others in the White House Legislative Affairs Office also played substantial roles in the legislative action, especially David Hobbs. From my post, I sat in on most of the White House meetings on the resulting legislation, including all the National Security Council's Deputies Committee Meetings in August and September 2004. As Congress took up legislation, I was the White House representative in dozens of congressional meetings. As the legislative drafting narrowed to a small group, I sat in on most, if not all, of the "Big Four" meetings that hashed out the final legislative text of the Intelligence Reform and Terrorism Prevention Act of 2004 (IRTPA). As a result, there are occasions in the text where my recollections are the source. To corroborate my memory, I have conducted many interviews to make sure I got the story as close to exact as possible. I also gave an opportunity to many of the key players to review the manuscript for accuracy. Although at the time I had only a couple of years of experience working in Congress, I was convinced that the legislative contortions and drama surrounding IRTPA were extraordinary. My sense was confirmed by many of the congressional veterans in the process. A fellow bystander marveled at the speed at which major issues were being considered and the exceptionally balkanized factions in pitched battle: the perceived alliance between the Defense Department and the

Armed Services Committees against the White House and the president and the split in the House among Republicans, some of whom supported the Senate approach. I thought in 2004 that the legislative drama would be useful to students of government in trying to understand how the legislative process works. I have tried to paint a portrait of the personalities and pressures that impact legislation, while also seeking to illuminate aspects of the legislative process that are typically unseen, particularly the machinations of the congressional leadership and the role of the White House in influencing legislative outcomes. Since 2004, it became apparent that due to the unique circumstances of IRTPA's passage, many were interested in how we ended up with a director of national intelligence (DNI) and a National Counterterrorism Center (NCTC), and, in particular, how and why some specific statutory provisions came about. In this work, I have focused on the main issues that dominated the debate, especially the authorities of the DNI and the NCTC. I also briefly discuss how the FBI fared throughout the process, although because of space limitations this and many other statutory provisions that were the subject of controversy and strenuous negotiations do not receive exhaustive treatment.

The aim of the book is to be the definitive history of this chapter of the tremendous change in our government after September 11, 2001. I hope it will inform any future efforts to reorganize the national security functions of our government. At the very least, it should serve as a guide for future efforts to reform intelligence. This book is primarily about the legislative history. It ends with a brief discussion of IRTPA's implementation, but a first attempt at its definitive history will be for others. Although the implementation review is brief, it does not cover Director Jim Clapper's tenure. I had to stop somewhere, and as Director Clapper was the incumbent when I became staff director of the House Intelligence Committee (with an oversight role of the DNI), this seemed to be a good place to stop.

A Note on Intelligence and Its Terminology

Intelligence is information collected and analyzed to ensure our policymakers and war-fighters have the best possible picture of world events. Raw, or unevaluated, intelligence may derive from many sources, including: human agents (spies), communication signals (intercepted phone calls and e-mails), measures and signals (technical data), and imagery (pictures) from satellites or planes.

In 2004 the vast majority of Intelligence Community assets resided in the eight Department of Defense intelligence entities: the National Security Agency (NSA), the Defense Intelligence Agency (DIA), the National Geospatial-Intelligence Agency (NGA), the National Reconnaissance Office (NRO), and the intelligence elements of each of the military services. The Intelligence Community also included elements of: the Department of Treasury, the Department of Energy, the Department of State, and the Department of Homeland Security. It also included parts of the FBI and, of course, the CIA. The nominal head of the Intelligence Community was the CIA director, who was known as the director of central intelligence (DCI).

Each organization has a director, with the DCI also serving as the president's principal intelligence advisor. The three most prominent Department of Defense intelligence agencies—DIA, NSA, and NGA—are sometimes referred to as the Combat Support Agencies (CSA) to signify the military aspect focus of their missions. As part of the Department of Defense, they were under the authority, direction, and control of the secretary of defense, although other authorities gave the DCI the power to task their intelligence assets and to develop their annual budgets.

A Short History of the Intelligence Community

Just four months after the victory over Japan in World War II, President Harry Truman convened a special lunch. The occasion was the creation of the National Intelligence Authority, a new system for managing U.S. intelligence. The system included a director of central intelligence responsible for "coordination and analysis."[1] To mark the occasion, President Truman bestowed upon his top spies black hats, black coats, and wooden daggers and christened its leader the "director of centralized snooping."[2] This lighthearted moment marked the beginning of a multidecade effort to bring unity of purpose to the system of interdependent national security agencies known as the Intelligence Community (IC). The issue of how to manage and coordinate intelligence across the U.S. government had been around since Pearl Harbor. The Japanese sneak attack was proof that the system had failed, and subsequent investigations concluded that it had been "presaged by a mass and variety of signals" that got lost in the noise of competing intelligence, imperfect dissemination, and other ambiguous information.[3]

President Truman sought to bring cohesion and unity to U.S. national security efforts by pursuing legislation to create a new national security system. As commander in chief at the close of World War II, Truman strongly felt that the United States "needed a more centralized and powerful state apparatus for the management of national security."[4] The result of his efforts was the National Security Act of 1947. It created the modern national security organizations by establishing the Department of Defense, the National Security Council, and the Central Intelligence Agency (CIA).

The formal creation of the CIA laid the foundation for the "permanent national intelligence structure."[5] This structure's guiding principle was to guarantee there would be no more Pearl Harbors and "to ensure through CIA that never again would the U.S. government be disadvantaged because it failed to consider as a whole all the information available to its parts."[6] During consideration of the National Security Act of 1947, President Truman's highest priority had been to unify the armed forces; his objectives for the unification of the Intelligence Community were modest. Truman's legislative proposal had been for a director of central intelligence (DCI) whose duties would be to "coordinate, evaluate, and disseminate intelligence." The final legislation reflected as much, not giving the new DCI the power to manage the more established intelligence agencies, which were primarily military in character.[7] The CIA's historian later called the CIA's coordination functions an "ambiguous mandate."[8]

In addition to coordinating and evaluating intelligence, the new CIA took, almost by default, a second mission, clandestine operations, for which it would become famous. The Office of Strategic Services (OSS) had been the intelligence operators in World War II, parachuting behind enemy lines to sabotage the German war machine and creating and running networks of foreign spies. Now, after the war, they needed a home. Their founder, William "Wild Bill" Donovan, lobbied hard to retain the OSS's expertise, and the organization was placed in the CIA. The agency took on a new image, one "steeped in the security discipline and no-holds-barred tradition of World War II."[9] Over time, presidents seeking levers to influence world events (especially as the Cold War was developing) came to use the CIA frequently, and covert action came to be the function that CIA directors focused on the most.

While the National Security Act had given the DCI the job of "coordinating the intelligence activities of the several government departments and agencies," it had "provided no language compelling these various agencies to cooperate. The director of central intelligence, who headed the CIA, had no levers—no general budget authority, no overall intelligence personnel authority, no exclusive access to the president, to force inter-agency collaboration."[10] Since "clandestine operations are sexy [but] correlation and evaluation are not,"[11] the community-coordination role assigned to the DCI faltered. Thus the CIA was "centralized in name only."[12] Although the covert action mission flourished, the coordinating of responsibilities, the inspiration for the "Central" in CIA, was hollow.

In spite of this, through the years, seeking efficiency and unity of effort, presidents and Congress modestly strengthened the DCI's management role over the Intelligence Community. Intelligence agencies came to have two masters: the DCI for some general budgetary and management matters and the particular cabinet secretary leading whatever department they called home. Still, most analysts—especially numerous Intelligence Community study groups—agreed that there was a gap between the DCI's responsibilities and actual authority. "The director of central intelligence was originally expected to coordinate spending, but no DCI has actually ever done so."[13]

Indeed, the DCI's impotence in its coordination function was just how many of the more established cabinet departments wanted it. This was especially the case for the military services, who routinely opposed more centralization in the DCI because they saw their own direct control over intelligence programs as essential.[14] The armed services needed their military intelligence elements for operations, so a system that was decentralized, more of a confederation of intelligence agencies, seemed to be optimal. One observer noted, "Defense fights hard to assert control over certain technical collection assets in peace because it will need them in war."[15]

The main conclusion posited by numerous studies before September 11, 2001, was that the Intelligence Community is an "inter-agency construct governed more by consensus than by administrative fiat and this reality has significant implications for how the IC is directed and how it acts."[16] To force unity of effort, commentators recommended a stronger manager of the Intelligence Community; the current system was thought to be uncoordinated for lack of authority in the DCI and because the DCI did not have time to run the IC, as the CIA alone was a full-time job.

CHAPTER ONE

Blow Up

On Saturday, November 20, 2004, just four months after the 9/11 Commission had issued its report and recommendations, the U.S. Congress was gathering for a special session. It was Rivalry Saturday in college football—Alabama would play Auburn, Harvard would confront Yale—and after weeks of campaigning for reelection, no member of Congress could have relished having to return to Washington the weekend before Thanksgiving. But there was urgent business at hand, a historic piece of legislation meant to fundamentally reorder the Intelligence Community.

The Central Intelligence Agency was created in 1947 to prevent another Pearl Harbor. Now a blue-ribbon panel of nationally prominent men and women proposed a new leader of the Intelligence Community, an empowered leader called the director of national intelligence (DNI) who could fix America's "dysfunctional" intelligence system by uniting the nation's scattered intelligence bureaucracies into a seamless enterprise capable of warning of a surprise attack, and of taking on the enemies of a new, post-9/11 world. A senator likened the report to a man on a shining white horse arriving to save the day.[1] Heralded as the recommendations of selfless statesmen who with an "aura of impartiality and legitimacy" had transcended partisanship for the good of the country,[2] the 9/11 Commission's proposal to create a DNI barreled through Congress in the months before the 2004 presidential election. Although the measure had met some resistance from friends of the Department of Defense, a deal seemed close enough that attention turned to Capitol Hill for passage of a landmark reform of U.S. national security.[3] Senator Joe Lieberman, an orthodox Jew, had sought a "national security waiver" from religious authorities permitting him to work on the Sabbath to vote for the bill.[4]

But inside the Capitol, an insurrection was afoot. The House Republican leadership, which usually kept its disagreements safely behind closed doors, was split. The number two Republican in the House, Tom DeLay, had given cover to two powerful committee chairmen to oppose the bill, supported though it was by the Senate, the White House, and even DeLay's boss, the Speaker of the House, Dennis Hastert. Hallway talk for years held that DeLay was the real power behind the throne; the truth was DeLay and Hastert were rarely in disagreement. But in the pre-election weeks, when the Speaker and other members of Congress were away campaigning for reelection, the Speaker's chief of staff had negotiated a compromise with the Senate and the White House that neither Congressman Jim Sensenbrenner, chairman of the House Judiciary Committee, nor Congressman Duncan Hunter, chairman of the House Armed Services Committee (HASC), could support. Congressman DeLay went to the Speaker's office and argued for putting off the vote, and their staffs feuded nearby. This day would be a test of congressional power politics: Could the Speaker marshal his troops behind a compromise with the Senate? Could the Speaker overcome the concerns of two committee chairmen and carry the day?

The full House Republican conference gathered in Room HC-5 in the basement of the Capitol, two stories below the House floor. This was the first gathering of the Republicans since their reelection victory and the members were fresh and excited, even rowdy. Those already seated could see their colleagues as they entered through a doorway at the front of the room. They cheered as popular members came into view.

Speaker Hastert, affectionately referred to as "the coach" for keeping the team together, called the rambunctious room to order. Earlier that morning, as it became clear that Hunter and Sensenbrenner were asking members to reject the compromise, the Speaker's staff had scrambled to save the bill. They had managed to cobble together talking points for the Speaker's use to show that he had gotten his colleagues a good deal. To begin with, Hastert appealed to his colleagues' disdain for the Senate. In their view, the Senate had merely parroted the views of the 9/11 Commission. But, the Speaker explained, through weeks of negotiation, the House had made a bad Senate bill into something better. Republicans wanted to tighten immigration laws and protect the military from undue intrusion by the new DNI. And while the House had not gotten all it wanted from the Senate, the compromise did have some immigration provisions that should please the House Republicans. Hastert called the compromise effort a "good bill." As for the 9/11 Commission's proposal to create a new intelligence czar—at that time called a national intelligence director and known by its unfortunate acronym, the NID—he declared it the culmination of national efforts to make the country safe after 9/11. In all, the Speaker asked his members to support the compromise package. Given the usual give and take in highly charged legislative negotiations, the House had done very well. Still, in a nod to Sensenbrenner, the Speaker acknowledged that he was a "tough S.O.B."

Chairman Sensenbrenner rose to speak. A political bruiser, his occasionally cantankerous demeanor signaled to adversaries, "This is not going to be easy." Undeterred by the Speaker, Sensenbrenner gave a straightforward account of his own dealings with the Senate. The House had sent over to the Senate a bill containing many important provisions to close loopholes in immigration law that might be exploited by terrorists. With all his might, he had tried to get these sensible provisions into the compromise measure negotiated with the Senate. But the House's position had not been taken seriously; the Senate had displayed a "condescending attitude."[5] He claimed that Senator Susan Collins, a moderate from Maine, had refused even to negotiate with the House Republicans, leaving the House to deal with an arch-liberal Democrat, Senator Richard Durbin of Illinois, who rejected almost everything that would make a difference. The dour chairman got his message across; the members hooted and jeered the Senate.

Next, Chairman of the House Armed Services Committee Duncan Hunter stood up to cheers. While affable and utterly without pretense, he would relentlessly pursue something important to him. During the weeks of negotiations, he had proved impossible to circumvent. A former Army Ranger who had served in Vietnam, he was respected by his fellow House Republicans on all matters pertaining to the military. As he stood before his assembled colleagues, one witness later recalled that Hunter seemed almost sorrowful as he declared, "I can't support this bill." The Senate had been unable to address his concerns that the troops in the field would have the intelligence they needed. Watching Hunter, a DeLay leadership staffer wondered whether out of deference to the Speaker he would deemphasize his objections. But when a member asked whether the troops in the field would be worse off than under current law, Hunter's ardor was stirred. He wanted to make sure the fighting men and women in Iraq, including his son "Dunc," who had fought in the First Battle of Fallujah, had adequate intelligence support. His passion summoned and his voice rose, "If Dunc needs to see what's over the foxhole he's in, we don't want to have him calling back to Washington to get some bureaucrat—*some NID*—on the phone to ask permission to move a satellite." And the roar had come.

It sounded like the House of Commons shouting affirmation to the prime minister during Question Time. The Speaker was sunk. His staff sat in the back row; one held his face in his hands.

The Speaker's lieutenant, Peter Hoekstra, the chairman of the House Intelligence Committee, spoke up, but he could not stem the tide. The staff looked at their shoes. The venerable chairman Henry Hyde, failing in health, murmured something. "What was that, Henry?" someone asked. "Henry should be recognized," another shouted. The members shifted their attention to the aging chairman. Hyde was unable to stand to address his colleagues, so Congressman Jim Leach rose to relay his words. "Henry says, 'The House and the Senate are a lot alike: both have about a hundred stupid members.'" The crowd bellowed with delight. The rout was on.

Perhaps the only member who could reverse the tide was Tom DeLay. The brash Texan had earned his nickname—the Hammer—in situations like this: when the votes were down, DeLay would hammer his colleagues until they supported the leadership. Speaker Hastert, the man DeLay had nominated for the job, was out on a limb. DeLay rose to speak. He was uncomfortable with this bill but understood that keeping a majority in the House often meant maintaining unity among the leaders at the cost of his own policy preferences. "Don't let the perfect be the enemy of the good" was a favorite justification around the Capitol. But today DeLay said only, "The Speaker has a tough decision to make," sealing the fate of the intelligence compromise.

Hastert's gamble had failed. With the majority of his members against him, the Speaker announced, in House parlance, that he was "pulling the bill." David Hobbs, the president's lobbyist, who helped broker the compromise with the Senate, was furious. Assuming that some Republicans would have supported the president and the Speaker and voted yes, their votes combined with those of the Democrats, who were nearly unanimous in favor, would have passed the compromise. But this was not smart party politics. A speaker who repeatedly ignores his constituents—the Republican members who elected him Speaker—will be out of a job. Back in the

Speaker's office after the meeting, Hastert and DeLay had a tough exchange about how they had gotten into this predicament.

The news of the death of intelligence reform licked through Congress like a flame. The air thickened with invective and blame. Senators took to the floor to blast the House leadership.[6] The House Democratic leadership lambasted "extremist House Republicans" who "subvert[ed]" the bill.[7] The 9/11 Commission's chairman blamed the Pentagon. Senator Lieberman told the press, "Talk about the interest of the war fighter, the commander-in-chief in the middle of a war has said he needs this bill to help carry out his duties to protect the American people and the war fighter and a small group of people in the House are stopping the commander-in-chief from getting what he wants. It is particularly shocking after the commander-in-chief has just been reelected."[8] The 9/11 commissioner, John Lehman, took to CNN: "The president now has been challenged directly by the leadership of the Congress and by the lobbyists and by the bureaucracy. Now he's got to show who's in charge."[9] Meanwhile, the House Republicans lauded Hunter and Sensenbrenner as heroes for standing up for the troops in the field. One conservative compared them to Horatius, "the legendary Roman who saved Rome by standing in front of a bridge and defeating an army that was sent to sack the city."[10] Another urged, "Stand fast, Duncan Hunter."[11] The White House, basking in its reelection glow, was jolted. The takedown was a "surprising embarrassment,"[12] and the media suggested that the president, just reelected, might now be "essentially a lame duck."[13] The night's broadcasts led with the story of the downfall.[14] Had the president failed to control his party[15]—or was he merely ignored? The 9/11 Families for a Secure America, one faction of family members of the 9/11 victims, said that the House Republicans "are going to have blood on their hands."[16] Deploring a "frightening breakdown in our democratic process"[17] and calling the denial of a vote "tantamount to tyranny,"[18] some 9/11 families members began a candlelight vigil at Ground Zero and elsewhere around the country to get a vote in the House of Representatives.[19]

CHAPTER TWO

The Making of a Juggernaut

The Origins of the 9/11 Commission and Its Recommendations

Two and a half years before the apparent demise of intelligence reform, the White House's legislative affairs team huddled past 11 p.m. near the floor of the U.S. House of Representatives. The House would soon vote on legislation to create a commission to investigate the September 11 attacks, and this team's job was to make sure a majority voted no. Each member of the team was a special assistant to the president assigned a group of Congressmen. They were the president's eyes, ears, and spokesmen on Capitol Hill. Called "specials" around the White House Legislative Affairs Office, they were to build a rapport with and know everything about their assigned members, so that when the president needed congressional support, the specials could deliver. A special was to shadow their congressional assignments: if your member was flying on Air Force One with the president, you went along for the ride; if your member was meeting with White House senior staff, you were there. Usually this meant the specials spent their days on Capitol Hill; if specials were hanging around the West Wing all day, they were not doing their jobs.

The specials were the tip of the spear for the White House on legislative business. For big votes that were expected to be close, the specials would break into zone coverage around the House chamber. From these positions, they tried to find persuadable Democrats or wavering Republican members of Congress and ask them to support the president. At least one special would be stationed on the east steps of the Capitol, one of the most traveled byways into the House. A second special might be down the stairs on the plaza to catch members coming into the Capitol through the carriage entrance, now the drop point for motorcades. But most were stationed on the perimeter of the House floor. If you took the underground subway to the Capitol, a special was stationed to receive you. If you were walking from the Senate across Statuary Hall to the House, a special was posted up nearby. This was the last chance for the White House to check a member before he or she voted. Sometimes, the presence of the staffers was symbolic: the White House was showing the flag, letting the members know the president was watching. It was known as "working the vote."

Some sixteen hours earlier at 8:30 a.m., the head of White House Legislative Affairs gave the specials their marching orders. There was a discussion about the strategy for the vote, and by 10 a.m. the specials had congregated on West Executive Avenue and piled into black White House sedans to be ferried to the Capitol.

That night's assignment for the White House specials was tough: to defeat an amendment offered to pending legislation that would establish in law a commission to investigate the attacks on the World Trade Center and the Pentagon. Tim Roemer, an aggressive young Democratic congressman from Indiana, led the effort to pass the amendment. As a member of the House Intelligence Committee, Roemer was participating in a joint congressional effort, the Joint Inquiry into Intelligence Community Activities before and after the Terrorist Attacks of September 11, 2001, to investigate the 9/11 attacks. Roemer considered the congressional review that had proceeded in the first half of 2002 a "good initial push" but insufficient.[1] The Senate, led by Senators John McCain and Joe Lieberman, strongly favored a commission. The White House argued that an investigation by a new commission would be duplicative because Congress was already investigating the attacks. Congress's investigation, called the Joint Inquiry because the House's and Senate's intelligence committees worked together, had reviewed thousands of documents, interviewed dozens of witnesses, held numerous hearings, and would eventually summarize their findings in a report. Positing that it would distract the intelligence agencies from hunting down al Qa'ida,[2] the White House contended that the intelligence committees were the "proper forum" for such a review because they had experience dealing with classified information. Their staff had expertise on intelligence matters, top-secret security clearances, and offices equipped with secure facilities.[3]

Angered by the opposition to a commission, the 9/11 Families, Congressman Roemer, and Senators John McCain and Joe Lieberman made common cause. They began a campaign to create a commission to investigate the attacks, believing "politics was at play."[4] Roemer untiringly canvassed the offices of moderate northeastern Republicans, considering them the most likely to defect from their leadership and support a commission. A group of 9/11 families, especially Carie Lemack, Beverly Eckert, Carol Ashley, and Mary Fetchett, joined Roemer's lobbying efforts, often traveling by train from Boston, New York, and New Jersey on short notice when Roemer needed help.[5] When the White House explained that the country needed to look forward and support the troops in harm's way, the family members were incredulous.

A commission to investigate the attacks posed a dilemma for the White House. On the one hand, it was politically dangerous in the short term to be seen opposing such an inquiry, especially with a highly visible group of victims' family members in support. And the chances of defeating the proposal were not good; all the Democrats and most Republicans in the Senate, and especially Senator McCain, strongly favored the proposal.

But in the longer term, the White House worried the inquiry could be turned into a political instrument against the president. Weeks before, Speaker Hastert had pulled the president aside in a White House meeting and warned that the commission could be "a very good set-up by the Democrats to pin the whole 9/11 issue on you."[6] The Speaker urged the president to beat Congress to the punch and create a commission on his own terms. For one thing, the congressional proposals under consideration would allow for an equal number of Republicans and Democrats, a more favorable ratio than in a Republican-controlled Congress. In addition, the commission would have the power to subpoena White House documents, a prospect that aroused fears of undue congressional meddling in executive branch affairs. And finally, the commission's hearings, which would be held in the months before the 2004 elections, could pin the White House down, responding to charges from hostile partisans hand-picked for commission membership by the Democratic congressional leaders. Tom DeLay declared that creating a commission "during a time of war is ill-conceived and frankly irresponsible. . . . We will not allow our president to be undermined by those who want his job."[7] The fear was of an unpredictable, runaway commission unfairly blaming the president for the 9/11 attacks on the eve of the 2004 presidential election.

These arguments carried the day at the White House. The president chose to fight in Congress. The specials had worked with their leadership colleagues all day on a whip count—a confidential list of how each Republican member planned on voting: yes, no, undecided. They gleaned it from analysis of voting patterns and intelligence collected in the halls of Congress, especially from staff and other members. The whip count looked bad; many moderate Republicans and members from northeastern districts, especially those that had been directly affected on 9/11, were planning to defect and support the Roemer amendment. Armed with this information, the specials knew which members were "problems."

Frequently, the White House, opening up every avenue of pressure, had worked hand in glove with the House Republican leadership and pulled out last-minute victories on the House floor. But victory was not in the cards tonight. At 1:58 a.m. the vote was called: 25 Republicans joined 193 Democrats and 1 Independent to give the Roemer amendment a one-vote majority. [8]

With the fight lost in the House, the commission was now certain to pass in Congress. The commission would be established by law in November 2002 after protracted negotiations between the Congress and the White House.

The House vote marked the first big victory for the 9/11 Families. One former senator called the Families the most powerful lobby group he ever came across in his career.[9] The 9/11 Families had become a political force.

• • • • • • • • • • •

Even before the Commission was in business, the Intelligence Community and Congress had begun to dissect what went wrong on 9/11. In particular, three episodes—George Tenet called them "pillars of conventional wisdom"[10]—from the 9/11 plot became shorthand for intelligence failures.

On December 4, 1998, in a top-secret directive to the Intelligence Community, George Tenet, the director of Central Intelligence, declared, "We are at war. I want no resources or people spared in this effort, either inside CIA or the community."[11] It was some months after the al Qa'ida bombings of the U.S. embassies in Tanzania and Kenya. Carried out within five minutes of each other, the bombings demonstrated the terrorists' new organizational ability and reach. For many, this was "the moment when [CIA and NSC] realized Bin Laden was waging war against the United States."[12] The declaration was a testament to George Tenet's foresight and recognition of the threat posed by al Qa'ida. However, the episode would come to signify something different. Since the memo went unnoticed and did not result in a surge of personnel or funding befitting a war, observers held it out as further confirmation that outside the CIA, which was under Tenet's direct control, the DCI lacked authority to back up words with deeds. The DCI's war memo came to symbolize the weak management of the Intelligence Community.

A second set of episodes supported the widespread conclusion that agencies of the U.S. government did not share information, especially the FBI and CIA, and that their rivalry, as well as real and perceived legal issues, had contributed to a failure to "connect the dots." In January 2000 CIA surveillance teams on the streets of Kuala Lumpur were watching three suspected terrorists at a safe house.[13] This was significant enough that the CIA's Counterterrorism Center briefed the CIA leadership on the terrorist cadre; the leadership in turn passed the information along to the president's national security advisor.[14] When the trio suddenly left for Thailand, the CIA teams in Kuala Lumpur cabled ahead to their colleagues in Bangkok, but otherwise the trail went cold. In March 2000 the CIA discovered that one of the three terrorists—Nawaf al-Hazmi—had departed Bangkok for Los Angeles.[15] He would go on to become one of the 9/11 hijackers. Another hijacker who attended the Kuala Lumpur meeting—Khalid al Midhar—was known by the CIA to have a U.S. visa and to have transited in and out of the United States between June 2000 and July 2001.[16] The CIA did not formally transmit the information about these individuals to others in the U.S. government for some months[17]; in the interim, the FBI might have initiated an investigation and uncovered the 9/11 plot. And, even when the FBI obtained information related to the Kuala Lumpur meeting, it did not share the information between the intelligence and criminal sides of its own house based on a misunderstanding of the applicable laws and procedures known as the "wall."[18] These failures took on tremendous significance in all of the post-attack investigations and formed the basis of one of the lessons learned from 9/11: agencies within the U.S. government failed to share information—both internally and amongst agencies—because of incompetence, real or perceived legal barriers, or bureaucratic rivalry. Two catchphrases sprung from this analysis. First, that a "foreign-domestic divide" hindered CIA and FBI cooperation in the pursuit of suspected terrorists. And in the chief slogan of the day, the Kuala Lumpur episode was a "dot" that, if it had been correlated to other "dots," might have contributed to a picture of the unfolding plot.

"Connect the dots" became more popular as shorthand for the problems that led to 9/11 when a series of FBI domestic actions came under scrutiny. In July 2001 the Phoenix, Arizona, FBI field office sent a memo to headquarters "identifying a pattern of Middle Eastern males with possible terrorist connections attending flight schools in the United States."[19] Apparently, no one at FBI headquarters connected that revelation to the increasing concern of a terrorist attack in the summer of 2001.

That same summer, agents in the Minneapolis FBI field office arrested Zacarias Moussaoui. They were concerned about the possibility of a larger plot to target airlines and shared those apprehensions with FBI headquarters and the CIA.[20] "Neither FBI headquarters nor the [CIA] apparently connected the information to warnings emanating from the [CIA] itself about an impending terrorist attack, or to the likely presence of two al Qa'ida operatives from the Kuala Lumpur meeting, al-Mihdhar and al-Hazmi, in the United States. The same unit at FBI headquarters handled the Phoenix electronic message and the communication about an airline attack, but still it did not sound any alarm bells."[21]

To post-attack investigators, this failure to "connect the dots" seemed further evidence that the U.S. government had significant pieces of information that, if they had been correlated with other pieces of intelligence around the Intelligence Community, might have foretold the 9/11 plot. These pieces of information resided in different pockets, and their possessors were "stovepiped," meaning that they passed information up their chain of command but not across interagency (and sometimes *intra-agency*) boundaries. The idea began to germinate that the Intelligence Community needed a leader with power to "smash stovepipes" and to "force agencies to work together."

Finally, the FBI's handling of the Zacarias Moussaoui case, including its inability to search his laptop, pointed to similar problems. First, upon arresting Moussaoui in August 2001 on an immigration charge after learning of his odd activities in flight training and recognizing his potential as a hijacker, the FBI sought to search Moussaoui's laptop.[22] Unfortunately (and likely incorrectly), the FBI believed it needed a court order to search the laptop and determined that it lacked sufficient information to obtain either a criminal or Foreign Intelligence Surveillance Court order to do so, even after it obtained information from a foreign government linking Moussaoui to a rebel leader in Chechnya.[23] Indeed, in the course of obtaining information from the French and British governments about Moussaoui, it became clear that the CIA believed he might be a suicide hijacker; at the same time, however, when the FBI sent information about Moussaoui to the CIA and the FAA, among others, no mention was made of the FBI case agent's personal assessment (much less the CIA's view) that Moussaoui planned to hijack an airplane.[24] Yet again, another opportunity to learn more of the then-unfolding plot was lost.

These episodes would play prominent roles in reviews of the Intelligence Community by a White House External Review Board, in the congressional Joint Inquiry into 9/11, and in a Bush White House effort to revamp intelligence analysis after 9/11. These reviews revived the idea of centralizing management authority in the Intelligence Community and put it squarely on the policy agenda.

• • • • • • • • • • •

Brent Scowcroft, a former Air Force lieutenant general and national security advisor to President George H. W. Bush, received a call in the early days of the administration of President George W. Bush. Would he be willing to lead the President's Foreign Intelligence Advisory Board (PFIAB, pronounced "piff-ee-ab"), which met in secret and advised the president on sensitive intelligence matters? Scowcroft was also enlisted in early 2001 to lead a second secret group, the External Review Board, charged by the president in a National Security Presidential Directive[25] "to review major structural issues." Condoleezza Rice recalled, "Everyone knew we had intelligence problems and intelligence gaps.... Intelligence reform had just been on the agenda for as long as I could remember."[26] After 9/11, the External Review Board's work took on additional significance; Rice asked Scowcroft to also consider what changes were needed to improve intelligence inside the United States. By March 2002, Scowcroft produced a classified study of the Intelligence Community that became known as the Scowcroft Report. Although its conclusions were not widely known, the report played a key role in developing the post-9/11 intellectual case for what became the two chief recommendations of the 9/11 Commission: a DNI and a National Counterterrorism Center.

The Scowcroft Report reignited a long-running battle between intelligence reformers seeking greater centralized management of the IC and defenders of defense primacy in intelligence. By proposing to effectively transfer the Department of Defense's intelligence agencies—the National Security Agency (NSA), the National Geospatial Agency (NGA), and the National Reconnaissance Office (NRO)—to the DCI, the report's authors aimed to "strengthen the director of central intelligence to be the unambiguous leader of national intelligence."

General Scowcroft's recommendations challenged the basis of the National Security Act of 1947. That law created a system whereby intelligence agencies within cabinet departments would report both to their cabinet secretary and to the head of the Intelligence Community, the DCI. The most familiar arrangement of this "dual masters" system mandated that, as "combat support agencies," the electronic eavesdroppers of the National Security Agency would report to the secretary of defense for tactical military matters but to the DCI on "national" intelligence issues of interest to more than one cabinet department.

The Department of Defense viewed the intelligence agencies as first and foremost critical combat support to their warfighters. But to Scowcroft, the "tactical military requirements have had a tendency to dominate the tasking of the national system; as a result, collection and analysis have not responded promptly to changing security challenges." Scowcroft cited the unification of the Army, Navy, Air Force, and Marines under the secretary of defense as a model for uniting the sixteen intelligence agencies under an intelligence chief. Before Congress enacted its landmark defense reforms in 1986, the Defense Department's service secretaries had maintained tremendous authority to the detriment of the authority of the secretary of defense and the generals in the field. The Goldwater-Nichols Act "made the secretary of defense the unambiguous leader of the department," whereas in the Intelligence Community the combat-support agencies "act with autonomy."

The Scowcroft Report recommended a second mechanism to force increased centralization within the Intelligence Community. The National Counterterrorism Center should be created specifically to "effectively collect, analyze, and disseminate all terrorism-related foreign intelligence, whether gathered domestically or abroad." The Scowcroft Report marshaled the information-sharing problems discussed earlier on behalf of an NCTC. The government had not shared terrorism information about the 9/11 plot properly in at least two important ways: information collected abroad by the CIA and other IC elements had not been appropriately shared with the FBI or other domestic agencies, and information the FBI collected was not accessible by intelligence agencies.

The arguments in the Scowcroft Report for increased centralization in the Intelligence Community are strikingly similar to the language later used in the 9/11 Commission Report in support of a DNI. The Scowcroft Report is also significant because, of all the reform proposals since 1947, its solution—moving the combat-support agencies out from the direction, control, and authority of the Department of Defense—was the most far-reaching.

Although the similarities in tone, language, and substance make the Scowcroft Report an antecedent of the 9/11 Commission Report, its proposal to vest maximum authority in the Intelligence Community chief would prove too radical for the 9/11 Commission and its solutions exceeded the policy prescriptions of its post–9/11 contemporary, the Joint Inquiry.

Scowcroft's challenge was to convince an administration in the throes of a war on terrorism and fighting in Afghanistan that a reorganization of the IC was necessary. In particular, Scowcroft understood that Secretary Donald Rumsfeld and Vice President Dick Cheney, a former defense secretary, would fiercely oppose transferring the national intelligence agencies from the Department of Defense. In the 1970s, during his first tour as secretary of defense, Rumsfeld rejected a suggestion that he transfer satellites to the control of the CIA. "If they're in my budgets, I'll run them."[27] Vice President Cheney had equally entrenched views on Intelligence Community matters. As a member of the House Intelligence Committee in the 1980s during his tenure as a congressman from Wyoming, Cheney had long followed the question of intelligence reorganization.[28] At least as early as 1992, when he was secretary of defense, he had flatly opposed intelligence-centralization efforts. At that time, he had called the idea of a DNI "unwise." Citing the intelligence needs of the "war-fighting commanders," Secretary Cheney wrote that a DNI would "seriously impair the effectiveness" of existing arrangements by "assigning inappropriate authority to the proposed director of national intelligence, who would become the director and manager of internal DOD activities that in the interest of efficiency and effectiveness must remain under the authority, direction, and control of the secretary of defense."[29] Cheney was opposed to greater centralization in the IC, in part due to a specific episode during the first Gulf War. To dislodge Saddam Hussein from Kuwait, the plan was to conduct an extensive aerial bombing campaign to destroy 50 percent of the Iraqi tanks before sending in ground troops. A "shoot-out" broke out in the West Wing on whose intelligence would determine whether the 50 percent mark had been met. DCI William Webster insisted that for a tank to be considered destroyed, the turret needed to be blown off. The DCI favored this metric because his principal intelligence collection mechanism was satellite imagery and a blown turret would be clearly observable. DoD claimed that many more tanks had been rendered useless although their turrets may still be attached to the tank. They were able to carry the argument because DoD's planes flying over Iraqi airspace could more easily spot tank damage than a satellite. Secretary Cheney drew the lesson that more centralization of intelligence assets was a bad way to go because a question of strategic importance was settled because DoD had its own assets available to inform the decision.[30]

DCI Tenet was asked to collect the written views of the president's senior national security advisors on the Scowcroft Report. Secretary Rumsfeld sent a note to the Office of the Vice President to make sure the vice president would weigh in. The vice president had his counsel submit a highly classified response to DCI Tenet, which opposed the recommendations for a more powerful DCI, emphasizing the importance of unity of command in the secretary of defense over the defense intelligence elements.

Defense intelligence advocates believed centralization proponents ignored or discounted the secretary of defense's specific statutory obligations to ensure that the intelligence agencies in the Defense Department—the DIA, but especially the NSA and NGA—were attuned to meeting the intelligence requirements of operational military forces.[31] It was incumbent upon the defense secretary to ensure that intelligence also served the tactical needs of operational military commanders. The combatant commanders, especially those in ongoing military actions, needed details on the number and types of troops arrayed against them, as well as the enemies' weapons and battle plans—the kind of intelligence needed to fight a war.[32]

Proponents held out as evidence the "profound repercussions"[33] of the Persian Gulf War, which the chairman of the Senate Armed Services Committee called a "watershed event."[34] The high-technology precision weapons used in the Gulf War changed the nature of warfare. The "tempo" of war had increased, and "in order to remain relevant to this accelerated process of war, battlefield intelligence had to be acquired, processed, analyzed and disseminated with incredible speed."[35] Amid praise for the military's defeat of Saddam Hussein in the "one-hundred-hour war" to expel Iraqi forces from Kuwait, Gen. Norman Schwarzkopf, USA (Ret.), the conflict's celebrated military commander, cited tactical intelligence as one major shortcoming in the military's performance. In Schwarzkopf's view, the U.S. intelligence assets were preoccupied with collecting national intelligence in response to a "directive out of Washington." The United States needed an intelligence system that would "be capable of delivering a real-time product to a theater commander when he requests that."[36]

The successful use of precision-guided munitions in the Persian Gulf War signaled the military's greater reliance on intelligence assets.[37] U.S.

precision-guided weapons "were the way of the future and placed a premium on the availability of intelligence and disposition of hostile forces."[38] The lesson of the Persian Gulf War was that "battlefield commanders should receive better national and organic intelligence support in future conflicts."[39]

To the defense proponents, military operations and intelligence became even more inextricable after September 11, 2001. Intelligence is absolutely vital to military action against terrorists and insurgents. Surveillance and reconnaissance aircraft were critical in the campaigns in Iraq and Afghanistan, often a prerequisite to military action by special operations forces. The Defense Department's greater reliance on intelligence began to be reflected in their budget submissions to Congress, in which their requests for intelligence systems drastically increased.

Once his report was complete, National Security Advisor Condoleezza Rice urged Scowcroft to personally make his pitch to Rumsfeld. According to one participant, "It was one of those meetings that don't go well. I'm here to sell you something you don't want to buy."[40] Rumsfeld took a call from Tenet during the meeting with Scowcroft. He was following up on a matter that had arisen during Tenet's morning intelligence briefing with President Bush. Rumsfeld announced to Scowcroft: "Now that is what I need, a DCI that will get me information."[41] A Scowcroft staffer saw the comment as telling, Rumsfeld thought an ideal DCI was subordinate to the secretary of defense.[42] Addressing Scowcroft, Rumsfeld dismissed his proposal. "First, it will never happen. And second, if it happened I would have to be the DNI because of the equities Defense has in this are so important to me." Scowcroft remembers saying, "Don, let me tell you something. If our positions were reversed, and I was secretary of defense and you were briefing me on this, I know you would be telling me the same thing I am telling you." Rumsfeld "just harrumphed."[43]

Later, Vice President Cheney told Adm. David Jeremiah, a member of the Scowcroft review group, "You are just rearranging the deck chairs on the Titanic, nothing useful will come of it, I will oppose it."[44] Afterward, Rice told Scowcroft that moving the national intelligence agencies out of the Department of Defense was just too hard and that Rumsfeld would not have any part of it. "Then it got put in a drawer and that was the end of it as far as I know."[45] Condoleezza Rice recalled that "Brent recommended the alternative model. For me, the issue was that we're right in the middle of the 9/11 stuff, right in the middle of the Iraq war, we still had Afghanistan, and I was rather skeptical about moving the boxes in the middle of a global war."[46] At the Defense Department, Secretary Rumsfeld and his lieutenants saw a threat in the Scowcroft Report. They drew a lesson: the secretary should draw the defense intelligence agencies more tightly under his control or risk losing them in an intelligence reorganization.

The Joint Inquiry confirmed for them that the Intelligence Community needed radical change, concluding in late 2003 that "prior to September 11, the Intelligence Community was neither well organized nor equipped, and did not adequately adapt, to meet the challenge posed by global terrorists focused on targets within the United States."[47] In their report, they concluded that the DCI was "either unwilling or unable to marshal the full range of Intelligence Community resources necessary to combat the growing threat to the United States."[48] They posited that the DCI's failed efforts to marshal resources from across the community against al Qa'ida "suggests a fragmented Intelligence Community that was operating without a comprehensive strategy for combating the threat posed by Bin Ladin, and a DCI without the ability to enforce consistent priorities at all levels throughout the Community."[49]

Armed with their diagnosis of 9/11 and noting the large role of the Defense Department, the Joint Inquiry recommended further centralization of the Intelligence Community in the form of a director of national intelligence. The DNI would be the president's principal advisor on intelligence "and shall have the full range of management, budgetary and personnel responsibilities needed to make the entire U.S. Intelligence Community operate as a coherent whole." It stressed that the same person could not be both DNI and head of the CIA.

Seizing on the "connect the dots" metaphor, the Joint Inquiry formalized the conclusion, noting that "the U.S. government does not presently bring together in one place all terrorism-related information from all sources."[50] It recommended that an all-source fusion center be created in the new Department of Homeland Security and that the FBI increase its capabilities in domestic intelligence.[51]

The Joint Inquiry's concerns were similar to the predominant school of thought among the Community Management Staff at the CIA—the staff who performed the DCI's community management functions. The Executive Director for Intelligence Community Affairs, Larry Kindsvater, argued for reorganization in 2003. Citing a "strange and dangerous managerial situation," he wrote that "the Community is not managed or organized to directly address national security missions and threats" and that the DCI "must truly be the head of the entire Community."[52] Kindsvater's dissatisfaction was significant because it came from within the Office of Community Management, the entity whose head Congress had elevated to deputy director of the CIA in statute in 1997 for the express purpose to "provide an emphasis to work issues across the community, across programs, and across intelligence disciplines that had not previously existed."[53] Kindsvater's arguments were interpreted as the formal acknowledgment that the elevation of community management within the CIA in 1998 had not had the desired effect.

• • • • • • • • • • • •

In 2002, the White House began to consider reform proposals. Condoleezza Rice noted that "when you think about the implications of 9/11 the biggest intelligence gap was between domestic intelligence and foreign intelligence. It actually wasn't that the CIA didn't coordinate with the NSA, it was that the CIA did not coordinate with the FBI."[54] Before 9/11, a CIA briefer provided daily intelligence to the president. Although the DCI was there to provide context, along with the vice president, national security advisor, and chief of staff, the FBI was not represented. After 9/11, FBI Director Robert Mueller and Tom Ridge, the head of the White House Office of Homeland Security (OHS), joined for President Bush's daily terrorism briefing. Including Mueller and Ridge would guarantee that any foreign intelligence regarding attacks to the homeland could be briefed immediately to the officials charged with security within the United States.

But fusing intelligence information in the Oval Office was an imperfect institutional solution to the problem of bridging the foreign-domestic divide. There were questions of what to tell the president: did he need to hear about every threat no matter how minor or unreliable? The president had been forced to become the "Connector in Chief," a less than optimal way to meld intelligence from around the Intelligence Community.[55]

General John A. Gordon, USAF (Ret.), pulled Directors Tenet and Mueller aside after an Oval Office session with the president: "We've got to fix this."[56] Seeking a solution, the White House chief of staff convened a series of meetings with designees from the CIA, the Defense Department, and the FBI. The White House sponsorship of the meeting suggested to its participants that the creation of a new intelligence fusion center was inevitable—the question was where it would be located bureaucratically. The CIA wanted to preserve the role of its Counterterrorism Center, which included representatives from all other relevant IC agencies and whose mission was to hunt terrorists. The CIA sought to limit the scope of the new fusion center, believing that operations to hunt terrorists overseas should remain at the CIA, as would the agency's role in analyzing the nature of the terrorist threat. The CIA rejected the name Terrorist Threat Analysis Center. The CIA did not want there to be an analytical function "because only the CIA's Directorate of Intelligence does that."[57] The CIA successfully argued for an entity whose mission was merely the *integration* of terrorism threats across the foreign-domestic divide. The new center should not even contain the word *intelligence* in its title, lest some misinterpret its mission as replacing the CIA as the primary analysts in intelligence.[58] Finally, the new entity would report to the director of the CIA. The interagency working group sponsored by the White House came up with a fusion center that would be called the Terrorist Threat Integration Center, called "T-TIC."

The proposal was closely held until the 2003 State of the Union address. From the rostrum on the floor of the House of Representatives, President Bush announced his latest initiative to fight terrorism:

> Since September the 11th, our intelligence and law enforcement agencies have worked more closely than ever to track and disrupt the terrorists. Tonight, I am instructing the leaders of the FBI, the CIA, the Department of Homeland Security, and the Department of Defense to develop a Terrorist Threat Integration Center, to merge and analyze all threat information in a single location. Our government must have the very best information possible, and we will use it to make sure the right people are in the right places to protect our citizens.

• • • • • • • • • • •

Secretary Rumsfeld observed the nascent congressional activity and worried that reorganizing intelligence would gain momentum. In a memo to his staff he wrote, "It is pretty clear to me that at least [Senator] Graham and maybe [House Permanent Select Committee on Intelligence Chairman] Goss, although I don't know that, have it in their minds that they want to be sponsors of a massive reorganization of the intel community . . . moving intel authority over to the DCI. . . . I am persuaded that rather than wait until the pressure builds on this, we should get all of the arguments and the people who understand this marshaled, so we can stop it from getting a good head of steam, rather than having to defeat it after it already has a good head of steam."[59]

Meanwhile, Secretary Rumsfeld sought greater control over the Defense Department's intelligence enterprise. In the spring of 2003, after receiving authorization from Congress, Secretary Rumsfeld created an undersecretary of defense for intelligence (USDI).[60] In an answer to congressional questions before his confirmation as the first USDI, Steve Cambone explained that in holding the position he would exercise "authority, direction, and control" over the defense intelligence agencies to be able to discharge better his duty to assist the DCI with the provision of intelligence across the federal government.[61] Many saw making a USDI the primary interlocutor with the DCI as a greater assertion of control by the Defense Department over the defense intelligence agencies at the expense of influence from the DCI. Cambone would later reject the suggestion that the USDI's creation was a frustration for the DCI, emphasizing instead that "the secretary needed to get his arms around his legal obligations for military intelligence. Someone has to make sure all that works. . . . There is a responsibility to make sure the services and the commands around the world have intelligence . . . and he has his own requirement as second in command behind the Commander-in-Chief for the maintenance of an intelligence capability for the purposes of the conduct of military options."[62]

Both the Joint Inquiry and the Scowcroft Report set the stage for consideration of intelligence-reform legislation after the 9/11 Commission's recommendations in July 2004. They were among the first formal articulations of the idea of a multi-agency fusion center. The Joint Inquiry Report also revived congressional support for the idea of increased centralized management of the Intelligence Community. Members of the Joint Inquiry, including Tim Roemer, Jane Harman, Barbara Mikulski, Bob Graham, and Dianne Feinstein, became strong supporters of intelligence reorganization, providing a congressional base of support for the creation of a DNI. The Joint Inquiry's endorsement put the issue of increased centralized management of intelligence on the table as the 9/11 Commission began its work.

Two new accelerants for intelligence reform were about to be introduced: another intelligence failure, this time in Iraq, and the "national theatre" of televised hearings regarding the 9/11 attacks.[63]

CHAPTER THREE

Tenet

Quite apart from his duties as DCI, some called George Tenet the best *CIA director* anyone had ever seen. In large measure, the CIA director's job is to manage the CIA's relationships—with Congress, with the White House, and with foreign intelligence services. Despite the CIA's considerable overseas presence, it needs the cooperation of the host nations to be effective. To deepen their relationships, CIA chiefs of station in countries around the world choreograph elaborate trips to Washington for the heads of foreign intelligence services. The heads are briefed, business is done, and they sometimes visit Congress; but frequently the most important part of the trip is dinner with the CIA director. Here, Tenet excelled. He would walk into a dinner with virtually no knowledge of his dinner guests, and a few hours later they would consider Tenet their best friend. "I'd see him at dinner with heads of other services, it did not matter who, whether they were Eastern or Western he was magnificent, always had a good joke, always good, I saw him with one Middle Eastern leader, soon they were smoking cigars, drinking Scotch, and having a great time together."[1] He would forge a bond with his counterpart. Gesturing around the room to all the officers who did the day-to-day work of intelligence cooperation, he would lean over to his counterpart, "If you ever need anything"—jabbing his finger at his guest—"you call me." One official recalled that "George had a natural penchant to be able to get the trust of leaders of foreign services."[2]

The CIA loved Tenet. He walked the halls at all hours, chomping on a cigar, dropping into the offices of his senior officers to ask them what they were working on. He strolled through the cafeteria and had lunch with junior officers. He would visit the offices of the special technical services employees, wowing them with his attention and interest. Tenet loved the cloak-and-dagger of intelligence operations. He so favored the agency's operational side that the standing joke was that Tenet was the best leader of the operations directorate the CIA ever had. There was subtle truth in the quip: his alleged preference for spying missions and intelligence collection was thought to leave less time for other CIA business—the development of intelligence estimates, the painstaking work of the CIA's analysts, and, especially, his role as the director of central intelligence, in particular its requirement that he manage the community outside of the CIA. An official observed, "The CIA director managed the CIA; it was the best job in the world. Managing the IC meant going out to the NRO and sitting through a three-hour meeting about satellite specifications. So it just was not done well."[3] Sources close to Tenet hotly dispute the narrative that Tenet did not manage the IC in his role as DCI. After the post–Cold War cuts to intelligence funding, the IC was in "chapter 11" bankruptcy. "There were more FBI agents in New York than intelligence officers abroad." Tenet's defenders point to Tenet's support of dramatic increases to the NSA's budget, including overhauls of recruiting, training, and rebuilding an intelligence cadre at the CIA.

Defenders of Tenet cite his employment of the entire IC against al Qa'ida. Assistant Director of Central Intelligence for Collection Charlie Allen, who worked frequently across the community on Tenet's behalf, remembered, "Tenet, that son of a gun, was always pushing me, I'd be in my office on the sixth floor, big knock on the door, and I'd say, Oh Christ, it is George again, and there'd be George chomping on a cigar, saying, What the hell are you doing, we've got to work hard, we've got to move this; he did that to everyone, he was all over the building telling them, 'Let's move!'"[4] Tenet called weekly meetings to dive deep into the hunt for Usama bin Ladin, creating a unit specifically dedicated to the search and frequently convening his senior officers to strategize in the pursuit of the terrorist leader. In the Clinton years, he reactivated the CIA's contacts in Afghanistan and brought locational data of Usama bin Ladin to the attention of the White House for decisions on military strikes. It was this fervor that led him to issue the Declaration of War (that would later be cited as evidence that the DCI had no authority in the Intelligence Community). In the summer of 2001, Tenet traveled nearly unannounced down to the White House to call attention to signs of an imminent terrorist attack. Tenet and his team knew something major was about to happen but did not know the timing or place of the operation. "We had the world buttoned-up overseas, U.S. embassies in Europe and Africa, the Fifth Fleet, all of Africa, but we didn't know it would be the homeland," remembered Charlie Allen. A former Tenet aide conceded that Tenet's efforts against al Qa'ida were necessarily "CIA-centric" because "George Tenet's only fighting platform he can command day-to-day is the CIA."[5]

On September 11 Tenet and his team saw the hand of Usama bin Ladin. Tenet briefed President Bush, who was then in a strategic command bunker in Omaha, Nebraska, that he believed the attacks were the work of al Qa'ida. Tenet was devastated on 9/11. Tenet's men were the first on the ground in Afghanistan nine days later, working with al Qa'ida's enemies and seeking information on the whereabouts of Usama bin Ladin.

As the months wore on and the investigation delved into the details of the 9/11 plot, Tenet would appear frequently in Congress to explain his agency's role in pursuing al Qa'ida before 9/11. Senator Richard Shelby, the chairman of the Senate Intelligence Committee, stepped up to the microphone and took aim. "There have been more massive failures of intelligence on [Tenet's] watch as director of CIA than any director in the history of the agency."[6] Shelby asked, "Why were we utterly unaware of the planning and execution of the September the 11th attacks? In other words, what went wrong?"[7] Senator Carl Levin catalogued for Director Tenet the CIA's failures on 9/11. "After months of investigation and numerous joint-inquiry hearings . . . a fair reading of the facts has led to a deeply troubling conclusion: Prior to September 11th, U.S. intelligence officials possessed terrorist information that, if properly handled, could have disrupted, limited or possibly prevented the terrorist attacks."[8] A 9/11 Family member thought Tenet "made many mistakes that had cost our husbands their lives, and we wanted people like him held accountable, not heralded as heroes."[9]

Tenet delivered a stout defense. In the midst of his twenty-minute peroration, the chairman of the Joint Inquiry tried to cut him off and Tenet bristled. "Well, sir," he said, "I have been waiting a year." The Joint Inquiry investigation would later conclude that the Intelligence Community did have information that was clearly relevant to the September 11 attacks and had failed to focus on it "and consider and appreciate its collective significance." Nor had the Intelligence Community "paid sufficient attention to potential for domestic attack," and as a result it "did not have a comprehensive counterterrorism strategy for combating Usama bin Ladin—the DCI was either unwilling or unable to marshal the full range of IC resources to combat the growing threat."[10]

Now that Congress had created a commission to investigate the 9/11 attacks, Tenet's CIA braced for another fusillade. The 9/11 Commission's executive director was Philip Zelikow, a historian at the University of Virginia. In addition to coauthoring a famous book about the Cuban Missile Crisis while at Harvard, Zelikow had cofounded a series of study groups on the operation of the Intelligence Community. He also participated in the president's Foreign Intelligence Advisory Board's adoption of the Scowcroft Report.

An early meeting between the CIA and the Commission's executive director left the CIA with the impression that the Commission had prejudged its investigation and would recommend a DNI.[11] One of Tenet's deputies recalled reporting back to Tenet afterward that Zelikow had begun the meeting by slapping the table and declaring: None of this would have happened if you had a DNI.[12]

For its part, the Commission viewed Director George Tenet with skepticism. Part of the Commission's mandate was to unearth the CIA's efforts to kill Usama bin Ladin during the years of the Clinton administration. The CIA claimed that Clinton had not given them "lethal" authority to kill bin Laden. The Clinton camp told the Commission that Tenet had received such authorization directly from the president on Christmas Eve 1998, and eventually presented documents supporting the claim. The Commission saw Tenet's denials as disingenuous: "How can you forget being with the president on Christmas Eve?"[13] Sources close to Director Tenet saw this as unfair because Tenet was out of town when the Christmas Eve authorization was given and claimed that because the authority lapsed after thirty days, Tenet would not recall it when meeting with the Commission staff years later.

From his interview with top CIA officials during the 9/11 Commission's investigation, Zelikow remembered that they "left a strong impression on me."[14]

Tenet said, and I believe him, that counterterrorism had become the number one national-security priority, maybe even as early as 1998. Then ask yourself, if you were running this forty-billion-dollar Intelligence Community and you believed the top national security priority is this, what would a management strategy to reflect a shift in priorities from Russia or China to this look like?[15]

Sources close to Director Tenet said he, too, was struck by the topics the

Commission pursued with him. They claim the Commission never asked him about how he spent his time managing the Intelligence Community prior to 9/11, much less his views on creating a DNI or reorganization generally. He thought the Commission's aim was "to play stump the dummy" rather than have a serious conversation on how to make intelligence work better. Had they asked, Tenet would have offered that he did believe that the DCI's job was too consuming for one person.

With mutual enmity, in the spring of 2004, Tenet twice appeared before the Commission. For his first appearance, the CIA released a thirty-seven-page defense of their record fighting al Qa'ida, including their pre-9/11 plan. The Commission's staff reported that the CIA's plan was great, as far as it went, but it was too narrow; it did not apply to the whole of U.S. intelligence outside of the CIA, and as a result there was "no comprehensive collection strategy to pull together human sources, imagery, signals intelligence, and open sources."[16] Tenet had not developed a management strategy to "monitor and rationalize [the Agency's] resources against priorities." In short, Zelikow concluded, "As a result, a question remains: Who is in charge of intelligence?"[17] The floating question did not sit well with Tenet. He declared that he had "serious issues" with the Zelikow's statement and called parts of it "flat wrong."[18] The CIA was willing to concede a need for a single place "where foreign intelligence and domestic information could be put together and analyzed quickly"[19] and that perhaps some changes were needed to help the DCI contend with his vast duties. But wholesale structural alterations would be wrong. Tenet testified that transferring community managerial functions from the CIA to a DNI who was without "operators and analysts" would be "throwing the baby out with the bath water."[20]

Even as the CIA defended itself for its pre-9/11 action, the Intelligence Community's National Intelligence Estimate on Iraq began to unravel. June 2003 ushered in the appointment of David Kay by Director Tenet to organize the faltering search for weapons of mass destruction in now-liberated Iraq.[21] That same month, the Senate Select Committee on Intelligence (SSCI) began a formal review of pre-war U.S. intelligence assessments on Iraq.[22] In July 2003 former ambassador Joe Wilson suggested that the Bush administration manipulated intelligence when the president said in his State of the Union address that Iraq had tried to buy uranium from Africa. The accusation engulfed the White House—and the CIA. Tenet seemed to take responsibility when he said "the CIA's approval process had broken down and that uranium in Africa intelligence should never have been included in the text written for the president."[23]

By January 2004, David Kay would repudiate the National Intelligence Estimate on Iraq's WMDs:

> Let me begin by saying, we were almost all wrong, and I certainly include myself here. . . . It turns out that we were all wrong . . . and that is most disturbing. . . . I believe that the effort that has been directed to this point has been sufficiently intense; that it is highly unlikely that there were large stockpiles of deployed militarized chemical and biological weapons there.[24]

After hearing Kay's conclusions, the White House let it be known that the president would appoint a commission to investigate the Iraq intelligence failure. Tenet would again rise to defend the CIA. In February 2004, in an extraordinary address at Georgetown University, his alma mater, he rejected Kay's contention that the search for WMDs was nearly over and gave updated, "provisional" judgments about where things stood. On the CIA's contention that aluminum tubes discovered in Iraq had been for a centrifuge program, he said that "we have additional data to collect and more sources to question." If Saddam had not reconstituted a nuclear program as the CIA contended, he "intended to." While they had not found bio-weapons, the CIA was still running down leads, and, nevertheless, Iraq "intended to develop biological weapons."[25]

Many Democrats in Congress believed that the president and vice president had misused the intelligence provided by the CIA. They believed that the CIA had either stood by and let it happen or had told the White House what it wanted to hear. The critiques were harsh. Senator Levin said, "I have no confidence in the CIA anymore because intelligence has been shaped and exaggerated and hyped so much now in this country by the CIA."[26]

Sensing an opportunity, Jane Harman, the ranking Democrat on the House Intelligence Committee, initiated a public campaign for intelligence reform. Citing the "urgent" threat of terrorism, and "misstatements" about intelligence by Bush administration policymakers, Harman introduced a bill to "fix the many problems that have plagued United States intelligence in the post–Cold War era."[27] Her bill would create a DNI with the existing powers of the DCI, but separated from the CIA. It would augment the authority on budgetary control, the tasking of intelligence collection, the authority to set information-sharing policies across the Intelligence Community, and the mandate to create "mission-based" centers.[28]

In appearances on Capitol Hill after the Georgetown speech, Democrats stepped up their criticism that the White House misrepresented the CIA's intelligence and hammered Tenet on whether he tried to stop the White House. "And if you didn't, why not?" asked Senator Edward Kennedy.[29] Senator Dianne Feinstein chastised, "It's a pretty bitter pill to swallow," since "people voted to authorize use of force based on what we read in these reports."[30] Senator Richard Durbin told Tenet that "our intelligence operations failed in a historic way."[31] Through it all, Tenet defended the CIA: "We're not perfect, but we're pretty damn good at what we do."[32]

Bob Woodward, the famous Watergate reporter and the author of a series of books on national security, quoted Tenet telling President Bush in the run-up to the invasion of Iraq that Iraq's WMD program was a "slam-dunk case."[33] For Tenet, this was when "the wheels came off the train."[34] Tenet wondered whether the president's advisors had convinced Woodward to shift the blame for Iraq to Tenet.[35] Tenet considered it "obvious" that the White House had fed "slam dunk" to the media and that this represented a "fundamental breakdown in trust."[36] Tenet decided to resign.

With Tenet's resignation on June 3, 2004, Harman pounced. President Bush announced Tenet's resignation on the South Lawn of the White House on the way to Andrews Air Force Base, and before the flight was airborne Harman had issued a press release her staff called "Tenet Out, DNI In." It stated, "We need a true director of the entire Intelligence Community—all 15 agencies—who has the necessary authority, responsibility, and accountability."[37]

All in all, the controversies swirling around the CIA in 2004 had an undeniable effect on the agency's standing with the public, with Congress, and with the 9/11 Commission. When the controversy began, Tenet had thought about resigning from the CIA, but the looming 9/11 Commission hearings made him think twice. They would be "contentious and politically charged" and Tenet did not want to leave his successor in the middle of that "mess."[38] Tenet called the hearings "grueling."[39] The 9/11 Commissioner John Lehman, who had been Ronald Reagan's hard-charging secretary of the navy, thought the case laid out against the CIA was "damning" and indicative of a "system that is broken, that doesn't function."[40] Lehman, pugnacious and indomitable, rebuked Tenet:

The attitude we . . . get from CIA institutionally, is that, hey, you know, we're the CIA. . . . A kind of smugness and even arrogance toward deep reform. . . . All the king's horses and all the king's men in CIA could not corroborate what turned out to be true, and told the president of the United States almost a month before the attack they couldn't corroborate these reports. That's an institutional failure. And I am here to tell you, and I'm sure you've heard it before, there is a train coming down the track, there are going to be very real changes made. You've done a terrific job in evolutionary change, but it's clearly not been enough. Revolution is coming.[41]

CHAPTER FOUR

Revolution Is Coming

The 9/11 Commission's hearings from 2003 to 2004 gained a national following. The 9/11 Families attended all their hearings and in frequent media appearances echoed the Commission's demands for a full and thorough investigation. Sparring with the Commission had become a political liability for the White House, forcing it to give access (albeit limited) to the president's daily intelligence briefing (PDBs) to the Commission and arrange for an interview with President Bush. The Commission was gaining clout and its hearings in the spring of 2004—which featured a duel between Richard Clarke, a former White House staffer for Presidents Clinton and Bush, and Condoleezza Rice, the president's national security advisor, on whether President Bush had done enough to protect the country from terrorism before 9/11—dramatically increased its profile.

Tenet's deputy, John McLaughlin, now acting DCI, embarked on a mission to salvage the CIA director's role as head of the Intelligence Community from the "coming revolution" promised by 9/11 Commissioner John Lehman. "We get it," John McLaughlin announced to the press assembled at CIA Headquarters in Langley. The Senate Intelligence Committee had just released a report that debunked the CIA's analytical assessments of Iraq's WMD programs. The Senate called the CIA's analytic tradecraft weak and faulted the Intelligence Community for "groupthink." It derided the CIA for not explaining to policymakers the uncertainties in the intelligence presented. The CIA had demonstrated "serious lapses" in relying on a German intelligence source, code-named Curveball, who had falsely claimed that Saddam Hussein had mobile biological-weapons labs.[1] This criticism came on the heels of a tumultuous series of reports and hearings about the CIA's performance on 9/11. The agency's standing on the Hill was as weak as it had been in decades.

"We were being beaten like little baby seals on the beach," McLaughlin recalled.[2] Since the Congressional Joint Inquiry on 9/11 had recommended the creation of a director of national intelligence with "the full range of management, budgetary, and personnel responsibilities"[3] to govern the Intelligence Community, the idea of a DNI garnered a base of support in Congress. After the Senate Intelligence Committee WMD report, the coalition in favor of a DNI broadened to include conservative Republican SSCI member Trent Lott, who called Senator Feinstein's bill to create a DNI a "fundamental reform of the Intelligence Community."[4] An SSCI staffer remembered, "Everywhere we drilled down on the Iraq WMD intelligence we found problems. It was a staggering wake-up call to the Members."[5] The Senate Intelligence Committee WMD Report and the 9/11 Commission's "indictment" had been a one-two punch to the CIA. One reinforced the other, leading to the conclusion that the Intelligence Community was hopelessly dysfunctional.

McLaughlin had a delicate task. He needed to blunt the coming "revolution" by acknowledging that the Intelligence Community had fallen short but was well on its way to fixing the problem. He expected that the 9/11 Commission's report could call for separating the CIA from the central management of the Intelligence Community, thereby downgrading the CIA's centrality in intelligence. So McLaughlin chose to take the idea of a DNI head on. Iraq and 9/11 were not, insisted McLaughlin, reflective of a "broken system and a community in disarray" but were the result of "specific, discrete problems that we understand and we are well on our way to addressing or have already addressed."[6] The agency "could have done better," but the answer was not "additional layers of command or bureaucracy" in the form of an intelligence czar apart from the CIA. McLaughlin argued that it was better to modernize existing practices and increase the powers of the DCI to manage the community. With some "modest changes in the way the CIA is set up, the director of central intelligence could carry out that function well and appropriately."[7] The CIA was willing to concede the need for a single place "where foreign intelligence and domestic information could be put together and analyzed quickly."[8] But not wholesale structural changes.

The CIA's argument was that bureaucratic power in Washington flows from a strong institutional base. With the exception of Stansfield Turner, President Carter's DCI,[9] all of the former DCIs had strongly opposed divorcing the community-management functions from the CIA. In 1978 former

DCI George H. W. Bush testified that "the CIA director . . . should be the DNI. . . . In theory he could draw on all the community elements, but he needs CIA as his principal source of support to be most effective."[10] Bush continued, "Without the CIA as the "bulwark of support for the director,"[11] a DNI would be "kind of naked . . . just a figurehead with no real support."[12] Bob Gates, a former DCI, declared that an intelligence czar "divorced from direct control of the Central Intelligence Agency" would "be an intelligence eunuch."[13] Gates had long opposed such a change. As DCI, he had sought to "preserve decentralization of the Intelligence Community that [he] . . . believes is essential to ensure the responsiveness to the very diverse needs of the users of intelligence."[14] Judge William Webster, a former head of the CIA, testified to the Joint Inquiry, "I would strengthen the DCI. I would not have a head of the national intelligence unless that [head of] national intelligence was actually running something."[15] In 1995, as Congress debated what a post–Cold War Intelligence Community should look like, the former DCIs lined up before Congress to criticize the idea:

> If one is going to strengthen the authority of the director of central intelligence, it is not going to be achieved by dividing his assets. I think that one must think of ways to add to his bureaucratic authority if he is to be strengthened. If we are going to have a DNI and a DCI, both with overlapping and conflicting authorities, we are going to have less.[16]

The CIA view was shaped in part by its history. Former Director William Colby characterized it like this: "The very name of the Agency, Central Intelligence Agency, was designed to provide that kind of a service, not for the different departments, but for the president and the National Security Council. It was supposed to be above the other departmental intelligence centers. It wasn't a co-equal. It is a Central Intelligence Agency and not something off by itself."[17] In short, the CIA was special, seen as the "dominant agency" and charged with seeing the "broad general context" rather than succumbing to a "narrowly directed" bureaucratic focus.[18]

The CIA's view was also informed by its assessment of power relations in Washington, DC. Since the Department of Defense has the largest institutional base and a powerful constituency in Congress, any attempt to take the intelligence agencies from the Defense Department would be bound to fail.

Any attempt to vest community management outside of the CIA would run the risk of creating what one commentator described as "a czar with no

... throne, much less palace."[19] Brent Scowcroft concurred, "I have doubts whether [a DNI separate from the CIA] would be successful."[20] Echoing the ghosts of the CIA's past, McLaughlin, claiming that the CIA had authority over only 10 percent of the Intelligence Community budget, called for "modernizing the structures we already have" and creating a "true source of central intelligence" by enhancing the DCI's control over the national intelligence agencies.[21]

CHAPTER FIVE

Grand Vision

The adjective most used to describe Governor Tom Kean was "patrician." He came from an old New Jersey family and from old money, but he was the "humblest rich aristocrat you'd ever meet."[1] Kean had been a very successful governor of New Jersey, but by his own admission he was no intelligence expert. He relied on his colleagues for national security expertise, most of whom had storied Washington careers. What Kean brought to the table was a sense of strategy. He had served on a variety of previous commissions in his career and understood that the ultimate success of the 9/11 Commission was whether its recommendations were implemented. Kean concerned himself most with crafting the rollout of the Commission's ideas to maximize the prospects of enactment of their recommendations.

Recognizing that previous attempts to reform the IC had failed, Governor Kean wanted recommendations that were achievable. If they overshot their mark, it would be easy for the president and Congress to ignore the Commission's work. An absolute prerequisite was unanimity. A report with differing views on the way forward would likely be lost in the shuffle of a presidential campaign. "I worried about the recommendations; that's where I thought we would come apart."[2]

A second key element of Kean's strategy was timing. He had rejected suggestions that the Commission's recommendations be deferred until after the presidential election. He wanted the Commission's recommendations to come out *during* the 2004 presidential election campaign with the hope of producing a bidding war between the presidential candidates. A final key element was to ensure that the families of the 9/11 victims backed the Commission's recommendations. The Commission viewed them as a "moral force" and the key to public acceptance of its report. "If the 9/11

Families come out against us on this and this is simply ten commissioners saying, 'here is what we think,' it is going to be extremely difficult to get the Congress and White House to act on these recommendations."[3]

Long before the recommendations were finished, Kean, in tandem with a Washington, DC, public relations firm hired by the Commission, devised an "intimately choreographed" rollout plan.[4] It included hiring a New York publishing house who could deliver six hundred thousand copies of the report to bookstores across the country to be ready to go on sale at noon at the affordable price of ten dollars.[5] After the announcement of the report, the commissioners would fan out to Boston, Houston, Dallas, Chicago, Atlanta, Seattle, and Los Angeles to tout their new product. In fact, the Commission planned to stay in business as a private entity to lobby for the enactment of their recommendations.[6]

If the Commission could unanimously agree on its recommendations before the presidential election, sign up the Families, and announce their findings in a spectacular fashion, the Commission had a shot at remaking the Intelligence Community. There were a variety of complications surrounding the development of the Commission's recommendations. First, the Commission spent the vast majority of its time unearthing the story of 9/11. Active consideration of recommendations came late in the process as the Commission's deadline approached. There was also tension within the Commission between the ideal and what was achievable. A Commission staffer noted that most of the staff was historians and lawyers with few public policy experts schooled in "making things work."[7] The tension between academics and practitioners would color the Commission's decisions on the major structural issues before them.

Increasing Centralization in the Intelligence Community

For decades, other commissions and study groups had considered and recommended ways to centralize authority within the Intelligence Community. Most concluded that because of technological change, rapid growth in the Intelligence Community, and increasing bureaucratic complexity, the loosely confederated intelligence bureaucracies needed stronger management. Several of the commissioners had studied and accepted these judgments. Commission staff cited these conclusions favorably in a briefing for the commissioners titled, "We've Been Admiring the Problem for a Long Time."[8] The issue was less *whether* the 9/11 Commission would recommend further

centralization than it was *how much*. Would the nature of international terrorism lead the group to conclude that wholesale change was needed or
would a careful augmentation of powers within the existing structure be
enough? And would the Central Intelligence Agency, created as a central
repository for information and later vested with coordinating functions,
be given increased authority?

The Commission did not seriously consider going "whole-hog" in recommending the defense intelligence agencies be removed from the Defense
Department and placed under a new secretary of intelligence. The Commission sought to minimize the type of disruption they saw in the creation
of the Department of Homeland Security.[9] Deemed politically difficult, a
Department of Intelligence did not comport with the Commission's overriding aim that their recommendations be achievable.

But at the same time, seeking to vest more authority in the existing
DCI was unpalatable. Lee Hamilton remarked that "We're in a new world,
and we have to begin to think of ways to structure this. I have heard the
argument about strengthening the DCI for 35 years. . . . It's a move in the
right direction. But I don't think it gets us into the new era we're in."[10] At
a June 2004 Commission meeting, Jamie Gorelick called the CIA's community management functions "deeply broken, deeply dysfunctional." A
9/11 commissioner and former senator Slade Gorton said, "It is impossible
to recommend that the agency that has screwed up the most gets the most
power." Bob Kerrey, also a commissioner and a former senator, asked whether
the Commission should recommend "tearing the old thing down?"[11] Senator
Gorton remembers feeling at the time that he had lost confidence in the
CIA across the board, in "even their basic functions."[12] John Lehman had a
dim view of the Intelligence Community even before September 11, 2001.
In 2000, in a Washington Post opinion article, he recited a series of failures,
from the Yom Kippur War through the bombing of the USS *Cole*, decry-
ing "the obscene failure of intelligence."[13] Lehman's impression from the
Commission's hearings was that "we had over a thousand witnesses testify,
everyone from the president to the case officers," confirming his view "that
the IC is so dysfunctional."[14]

The CIA's approach to the Commission, contrasted with FBI Director Robert Mueller's open engagement, also influenced its recommendations. The
Commission saw Tenet's attitude as "when you people get smart enough [on
the facts leading to 9/11], you'll see we did the right things."[15] A Commission

staffer conceded that how an agency approaches an investigation could influence the Commission's ultimate recommendations.

· · · · · · · · · · · ·

With a Department of Intelligence and enhancement of the DCI's authorities off the table, Zelikow acknowledged that the idea of a DNI "was a sort of 'default' recommendation from the start because several commissioners had already come in with this idea foremost."[16] Vice Chairman Hamilton had testified before the Joint Inquiry in 2002 that, "We need a single cabinet-level official who is fully in charge of the Intelligence Community, a director of national intelligence or DNI" who "must be in frequent and candid contact with the president" and enjoy enhanced budgetary and appointments authority.[17] As a member of the Congressional Joint Inquiry into 9/11, Roemer had also previously endorsed a DNI explaining that "the current structure is not conducive to the management of the Intelligence Community as a coherent whole."[18] As the ranking member of the Senate Intelligence Committee in 1998, Senator Kerrey had lamented that "the law currently does not give the DCI the kind of management authority that the American people think the DCI has."[19] Zelikow later said he was "basically sympathetic, but this is the perennial answer."[20] "The issue was on the table; our role was to evaluate it and figure out whether to try and block it, encourage it, and/or mold it."[21]

For Commissioner Gorelick, at a minimum, the DNI was critical to solving the information-sharing problems of 9/11.[22] She also recalled that "our basic discussion was this: The DCI has had the authority to manage the community for decades and has been unable to do so in the face of opposition/control at DOD with the support of its authorizers and appropriators; thus, a new structure was needed."[23] Troubled by the "huge numbers of really first-rate people [who] were trapped in amber because of this bloated bureaucracy," Commissioner Lehman envisioned a DNI as a "terrible swift sword–wielder" to free the IC.[24] Roemer sought in a DNI a strategic thinker who could "articulate a vision for the Intelligence Community ten to fifteen years from now" and adjust spending priorities accordingly.[25] Roemer and Zelikow were especially moved by what they saw as the failures of the DCI. The irrelevance of Tenet's top secret "declaration of war" memo demonstrated the "limitations of the DCI's authority over the direction and priorities of the Intelligence Community."[26] Zelikow called the episode the most important reason for a DNI.[27] The question: where to put it?

The Commission understood that proximity matters. Commissioner Lehman proposed making the DNI a "top official in the Executive Office of the President."[28] A DNI near the center of executive power would ensure its effectiveness. "The intelligence management would be an enlarged and powerful White House staff operation, managing a committee system to set priorities and—empowered to receive the national intelligence appropriation—able to allocate resources across all the divides."[29]

Vice Chairman Hamilton strongly endorsed placing the DNI in the White House to ensure its bureaucratic gravitas.[30] He later explained, "If you've got him stuck out here somewhere in center field, he's not going to have the authority. He has to have the authority that comes with the presidency of the United States."[31] In later congressional testimony, Zelikow cited the need for proximity to the president and the "centrality of counterterrorism in contemporary national security management."[32] He considered the perils of a weak institutional base for the new DNI. Creating a new office, separate from the CIA and the White House, risked its becoming "a bureaucratic fifth wheel that would make the present situation even worse."[33]

The Commission proposed another feature to augment the DNI's managerial authority. Rather than transferring the defense intelligence agencies to the DNI, the newly created USDI at Defense would report to the DNI and the secretary of defense. The Commission relied on this mechanism (sometimes called dual-hatting because the intelligence official would report to two bosses) as a mechanism to strengthen the DNI's management authorities over intelligence agencies in other cabinet departments short of uprooting them. The CIA director would be the DNI's deputy for foreign intelligence. Either the FBI or the Department of Homeland Security intelligence head would also serve as deputy DNI for domestic intelligence.[34]

What Would the Commission's DNI do?
A Goldwater-Nichols for Intelligence

Vice Chairman Hamilton recalled a "feeling on the Commission that we had to break new ground and recommend a new structure rather than just readjusting. Something had to break the mold."[35] They sensed that the United States was in an epochal transition. To meet the moment, the Commission embraced a philosophy of Intelligence Community management based on the successful integration of the Armed Forces under the Goldwater Nichols Act of 1986.

The World War II generation had restructured the government to fight the Soviet Union. In a similar vein, the Commission sounded the call to combat a nearly invisible adversary that could effortlessly penetrate the nation's borders. "We needed to fight a network with a network," the Commission declared. This new world demanded joint action. "National intelligence is still organized around the collection disciplines of the home agencies, not organized around the joint mission." The 9/11 case had demonstrated the hazards of a system in which agencies did not work effectively together. To succeed against a new enemy, "seamless integration"[36] was critical. Mere cooperation was not enough; the new Intelligence Community had to overcome structural barriers which impeded "joint action."[37] Since "no one component holds all the relevant information,"[38] the balkanized U.S. Intelligence Community needed someone to break down stovepipes and "catalyze transformation in the Intelligence Community and . . . manage a transformed community afterward."[39] Corporate America provided a blueprint: the DNI should manage the entities of the Intelligence Community like General Electric had managed its vast empire of disparate companies.[40]

The Commission sought to transform highly specialized intelligence offices into more of a joint force, paralleling the Defense Department's transformation under the landmark Goldwater-Nichols Act. Since its creation in 1947, the Defense Department had been plagued by management problems. The secretaries of the Army, Navy, and Air Force and the commandant of the Marine Corps controlled their own troops and equipment. The ability of the secretary of defense to coordinate was weak. Despite mechanisms and efforts to force the services to work together, some suboptimal military performances—from the failed hostage-rescue attempt in Iran to the invasion of Grenada—were blamed on disunity stemming from an unclear chain of command and a weak secretary.

Goldwater-Nichols unified the Army, Navy, Air Force, and Marines in battle under a combatant commander who reported to a newly empowered secretary of defense. The service secretaries were the bureaucratic losers in the Goldwater-Nichols reforms. They were removed from the chain of command and their roles redefined as training and equipping their forces. To foster a new sense of jointness among the services, Goldwater-Nichols required officers to serve tours outside of their own services to qualify for promotion.

Goldwater-Nichols revolutionized the armed forces, and intelligence reformers took notice, adopting the slogan "We need a Goldwater-Nichols for intelligence." To foster a "collective mind-set"[41] among intelligence officers, the Commission recommended tours in different intelligence agencies before career promotion. The Commission saw the intelligence agencies as analogous to the military services and suggested they focus on training and equipping, in the case of the CIA, human intelligence officers. "The collection agency should have the same mission as the armed services do. They should organize, train, and equip their personnel." [42]

The Commission also saw an Intelligence Community parallel to the combatant commands created under Goldwater-Nichols.[43] The DNI would have authority to create centers of intelligence, drawing upon the intelligence professionals trained by the intelligence agencies.[44] For example, if a serious issue with China arose, the DNI would have the authority to pull together the China specialists from across the Intelligence Community—from CIA, DIA, and NSA—to array against an emergent threat. The Commission envisioned the centers as loci of cross-agency integration. Hamilton said, "A joint mission center on WMD and proliferation, for example, would bring together the imagery, signals, and HUMINT specialists, both collectors and analysts, who would together jointly on behalf of the mission."[45] The creation of centers would also, the Commission argued, give the DNI troops.[46]

• • • • • • • • • • •

To implement this transformative vision, the Commission recommended a DNI with powers—some old, some borrowed, and some new. The authorities which had been given to the DCI in current law would be transferred to the new DNI, including the titles of "head of the Intelligence Community" and "principal intelligence advisor to the president," and the key responsibility to protect intelligence sources and methods from unauthorized disclosure. The Commission's DNI would also retain rights to participate in the development of the Defense Department's tactical intelligence budget and to task intelligence collection assets such as satellites. Other new features for the 9/11 Commission's DNI were borrowed from previous commissions and study groups. Among these were augmentations of existing law pertaining to budgetary authority, flexibility to redirect spending to more urgent needs,[47] and powers to hire and fire.[48]

The Commission principally relied on enhanced budget powers as the cornerstone of the DNI's authority since "in intelligence, as elsewhere, money talks."[49] The Commission would recommend that the DNI possess authority to develop the budget submissions for the defense intelligence agencies and new flexibility to transfer money already appropriated by Congress.[50]

But the chief budgetary power recommended by the Commission was that the DNI would receive the appropriation directly from Congress.[51] This differed from current law, in which Congress appropriated the money to the Department of Defense for its disposition to the intelligence agencies, including the CIA. The Commission's recommendation to give the appropriation directly to the DNI acknowledged a bureaucratic fact of life: intelligence agencies listen to whomever writes the checks. But a direct money flow from Congress to the DNI required changing policies governing disclosure to the public of how much the United States spends on intelligence. For most of the previous fifty years, Congress had appropriated money to the CIA mixed in with the Defense Department's regular budget. The dollars for intelligence were "buried" in the Defense budget as a shield to prevent the nation's adversaries from being able to make judgments about U.S. intelligence capability based upon annual expenditures. But if the aggregate sum for intelligence were declassified, the money could be sent directly to the DNI instead of to the secretary of defense, thereby improving the responsiveness of intelligence agencies to DNI directives. Although the Commission cited combating "secrecy and complexity"[52] as its rationale for declassification of the top-line intelligence figure, another benefit was enabling a single direct budget appropriation to the DNI.

The Commission's second key goal was to have enhanced DNI influence in the selection of heads of intelligence agencies. As Commissioner Lehman said of Washington, "My experience in this town has been, there are only two things that matter in doing management and oversight.... You've got to have the ability to hire and fire the top people if they don't perform and pick the ones that do perform and promote the ones who do reform."[53] The Commission recommended greater "appointments" authority by giving the DNI formal duties to recommend and submit nominations to the president for the CIA and the defense intelligence agencies.[54]

In addition, the Commission agreed with the conclusions reached by several of its predecessors[55] that the head of the Intelligence Community should have greater authority to transfer personnel from their home agency to an intelligence center if required by a national security exigency.[56]

Another major recommendation was the creation of a National Counterterrorism Center, "strongly advocated by Zelikow."[57] The Commission thought that President Bush's Terrorist Threat Integration Center (TTIC) was the "right concept" but was in need of strengthening.[58] The NCTC was designed to foster counterterrorism intelligence sharing, citing the failure of the FBI to share information on Moussaoui with the director of the FBI or compare with other intelligence information collected by the CIA.[59] The NCTC would assume the duties invested in TTIC as the federal government's fusion center. But, in another borrowed idea from the military, it would assume a second role in planning the government's response to terrorist threats. Zelikow "cribbed directly from the joint staff manual" to ensure that the NCTC's planning mission would mirror that of the Joint Chiefs of Staff.[60] Zelikow called the Commission's vision for an NCTC "entrepreneurial."[61] The NCTC would not just be an intelligence entity; it would actually plan operations.[62] The Commission relied on details of the 9/11 plot as justification to invest operational planning authorities in the NCTC director. The Kuala Lumpur episode, discussed previously, Zelikow later explained, was a powerful "emblem" of the need for centralized planning in complex intelligence cases. If the NSA were to discover that a suspected terrorist was traveling to Bangkok and Kuala Lumpur, the Commission envisioned the NCTC would be akin to an attending physician at a hospital managing a team of specialists from across the IC to include assigning tasks to the CIA and asking the Special Operations Command to draw up plans for operations.[63]

This "typically complex" case required centralized management because it involved numerous foreign locations.[64] As a 9/11 Commission staffer put it, "The NCTC in Zelikow's mind was a stealth MI-5. MI-5 is a global counterterrorism service. It is highly tactical."[65]

What It Meant for the CIA

The 9/11 Commission's recommendations demoted the CIA. The separation of the Intelligence Community management functions from the CIA would in effect strip the agency of its status as the centerpiece of U.S. intelligence. The Commission cited two additional reasons for vesting cross-agency authority in a DNI separated from the troops in the CIA. First, 9/11 had driven home that terrorists ignored national borders and operated within the United States. To be effective against this new threat, the DNI would need to oversee intelligence collection within the United States. Given the CIA's history of "domestic spying" and other abuses aired in the 1960s and 1970s, the DNI should not also be head of the CIA, which by "law and custom" did not conduct activities within the United States. Second, like many of its predecessors, the 9/11 Commission contended that since the CIA was one of the "claimants" for funds, it was better for the DNI to be separate and avoid being both an advocate and a judge.[66] Finally, the DCI was overburdened. "No person can perform all three responsibilities [of]: running the CIA; running the Intelligence Community; and serving as the president's chief intelligence adviser."

Under the Commission's construct, the CIA director would no longer manage the Intelligence Community. Its analysts would be subject to transfer to intelligence centers by a DNI. And it would give up the coveted title of principal intelligence advisor to the president; its director would be a mere deputy to a new DNI. The agency's special authorities for covert actions, at least as they pertained to counterterrorism, were also in jeopardy. Since covert action was "highly tactical" and required "close attention," a DNI should rely on the relevant "joint mission center" to "oversee the details."[67] The CIA should "concentrate on building the capabilities to carry out such operations and on providing the personnel who will be directing and executing such operations in the field."[68] The Commission was proposing a substantially lesser role for the CIA in its most sensitive function, covert action. Suggesting that the CIA focus on training and equipping the personnel for covert action was reminiscent of the demotion the secretaries of the Army and Navy had received in Goldwater-Nichols, which removed them from the chain of command and defined their new roles as training and equipping. It seemed to imply that the CIA, which had enjoyed a direct relationship with the White House on covert action, would have at least two new intervening players in the mix, a DNI and a "joint mission center." Finally, the Commission recommended transferring the paramilitary branch of the CIA to the Department of Defense. While the agency would still execute covert action, it seemed its authority would be newly confined to "the field" while overall management of the mission would reside with the DNI. The Commission would have the CIA redouble its focus on its core missions. "Rebuilding the analytic and human intelligence collection capabilities of the CIA should be a full time effort" for the CIA director.[69]

Domestic Intelligence

As the CIA and the Commission battled over the 9/11 narrative, FBI director Robert Mueller took a different approach. Pointing to the FBI's history as a law-enforcement agency, some in Congress and some commentators favored a domestic intelligence service modeled on the United Kingdom's storied MI-5. The FBI's was a gun-and-arrest culture ill-suited for intelligence work. With the idea of a domestic intelligence service separate from the FBI being debated, Mueller pursued the Commission to head the idea off at the pass. Mueller struck a cooperative pose with the Commission. His attitude was, "obviously something went really wrong on 9/11 and I'm here to fix it with you."[70] Of course, the timing of his ascension to the FBI directorship facilitated this more cooperative approach; having come into the job the week before 9/11, Mueller was able to approach the Commission with a clean slate. Unlike Tenet, who had been at the job for four years on 9/11, Mueller did not have to defend the FBI's performance. He made enormous amounts of his time available to the commissioners and staff, forthrightly acknowledged the FBI's shortcoming, and pledged to remake the FBI into an intelligence service from within.[71] A Commission staffer saw Mueller as changing the bureau "in real time" through his interactions with the Commission.[72] Jamie Gorelick remembered that all this had a profound effect on the commissioners and stated, "George never did this, I don't know why."[73] Mueller fostered goodwill with the Commission through his personal involvement and cooperation with their investigation while Tenet made his case in public hearings.

The FBI benefited from an argument that they had not so much failed *on* 9/11 because domestic intelligence was not really part of their mission until *after* 9/11. While the CIA had been firmly in the foreign intelligence business for decades, the FBI was perceived as a law-enforcement agency. After 9/11 Mueller consolidated the bureau's intelligence functions in a Directorate of Intelligence and announced a series of measures to create an intelligence service within the FBI. Mueller also created field intelligence groups composed of intelligence analysts, linguists, and surveillance specialists. These initiatives supported an argument that the FBI should be given a chance to succeed in a new mission area while the CIA was forced to explain why it had failed at something that had been core to its purpose.

In any event, a new intelligence service that would operate inside the

United States was a tough sell. Ultimately, John Lehman was its only real advocate. Senator Gorton remembers that most commissioners decided that a domestic intelligence service was inapt for the United States after hearing from the United Kingdom's MI-5 chief that her job was made easier because she had only a small number of local police constabularies requiring coordination. Jamie Gorelick and Tim Roemer questioned whether a new domestic intelligence service could in practice "comport with the Bill of Rights."[74] The commissioners also found persuasive Director Mueller's argument that the connection between the FBI and the local police forces warranted vesting an intelligence mission in the FBI because they were best suited to take advantage of their "eyes and ears."

The Commission endorsed Mueller's reform plans and gave him a chance to make an "all-out effort to institutionalize change."[75] Mueller's long hours with the Commission paid off. Zelikow summarized that the Commission report "basically said we're betting on Bob Mueller."[76]

CHAPTER SIX

"The Fix Was In"

Initial Consideration in Congress and the White House

The night before the release of the 9/11 Commission's recommendations on July 22, 2004, Fran Townsend escaped to her car. A close advisor to the president, Townsend had been a mob prosecutor in New York under Rudy Giuliani; drawings of her in action in the courtroom, the kind rendered for use on the local news, adorned the walls of her low-ceilinged basement office in the West Wing. Townsend was a sharp dresser, frequently decorated in stunning diamonds. Previously advising former attorney general Janet Reno, in a testament to her survival skills, she had made it from head of Coast Guard Intelligence to a Republican White House. There, she rose quickly. The president appreciated her efficient, no-nonsense style. As the president's homeland security advisor, she managed the Homeland Security Council, a White House office modeled after the National Security Council, with staff managing coordination of border, aviation, and bio-defense issues as well as other hot post-9/11 topics.

As the car rolled down West Executive Avenue that night to exit the White House gates, Townsend's cell phone rang. It was her office: the White House had finally gotten an advance copy of the 9/11 Commission's report. Much of it had been reviewed for declassification purposes, but not the final two chapters containing its recommendations. The 9/11 Commission's chairman and vice chairman were coming to the White House the next morning to present the president a leather-bound version of the report, but someone needed to tell the president and the senior staff what it said. Almost to the gate, Townsend's car U-turned and headed back up the drive to read the Commission's report and begin preparing the White House's response.

· · · · · · · · · · ·

At the other end of Pennsylvania Avenue in the Capitol, the House Republican leadership was also preparing for a late night. On the steps of the east front of the House of Representatives, John Russell, assistant to the Speaker's chief of staff, paced across the long marble slabs. Like a riverbed, the stairs sloped in the middle, worn by decades of foot traffic. Russell lit a cigarette; the flame jerked his face out of the shadows. He was waiting for Philip Zelikow, the executive director of the Commission. The House Republicans had a poor relationship with the Commission, piqued by what it considered a strategy to put the president in a bad light by leaking the details of their negotiations over access to presidential documents. Speaker Hastert had opposed extending the Commission's deadline and had complained that the Commission's strategy to send the report to a publisher meant that "the publisher gets to see the report before the Congress." A Commission aide noted that their plans to use a private publisher had been featured in a recent *New York Times* article. "We don't read the fucking *New York Times*," the Speaker's office thundered.[1] Tom Kean later called his inability to work with the Republicans in the House his greatest failing as chairman of the Commission.[2] But tonight, to appease the Speaker, the Commission promised to deliver an advance copy of the report. Once Zelikow arrived and made the handoff, Russell rushed back into the Capitol, across Statuary Hall, and into the Speaker's office where the Speaker's chief of staff and national security aides stood by. Zelikow had only delivered one copy of the report. The group tore the book into fourths so they could all simultaneously begin reading it, swapping sections as they read.

• • • • • • • • • • •

In the weeks before the report's release, staff for Senators Susan Collins and Joe Lieberman had been petitioning the Senate leadership. They ran the Senate Homeland Security and Governmental Affairs Committee (SHSGAC). The committee oversaw the postal service and governmental procurement practices. However, their jurisdiction included the reorganization of executive branch departments and agencies. This feature had been used to great effect in 2002 when they sponsored legislation that created the Department of Homeland Security, combining agencies from across the federal government into a new terrorism-fighting department. Foreseeing that the 9/11 Commission was likely to recommend some restructuring of the Intelligence Community, Collins and Lieberman hoped to have some role in the coming legislative action, although displacing the mighty Appropriations, Armed Services, and Intelligence Committees seemed far-fetched.

• • • • • • • • • • •

At 9 a.m. on July 22, 2004, Kean and Hamilton showed up at the White House to deliver their report to the president. But a few blocks away, perhaps the most important meeting of the day, between Roemer and the 9/11 Families, would soon begin. Although Roemer was their closest ally, the relationship had been occasionally tense. The Families had often reproached members of the Commission at their hearings for being too easy on the witnesses. Interested in accountability, the Families had pressed the 9/11 Commission to name names and, in some cases, to recommend firings. The 9/11 Commission had decided against such an approach, and Roemer worried that the Families would reject the Commission's work on those grounds.

Roemer stood before a group of several dozen family members in an anteroom adjoining Washington's Mellon Auditorium. The staff handed out copies of the report to the Families. Roemer detailed the Commission's findings and recommendations. "We told them how difficult the process had been, I remember telling them this is as far as we could push it, we were pushing for vast and comprehensive reorganization, brand-new ideas for our government, that everybody was going to be held accountable from presidents to Congress, and especially Congress to make reforms that we need to make to executive agencies, we are looking at every branch of government."[3]

The Families began to ask questions. Roemer thought it was touch-and-go. He was uncertain whether he had convinced them that the Commission had been "tough enough, accountable enough, comprehensive enough, and reform-oriented enough."[4] The briefing ended and as Roemer stood, the Families still did not exhibit an observable reaction. Finally, one family member approached and asked him to sign his copy of the report. The others joined. The Commission had brought the Families aboard.

Minutes later, at 11:30 a.m., the commissioners assembled in the Mellon Auditorium. Tom Kean and Lee Hamilton stood before the assembled press and Families. The networks broke into regular daytime programming to cover the event live.[5] ABC's reporters read from the 9/11 Report and remarked on its unanimous findings.[6] The auditorium's fourteen gold-leafed columns soared toward a gilded ceiling sixty-five feet above. The grand venue had been selected for its historic pedigree. In 1949 President Truman had stood here to witness his secretary of state and eleven foreign ministers sign the North Atlantic Treaty creating NATO. NATO's founding marked the beginning of the Cold War era; the 9/11 Commission was marking a new age of asymmetrical threats. Just as the United States had relied on NATO to bolster its post–World War II security, the 9/11 Commission offered new measures to safeguard peace and prosperity.

The 9/11 Commission's message was designed to be broadly understood. The effort against international terrorism lacked discipline. John Lehman cited a "deep fundamental dysfunction" in the intelligence system.[7] Gorelick commented that there were no incentives for agencies to work together; there was no one in charge. The country needed a quarterback.[8] Hamilton stated,

> A critical theme that emerged throughout our inquiry was the difficulty of answering the question, Who is in charge? Who ensures that agencies pool resources, avoid duplication, and plan jointly? Who oversees the massive integration and unity of effort necessary to keep America safe? Too often the answer is no one.[9]

Just as the setting was designed to evoke an epochal transition, the Commission's message was intended to provoke congressional and executive action. Their recommendations were "urgent." "We don't have time to waste with another attack looming," warned Roemer.[10] They raised the specter of the election to prod the politicians. Commissioner Jim Thompson added that the recommendations "need to be enacted speedily, because if something bad happens while these recommendations are sitting there, the American people will quickly fix political responsibility for failure and that responsibility may last for generations, and they will be entitled to that."[11]

The commissioners briefed the Democratic nominees for president and vice president by phone. Appearing with Kean, Hamilton, and Senator Lieberman, Senator John McCain declared, "The sooner we act on this Commission's recommendations, the better off we're going to be."[12] Warning that "the lives of the American people are on the line," Senator Lieberman called for a special session of Congress to enact the Commission's recommendations.[13] He also declared he was "accepting the torch from the 9/11 Commission, from Tom Kean and Lee Hamilton. And we pledge to carry it forward until the work is done."[14] Congresswoman Nancy Pelosi, the Democratic leader in the House, urged swift action. Jane Harman picked up on the theme: "We're at a heightened threat level, there may be attacks sometime during this political season."[15] Roemer joined in. "We have the perfect storm. The eyes of history are on our backs, the claws of al Qa'ida are on our shoulders, the grief of 911 is still in our hearts. That will compel Congress to act."[16]

Release of the recommendations galvanized the 9/11 Families. One commissioner said that the Families had "lectured us to be aggressive, they wanted scalps, and we weren't giving them scalps, we weren't saying someone should go to jail, and so-and-so should be fined. They were mad about that," but then they pivoted from that to "let's take this and make it happen."[17]

. . . .

On the day of their announcement, the Commission received another boost: Senator John Kerry, the presumptive Democratic nominee for president, unreservedly endorsed their recommendations.[18] While Senator Kerry had previously expressed support for a DNI,[19] a blanket endorsement of the 9/11 Commission's recommendations could be good presidential politics. President Bush's rationale for reelection was that he had kept the country safer after 9/11. Republicans traditionally enjoyed an advantage on national security issues over the Democrats. If Kerry quickly seized the popular Commission's recommendations, he might put Bush on the defensive unless the president, too, endorsed them.

A few days later, the Kerry campaign pulled together an event to capitalize on the 9/11 Commission Report.

> Now that the 9/11 Commission has done its job, we need to do our job. We understand the threat. We have a blueprint for action. We have the strength as a nation to do what has to be done. The only thing we don't have is time. We need to do it now.... Because this threat won't go away and the recommendations of the Commission make sense and they should be implemented now.[20]

Kerry promised an "emergency security summit" if he was elected president and the recommendations had not been implemented.[21]

The 9/11 Commission had calculated correctly. Instead of the recommendations getting lost in the shuffle of an intense presidential campaign, their report now became an issue. The argument had been framed. Senator Kerry and the 9/11 Families' quick endorsement of the Commission's recommendations helped fuel a media frenzy about the report. And if

Bush didn't support the Commission, Kerry was determined to use it to bludgeon the president.

• • • • • • • • • • • •

Back in the Capitol, Senate Majority Leader Bill Frist saw that there would be a political imperative to legislate the recommendations. Frist and the Republicans had carefully sketched out a legislative plan for the fall before the elections, but now the ground had shifted. To neutralize the potential that the 9/11 Commission recommendations would be used against Republicans, Frist sought to ensure that the recommendations would be treated in a bipartisan manner and by a committee that was seen as impartial. Senators Collins and Lieberman had a history of working effectively together. Vesting responsibility for considering the recommendations in their committee was politically shrewd. Lieberman had helped push the legislation creating the Commission through the Senate. They would be seen as sympathetic to the 9/11 Families and the Commission, thereby immunizing the Senate from charges that it had buried the recommendations. Collins and Lieberman could "meet the moment."[22] And the leadership could stay focused on its game plan in the months before the 2004 election without letting Senator Kerry drive the message.

While politically ingenious, assigning a reorganization of the Intelligence Community to a committee without intelligence expertise was a rather extraordinary step. The Senate's experts were the Intelligence and Armed Services Committees. The Senate Homeland Security and Governmental Affairs Committee had now vaulted ahead of two powerful national security committees. Many in the Senate and the House leadership were aghast. Frist's decision was mocked: "national security novices" whose legislative portfolio included overseeing the postal service, were suddenly in the lead. The Senate cast aside its usually sacrosanct August recess and announced a series of hearings, to begin the morning after Senator Kerry's acceptance speech at the Democratic National Convention.

Not to be outdone, the Democratic leader in the House, Nancy Pelosi, called for Congress to return to Washington to begin acting on the legislation. The *New York Times* reported that "[The Democrats] are also hoping the issue will help them recapture a majority in the House in November."[23] The House Republican leadership was less enthusiastic: "I will ask our committee chairmen to hold hearings on these recommendations over the next several months so that we can act on them as quickly as possible." He cautioned that the Republicans were "going to be deliberate and not rushed. We're going to make sure that it really solves the problems."[24]

• • • • • • • • • • •

As the Democrats called for abandoning the congressional recess to return to Washington to enact the 9/11 recommendations, President Bush departed for his ranch in Crawford, Texas, for what was traditionally a period of downtime during the rival party's convention. While the Democrats convened to formally nominate Senator John Kerry for president, President Bush's chief of staff, Andy Card, assembled the president's White House advisors for a Saturday meeting on the 9/11 Commission's intelligence recommendations. The president's advisors had been on television over the previous days welcoming the 9/11 Report. The president's communications director, Dan Bartlett, characterized the president's attitude: "I think the best way is to say it's not a matter of if, it's just a matter of when and how."[25]

At the White House that Saturday was Vice President Cheney; Condoleezza Rice; Steve Hadley, Rice's Deputy; Fran Townsend, the president's Homeland Security advisor; and Dan Bartlett. Given the momentum building for action on the Commission's recommendations, the White House would need a substantive response by the time the spotlight shifted from the Democrats' nominating convention. A senior advisor to President Bush remembered that Kerry's quick endorsement was seen as crassly political. "I can tell you that Kerry's quick endorsement moved no one, it was subject to derision among the president's staff; he could not possibly have read it."[26] Another quipped, Kerry "either knew what was coming out ahead of time or it didn't make any difference."[27]

Vice President Cheney warned against jumping on the bandwagon. "We can't go on Congress's schedule; we can't fall to pressure and do the wrong thing."[28] In the months prior to the release of their report, the White House had worked to portray the president as open-minded to the Commission's ideas. In truth, the White House was pleasantly surprised by the report. The Commission had not adopted Richard Clarke's views on blame for 9/11, instead citing a "failure of imagination" and listing missed opportunities for killing Usama bin Ladin, many that spanned the years prior to Bush's taking office. The White House saw the vast majority of the Commission's recommendations as an endorsement of items on President's Bush agenda, even when it came to intelligence. Two of the recommendations—to create a national intelligence director and a national counterterrorism center—were new, but otherwise Andy Card directed publicizing that President Bush endorsed the vast majority of the recommendations off the bat.

On Monday morning, the president's national security team assembled in the White House Situation Room in the basement of the White House. Called the Sit Room, it is the nerve center of the national security aspect of the modern presidency. The staff congregated around a conference table and looked toward a television screen connected to the president's communications trailer at his ranch in Crawford. This customized pod, stationed near the ranch house, was the president's link back to the White House, a secure two-way connection to allow classified discussions and briefings. President Bush appeared on the screen and called the meeting to order; he gave guidance to his national security team: "We should be open to the Commission's recommendations. We're for reform. If there is a better way for the intelligence system to work, we should do it." Before departing, the president directed the group to produce recommendations by the end of the week.[29]

Vice President Cheney urged caution: just because it is called reform does not mean it will be useful. Andy Card remembered that the vice president was "unshackled because he did not care about the politics."[30] Secretary Rumsfeld was opposed to the recommendation for a DNI and an NCTC but saw the uproar caused by the reaction to the 9/11 Commission report as a tremendous chance to remake the whole U.S. government. Soon after the Commission released its report, Rumsfeld dashed off a quick memo to the president, stating, "This is an opportunity. We should seize it."[31] He urged the creation of a small working group to consider modernizing the U.S. Information Agency, securing money to fund Pakistani schools to compete with Islamic madrassas, reshaping and motivating the federal government's stultified bureaucracies, and remaking the committee system in Congress. John McLaughlin urged restraint. The country was still at war. The 9/11 Commission had failed to consider the changes implemented since September 11.

Andy Card ended the meeting by directing that the National Security Council staff begin drawing up executive orders to implement the 9/11 Commission recommendations in so far as possible without congressional action. This would appease the popular demand for immediate action on the 9/11 Commission recommendations. Some in the White House thought that maximization of the DCI's authority via executive action might forestall the need to legislate solutions in Congress. Andy Card indicated the president would need to be able to speak to the recommendations by Monday, August 2.

The president's three closest White House aides on national security matters favored the Commission's recommendations. Condoleezza Rice was open to the idea of a DNI because, during her time in the Pentagon, she had seen the success of Goldwater-Nichols: "I was favorable to the better unification of the intelligence mission through an intelligence advisor to the president, a singular person, like a DNI, paralleling the chairman of the Joint Chiefs."[32] Steve Hadley had served on a CIA advisory board in the 1990s and developed the view that the "Intelligence Community is not working as a single enterprise" and that the DCI's roles should be severed from the management of the CIA.[33] Townsend shared this view and had previously urged the president to embrace reform because 9/11 exposed problems that "needed someone's full-time attention." Since running the CIA was a full-time job, better to create a DNI whose job it was to worry about blending the different mind-sets into a common approach.[34]

President Bush recalled that the "intelligence failure was on my mind at this point, [but] I was open-minded and my style was to listen to opposing views."[35] The president named his chief of staff to head an internal working group to consider the recommendations. Its first order of business was to produce a document outlining the substantial commonality between the Commission's recommendations and administration policy. But the attention was on the Commission's recommendation to redesign the Intelligence Community. At a press briefing, the White House chief of staff admitted, "We are making good progress and expect to have recommendations to the president soon. I'm sort of staggered at how quick people are to endorse wholesale the Commission report without some considered reflection on it."[36]

• • • • • • • • • • •

The Commission's report had staying power. In the coming weeks, the country's leading papers would editorialize in favor of the recommendations by a margin of 6 to 1.[37] It rose on the best-sellers list. The *New Republic* called it "novelistically intense." John Updike raved that the King James Bible was the English language's "lone masterpiece produced by committee, at least until this year's 9/11 Commission Report."[38] Its tone was "evenhanded and nonpartisan" and described the "bland evil of the plotters, the Hamlet-like indecision of government officials, the bravery amid chaos of the firefighters."[39] The publisher printed another half million within a week of the report's release, and millions more were downloaded from the web.[40] It had symbolic power. John Kerry kept it within reach during media interviews.[41] Vice President Cheney quoted it extensively on campaign events,[42] and he gave reporters an update on how far he had read.[43] The White House announced that Condoleezza Rice was flying to the president's ranch "to work on the recommendations."[44] It had become a campaign issue. Kerry used his acceptance speech in Boston on July 29 to embrace the Commission's recommendations: "The 9/11 Commission has given us a path to follow. . . . As president, I will not evade or equivocate; I will immediately implement all the recommendations of that Commission." The 9/11 Commission was upping its rhetoric in appearances before Congress. Governor Kean told the Senate, "The present system is unacceptable and doesn't work. Just that simple: does not work."[45]

As members of Congress and the media got on the Commission bandwagon, Secretary Rumsfeld was worried: "I got the feeling that [their attitude was] just don't stand there—do something. We are in the middle of a war that is complicated and different and we're rearranging the deck chairs of the Titanic. And when those amateur brain surgeons took over in the Senate I got even more worried."[46] In addition to written notes to the president, Secretary Rumsfeld was eager to make his case directly. Card reassured him he would have his chance. "'I am not preventing you from telling the president what you think' . . . I remember literally having that conversation with him."[47]

Townsend remembers the president's attitude toward the recommendations: "Given the timing of it, all that's going on, we're going to end up doing it. . . . I would say he was open to it; I would not describe him as enthusiastic."[48] Rice recalls, "The president was just attracted and said to himself we've just had these massive intelligence failures, how could we not make these kinds of changes."[49] Recognizing the congressional enthusiasm, Card argued to the president that, "if we don't lead, they'll do it to us."[50] "I was not in the 'thank you very much for your recommendations 9/11 Commission but we think we know better' . . . school."[51]

Three distinct camps emerged. The first camp consisted of the president's White House advisors who favored the 9/11 Commission's formulation for a strong DNI with budget and appointment authority to manage the Intelligence Community, including Rice, Hadley, and Townsend.

John McLaughlin now argued that the 9/11 Commission's goals could be best achieved through vesting increased authority in the DCI, who retained the day-to-day management of the CIA.[52] He contended that the Commission's suppositions were flawed. While existing law did not give the DCI enough authority to manage the Intelligence Community, the DCI was not as weak as posited by the Commission. McLaughlin believed that "George [Tenet] had a lot of authority based upon seven years of being in the job and building personal relationships with everyone in the community." In fact, McLaughlin argued for moving the national-defense intelligence agencies under the authority of the DCI. This might be an opportunity to give the Intelligence Community a firmer foundation by removing the intelligence functions from the Defense Department. In one of the secure video sessions with the president from Crawford, McLaughlin remembers, he pressed the president on whether he wanted a mere coordinator or a "real director" as the head of the Intelligence Community, something that would only be possible by "empower[ing] the DCI."[53]

Vice President Cheney and Secretary Rumsfeld opposed a DNI and an NCTC on the grounds that it would adversely affect the ability of the secretary of defense to manage the Defense Department. Vice President Cheney, at the conclusion of one of the SVTCs with the president in Crawford, recommended against endorsing a DNI. For Rumsfeld, it was plain that the Defense Department was "the biggest user and biggest supplier" of intelligence.[54] Vesting a new Intelligence Community head with increased powers relative to the secretary of defense meant that the Defense Department would have less control over its own intelligence assets. This weaker hand would compromise the secretary's authority, potentially undermining his ability to ensure intelligence assets were available to the troops relying on those assets in combat.

Card assessed that the CIA's concept was a loser. "Their position was not tenable because Congress was not going to allow it to be tenable."[55] Given the hostility toward the CIA, a solution guaranteeing more authority for the DCI was a nonstarter. Moreover, moving the combat support agencies out of the Defense Department was also unlikely, given the constituencies for the Defense Department (particularly in Congress) and, especially, ongoing wars in Iraq and Afghanistan. McLaughlin would say later to colleagues that "I felt like a patient on a hospital operating table staring up at a bunch of people who'd never been to medical school."[56]

McLaughlin's "dominant memory" of this period was of a White House meeting on intelligence reform in which he argued against a DNI on the grounds that it would be another layer of bureaucracy: "People were just smiling at me, it was as if the fix were in, I can remember Fran Townsend sitting across the table from me, I was going through my argument one day and she was looking at Condi and smiling and I had the feeling, 'Why am I here? Why am I even trying?'"[57]

Vice President Cheney and Secretary Rumsfeld appealed directly to the president. A Defense Department intelligence official recalled Secretary Rumsfeld's bureaucratic methods: "Rumsfeld's style was to only engage once everyone's cards were on the table, and was generally quiet during meetings. Later he would pull someone aside, maybe Condoleezza Rice or the vice president, and give his view."[58]

Of course, although many of the president's key advisors supported the creation of a DNI, an undeniable new political imperative reigned. Rice notes,

> After the 9/11 Commission comes in, the opponents of a DNI are severely weakened because the 9/11 Commission carries a weight nationally and bureaucratically and to say we are going to reject the recommendation of how to get better intelligence agencies performance after two of the highest mess-ups in modern American intelligence history: you had 9/11 ...and the intelligence failure on Iraq. By now, you had to go with DNI. I was favorably disposed, anyway.[59]

President Bush recalled that "Rumsfeld was against it, but you've got to understand why, because he thought it was going to undermine the intelligence capabilities within the Department of Defense."[60]

Aboard Air Force One on a campaign swing through Ohio, West Virginia, and Pennsylvania, Andy Card reviewed the bidding with the president. Card remembers the president was favorably disposed to the idea and that their discussion was mostly about "personalities and bureaucracies" and wondering who would be the right person for the job.[61]

• • • • • • • • • • •

Monday morning, August 2, was the president's first day back in the West Wing in ten days. The Democrats had formally nominated Senator Kerry, who was hitting the campaign trail looking for post-convention momentum. The president would soon be leaving to campaign. Things were a little chaotic. Townsend and Rice reported to the Oval Office to brief the president on the NSC meetings regarding the Commission's recommendations. Townsend remembers the president was very much engaged on the questions

McLaughlin was worried about—Bush wanted to know the likely impact of reform; he did not want anything that would hurt the war effort in Iraq and Afghanistan and did not want to distract the CIA from its mission.

> He wanted to be sure whatever we did, did not harm the ongoing effort to rebuild after the peace dividend; if you think you can restructure in a way that helps them, okay, but first do no harm.[62]

Townsend noted the Defense Department's objections; the president was to speak to Rumsfeld that morning and Townsend was giving the president a heads-up on the issues Rumsfeld was sure to raise. President Bush put his hand up. "Listen, I've decided. I get it but I've decided."[63]

John McLaughlin arrived at the White House to give the president his daily intelligence briefing. Rice took McLaughlin into the anteroom outside the Situation Room to break the news. "I just want to tell you this morning that the president is going to announce support for a DNI and it is going to be out in the Rose Garden and you should stay for that."

McLaughlin asked, "So that game's up, right? We're done?"

Rice answered, "We're done."[64]

• • • • • • • • • • •

Symbolism counted. For his Rose Garden address, the president needed to have his national security team behind him. It showed that the administration was united behind the president. But FBI Director Robert Mueller did not want to join the political officers of the cabinet—Powell, Rumsfeld, Ashcroft, and Ridge—in the Rose Garden. While it was an announcement about national security, it might be perceived as political. The FBI director was not a cabinet member and was not considered a political officer, especially since the director of the FBI served a ten-year period designed to overlap presidential terms. But if Director Mueller would not join the Rose Garden announcement, then the acting CIA director—another non-political position—wondered how he could. Without the CIA presence in the photo implicitly supporting the president's decision, the conclusion would be drawn that the CIA did not support the new look of the Intelligence Community. A signal that the CIA was officially not on board would invite mischief in Congress.

The White House senior staff talked to McLaughlin and Mueller and prevailed upon them to join Ridge, Rumsfeld, Ashcroft, and Powell on the steps of the Rose Garden just outside of the Oval Office. But one White House aide remembered the "body language was horrible."[65] Director Mueller seemed to be staring off into the distance. As the president arrived and began his speech, thanking the 9/11 Commission for their "thoughtful and valuable" recommendations, to some observers McLaughlin and Mueller, on the far ends at either side of the president, were a step or two removed from the united front, about to step off into the bushes. President Bush recited the litany of innovations since 9/11 to fight terrorism, including reforms at the CIA and FBI and the establishment of the Terrorist Threat Integration Center. He continued,

> Today I'm asking Congress to create the position of a national intelligence director. That person—the person in that office will be appointed by the president with the advice and consent of the Senate, and will serve at the pleasure of the president. The national intelligence director will serve as the president's principal intelligence advisor and will oversee and coordinate the foreign and domestic activities of the Intelligence Community. Under this reorganization, the CIA will be managed by a separate director. The national intelligence director will assume the broader responsibility of leading the Intelligence Community across our government.[66]

For over fifty years, the director of the "President's Agency" had enjoyed the role as "head" of the Intelligence Community. Now the president embraced a more limited role for the CIA. McLaughlin apparently was not the only one surprised by the announcement that morning. When McLaughlin got back to his desk, his secure phone rang. "What the hell was that all about?" Colin Powell asked.[67]

But the president also delineated that the DNI would not direct the operations of the CIA and the Defense Department. Thus Cheney and Rumsfeld had won with the president their key point: the secretary of defense must retain command authority over all elements of the Department of Defense including intelligence elements, as unity of command is essential to success in warfighting. The president said,

> The national intelligence director will work with the respective agencies to set priorities. But let me make it also very clear that when it comes to operations, the chain of command will be intact. When the Defense Department is conducting operations to secure the homeland, there'll be nothing in between the secretary of defense and me.[68]

This was an important delineation that revealed how the president saw the

DNI fitting into the national security effort. The president elaborated in a press exchange that he envisioned the DNI as more the chairman of the Joint Chiefs (an advisory role) than directly in the chain of command to direct elements of the Intelligence Community.

The president also endorsed the creation of a National Counterterrorism Center as a "knowledge bank" whose duties would include delivering the Daily Terrorism Threat Report to the president. He envisioned a lesser role for the NCTC's "operational planning" mission: "the new center will coordinate and monitor counterterrorism plans and activities of all government agencies and departments to ensure effective joint action, and that our efforts are unified in priority and purpose."

His advisors amplified the president's point about the sanctity of the chain of command. Townsend noted that "the president was very clear today in his statement and in his intentions. That is to maintain the chain of command in each of those operating agencies. If there's a related military intelligence operation, he'll look to the secretary of defense on that."[69] The CIA, too, would maintain its direct covert-action relationship with the president. "And so if there was a covert operation ... that the president wanted implemented by the CIA, he would give that order directly to the CIA director, and the CIA director would be answerable to him."[70]

Rumsfeld and Cheney saw a DNI and NCTC with powers to command sub-elements of the Defense Department as a grave threat to the chain of command. The president's August 2 announcement, while endorsing the creation of a DNI and an NCTC, curtailed the change envisioned by the 9/11 Commission. The president's DNI was more of a priority-setter and an advisor, certainly not an operational quarterback directing operations.

The president's decision to maintain his direct control over the executive branch's operational assets would affect the powers of the DNI as an intermediary between the president and his "line operators" as well as the ability of the NCTC to manage sub-elements such as the FBI Counterterrorism Division, the CIA's Counterterrorism Center, or the Joint Special Operations Command (JSOC). To defense advocates, the president had made a very important decision. Any legislation creating a DNI and an NCTC would have to preserve the chain of command. Vice President Cheney and Secretary Rumsfeld had not been able to block the momentum for a DNI from reaching the White House, but they had secured important ground. Rice recalled, "For Don, I think he knew the devil would be in the details."[71]

CHAPTER SEVEN

Congressional August

Congressman Duncan Hunter was beloved by his colleagues for his lack of pretension. In Washington, the Californian drove an old, beat-up taxi cab, a Mercury Marquis station wagon that he bought for $600 and repainted. A colleague put a sign on it that read, "Do not tow. I am not kidding, this car is still operative." He rarely donned a suit, preferring slacks, a blazer, and tie. Hunter did not drink, smoke, or curse. If someone uttered a four-letter word with a lady in the room, Hunter would let you know you had crossed the line. He had been an Army Ranger in Vietnam but never talked of his tours of duty, offering only, "I had a very ordinary experience there." Once when his staff saw Hunter wearing what seemed like a new pair of shoes, they were surprised and moved in for a closer look. The shoes weren't new; he had worn his golf shoes to the office. As he entered his office, he frequently tossed his jacket like a banana peel across his messy desk and set about removing piles and stacks from the chairs so his visitors could sit down. The couch in his office looked as though he might have slept there the night before. There was a large map of the world on the wall and a picture of Hunter and Vice President Cheney with the inscription, "Duncan, when are we going hunting?"

Some called Hunter's support for the military "extreme."[1] Apart from his Vietnam service, he was the son of an artillery officer in the South Pacific during World War II and represented a congressional district that was home to retired military personnel and the Marine Corps Air Station Miramar, featured in the movie *Top Gun*.[2] Hunter believed that the Commission had done some good work in diagnosing the problem, "but when they made recommendations, they identified a problem here and shot the guy next door, and the guy next door was defense."[3] He was "concerned that some of the Commission's recommendations, if not carefully implemented, may increase the gap between the war-fighters and the national intelligence capabilities they rely on to protect our forces and defeat our enemies."[4] Hunter's son's experiences in Iraq colored his views as well.[5] In March 2004 four military contractors had been killed in Fallujah and their bodies burned, dragged through the streets, and hung from a bridge. The Marines were called in to take the city, which had become a lawless safe haven for insurgents. In house-to-house fighting in Fallujah, the best weapon the undermanned Marines had was the AC-130 Gunship.

But while the Marines fighting on the ground in Fallujah could communicate with the aircraft and request air support, they did not "own" the AC-130s flying overhead. A different military command controlled the AC-130s and during the battle pulled them from the skies over Fallujah to provide support to another mission. Without their guns in the sky, the Marines were disadvantaged. Duncan Hunter's son, Lt. Duncan Hunter, was livid and called his father to explain what had happened. To Chairman Hunter, the Marines' inability to keep the AC-130s in support of their mission "broke the code for me that ownership of assets was the most important part of military operations." What Hunter had learned from his son was something that experts had also observed about the military: "Both the Army and Marines strongly believed that owning indigenous assets was the only way to ensure that necessary support would be available when required. This . . . illustrates a fundamental tenet in most organizations: direct control over supporting assets is nearly always preferable to reliance on cooperative efforts from an outside entity."[6]

Hunter saw a more powerful DNI with increased control over the Pentagon's intelligence assets as a threat to the ability to fight and win wars. Hunter would seize on Hamilton's admission that "our report takes no issue with tactical support. . . . We wrestled with this. This is not an easy question, and I don't know that we've got it exactly right."[7] He said, "You want the assets enslaved to the war-fighting commander in a military operation; having an intelligence support structure serving another master is at the least inefficient and, worst, critical."[8] To Hunter, increased budget authority for the DNI would sever the military's ability to control intelligence assets.

Despite Hunter's misgivings, the media focused on the Senate, which largely embraced the Commission's recommendations. Senators Collins and Lieberman were early converts to the DNI and NCTC. At the Senate's first hearing on July 30, 2004, which featured Kean and Hamilton as witnesses, Collins announced that she supported the DNI "in concept."[9] Momentum had continued to build for action on the 9/11 Commission's recommendations during the August hearings, which were held, in the eyes of one senator, as a "statement of intensity."[10] Adding to the urgency was the oft-repeated sense that the intelligence failures on 9/11 and in Iraq had opened a "unique window of opportunity."[11] Of course, the election campaign also supplied undeniable political motivation, and some 9/11 Commissioners warned that the clock was ticking on another attack. But the looming election cannot completely account for the zeal for congressional action. In the three years since the attack, many in Congress had already reached the conclusion that dramatic action was critical.

Congressional sentiment at the time on intelligence reorganization can be divided into three principal strains. First, many in Congress believed that the attacks of 9/11 had ushered in a new era in U.S. national security. To move beyond the Cold War, the nation needed to prepare for asymmetric conflict. Threat alerts reminded everyone that the country was in a time of crisis and that it was time to recalibrate for a new fight. Senator Lieberman pressed, "We're operating in an emergency climate . . . we're in the middle of a war . . . we're under an imminent threat of attack now."[12] As the ranking Democrat on the Senate Intelligence Committee, Senator Jay Rockefeller, like many leaders on the Senate Intelligence Committee, had been a longtime critic of the Intelligence Community. He declared it a "Cold War artifact" based on a "fifty-seven-year-old . . . blueprint" and an inapt "arrangement for attacking an enemy that does not wear a uniform."[13]

Second, in the face of two massive intelligence failures, many in Congress rejected as unthinkable that a serious response was unnecessary—Congress must do *something*. Senator Lieberman found the 9/11 Commission's report to be an "indictment of the status quo."[14] In the wake of George Tenet's statement that the WMD case against Iraq was a "slam dunk," and revelations that the Iraqi defector gave fabricated information to Germany, Senator McCain dismissed reorganization skeptics: "For us to maintain the status quo is simply not acceptable" and "would not be satisfactory to my constituents."[15] The Iraq failure on the heels of 9/11 was critical to broad-based support in Congress for reform. Senator Snowe declared the Iraq failure "was basically what prompted me to support creation of the director of national intelligence."[16] A DNI would facilitate an "atmosphere of objectivity, connectivity, [and] information sharing."

One Democratic leader was blunt, "Intelligence failed us a second time."[17] The 9/11 Commission and the Iraq WMD reports led to the "inescapable conclusion" that the Intelligence Community needed a change.[18] In his confirmation hearing to become the DCI, former congressman and chairman of the House Intelligence Committee Porter Goss was pushed on whether he was enough of a "change agent."[19]

A third motivating factor for intelligence reorganization was frustration with the CIA. Senator Pat Roberts said, "To say that, quote, 'We get it,' and then imply that the problems with the Intelligence Community's WMD assessments were reasonable at the time, or to state that the problems with the pre-war Iraq assessments were isolated shortcomings, says to me that there are still those people that don't get it."[20] We were in an age in which "we've no longer come to trust" intelligence.[21] A corollary was that the CIA's human intelligence operations were seen as so broken that someone needed to spend full time rebuilding the CIA's morale.[22] A writer asked, "Can the CIA Really Be That Bad?"[23]

Senator Lieberman's examination of 9/11 led him to conclude that the Intelligence Community was plagued by "disastrous disconnects . . . a culture of rivalry rather than competition."[24] He later added, "In my own reaction, I found the Commission report so convincing that I would say not that my mind is totally made up, but that I would put the burden of proof on those who would argue with the major recommendations of the Commission."[25] Members of Congress increasingly accepted the 9/11 Commission's argument that "structure matters." Collins said, "The intelligence failures were not the result of individual negligence but of institutional rigidity."[26] "The time for action is now" was a common refrain from members of Congress.[27] For the Senate Intelligence Committee, the report confirmed what they had previously concluded in their Joint Inquiry and Iraq WMD reports: "The structure is defective." The "so-called director of central intelligence" lacked authority to manage, leading to a "flawed design [that] has contributed greatly to past intelligence failures."[28]

• • • • • • • • • • •

However, over at the Senate Armed Services Committee (SASC), some members expressed skepticism. Their reading of the report was that 9/11 had absolutely nothing to do with the performance of the Department of Defense, and yet the Commission's recommendations seemed aimed at reducing the powers of the secretary of defense over the NSA, NRO, and NGA. The chairman of the SASC, John Warner of Virginia, said that "the Commission correctly pointed out that our intelligence structure failed to connect the dots in terms of observing them and fusing together the indicators of a significant threat from al Qa'ida. Most agreed that the most significant problems were an unwillingness to share information on the part of some agencies and a structural inability to combine domestic and foreign intelligence." The recommended solutions, however, were to reorganize the entire community, not just to focus on parts that were unsatisfactory: "We must examine the reasons for these dramatic proposals by the 9/11 Commission and understand how the recommended solutions do or do not address the problems identified in the Commission's report."[29] Senator Levin said, "Nobody's been able to identify where the failure, the inability to control the budget led to the failures before 9/11. I don't see in the report how the issue over budget execution relates to the failures which were so dramatically laid out by the 9/11 Commission."[30]

The most comprehensible argument against vesting more control in a DNI was that troops were fighting two wars and we should avoid any action that might endanger the warfighter.

On the opposite end of the spectrum, others argued that the dual-masters approach, embodied in the current DCI arrangement and the 9/11 Commission's recommendation, had proven to be unworkable "because [the DCI had] bucked up against very powerful secretaries of defense through the years." Real institutional power required transferring the Department of Defense's "intelligence factories . . . the technical collection agencies—notably the National Reconnaissance Office, the National Security Agency and the National Geospatial-Intelligence Agency—" to the DNI.[31]

This approach appealed to the Senate Intelligence Committee, especially its chairman, Pat Roberts of Kansas. Like two of his predecessors,[32] he favored creating a new entity with all intelligence agencies under its thumb. Advocates of the "give him troops" approach believed that what bedeviled the DCI, and would come to plague the 9/11 Commission's DNI, was the lack of "authority, direction, and control" over the intelligence agencies in the Department of Defense. To achieve a command relationship over the national defense intelligence agencies, Senator Roberts announced support for what many described as a "Department of Intelligence" in August 2004.[33] His supporters wrote that "in particular, we feel strongly that the

DNI must have day-to-day operational control of all elements of the Intelligence Community performing national missions."[34]

Despite the popularity of the Commission, in the early churn of hearings on the report, two key features of the Commission's DNI were jettisoned. The first was the idea that the DNI be located within the executive office of the president. This recommendation had immediately drawn fire because of concern that intelligence might become politicized if the DNI worked in the White House. In the first substantive briefing from the Bush White House on their policy review the feature seemed sure to be dropped, and by August 2 the White House was opposed outright.[35] Many in Congress also spoke out against it.

Lee Hamilton, who supported the feature out of the deeply held view that the DNI needed to be substantially advantaged over the DCI, explained that "our intent with this recommendation was to make the DNI and the NCTC powerful forces in government. We believe that the agencies will work together effectively on terrorism, which is our most important national security issue, only if they are working directly for the president ... we think that the dangers [of politicization] arise from the functions and from the relationships that go with the job, regardless of where you are situated."[36] As noted previously, in testimony before the SHSGAC, the executive director of the Commission would explain the Commission's rationale:

> We recommended the executive office of the president because of the need for proximity to the president and the National Security Council, and because of the centrality of counterterrorism in contemporary national security management. If not put in the executive office of the president, one alternative would be to create a new agency as a home for the DNI and the NCTC. Lacking any existing institutional base, such an option would require authorities at least as strong as those we have proposed, or else it would create a bureaucratic fifth wheel that would make the present situation even worse.[37]

However, by September, the 9/11 Commission had backed away from locating the DNI in the White House. Hamilton told a congressional committee, "I think we've learned from our contacts with you."[38]

The second casualty was the 9/11 Commission's recommendation that the head of the CIA, the undersecretary of defense for intelligence, and the FBI assistant director for intelligence (or undersecretary of intelligence at

DHS) be "dual-hatted" as deputies to the DNI. The report, although sparse on justification, drew an analogy to the Department of Defense. The deputies, "like the leaders of the Army, Navy, Air Force, or Marines," would handle acquisition, training, and execution of operations planned by the national intelligence centers. The 9/11 Commission envisioned this as a mechanism to increase the power of the DNI over the constituent elements of the IC without giving the DNI explicit authority, direction, and control over them as a cabinet secretary might have over agencies in his domain. However, citing concerns about undermining the ability of a cabinet secretary to manage subordinate offices, the White House rejected dual-hatting.[39]

But the major takeaway from Congress's hearings on the 9/11 Commission's recommendations was that, most of all, the DNI needed control over the budget. A common refrain was "He who has the gold rules; there are only two things that matter in Washington: firing authority and who controls the purse strings." The impression was left that the explanation for the DCI's weakness was that "85 percent" of the intelligence budget travelled through the Defense Department on its way to intelligence agencies such as the NSA, NRO, and NGA. If the DNI's power over that money could be increased, to include having Congress send it directly to the DNI for disposition to the defense intelligence agencies, the result would be an increased management authority across the board, to reform information sharing, to break down "stovepipes," and to manage the IC more cohesively. Some thought President Bush's initial endorsement of the DNI was halfhearted with regard to budget authority, in part because his chief of staff briefed the press that the DNI's new role would be merely "*coordinat[ing]*" budgets, something commentators suggested was "a word that always raises eyebrows."[40] With the preponderance of early congressional opinion strongly in favor of the 9/11 Commission report, a new standard developed. The issue had become not just whether to create a DNI but whether to create a *strong* DNI; the litmus test for a strong DNI was whether the position would have "full" budget authority.

CHAPTER EIGHT

The Devil in the Details

NSC Consideration of a DNI and an NCTC

As the public debate focused on the DNI and budget authority, two of Rumsfeld's generals were privately making the rounds. General Michael Hayden, described by one reporter as "diminutive and bookish in appearance,"[1] was one of them. General Hayden later wrote,

> Many of us felt that if we were going to take direct control of the CIA away from the new head of the community, we really had to make sure that the legislation dealt the new office a very powerful hand and that it did it formally and specifically. . . . That's why Jim Clapper and I warned the House Permanent Select Committee on Intelligence (HPSCI) in late summer of 2004 that a "feckless" DNI would actually make matters worse.[2]

General Clapper, the head of the NGA, and General Hayden, the head of the NSA, favored what General Clapper later called "something akin to a Department of Intelligence."[3] In 2003, after the creation at the Pentagon of an undersecretary of intelligence, Clapper recalled that he and Hayden sometimes got conflicting guidance from their two bosses—the USDI and the DCI. Clapper called it "dueling banjos."[4] Years earlier, Clapper held the view that without a strong leader of the Intelligence Community, left to itself, it "cannot and does not make meaningful trades between and among collection disciplines" because it was "like piggies who came up to the trough." He explained, "Rather than going to three or four or whatever stovepipes, three different places to get your customer's satisfaction, you go to one place. You'd have one institution that would be responsible for collection."[5]

Hayden's view, similar to John McLaughlin's, was that the 9/11 Commission had gotten it wrong in underrating the DCI's management of the community. As head of the NSA, Hayden viewed George Tenet as a "booming personality" who frequently was called to directly manage the heads of the national intelligence agencies within the Department of Defense.[6]

• • • • • • • • • • •

McLaughlin, Hayden, and Clapper began meeting to coordinate positions and quietly to work the Congress and the White House. Clapper and Hayden also went to the White House and had a secret meeting with Fran Townsend. The meeting was "off the calendar" and held in the executive private dining room off the White House Mess.[7] The precautions were taken to prevent Secretary Rumsfeld from discovering that they were seeing the president's staff behind his back.

John McLaughlin, as acting DCI, had no such restrictions on what he could advocate to the White House. In a letter to the president that August, he argued that "a significantly empowered director of central intelligence could fulfill the spirit of the 9/11 Commission's recommendations."[8] But once the president had endorsed the creation of a DNI, McLaughlin argued that as long as the president was "going to do this, don't do it halfway."[9] McLaughlin advocated to President Bush that the president should "give [the DNI] command and control authority over core national intelligence agencies—the CIA, NSA, NGA, and NRO."[10] As noted, McLaughlin worried that the 9/11 Commission's DNI "would be creating a layer of bureaucracy that if not empowered will just be a creator of work, not an enabler of work."[11]

Loss of the defense intelligence agencies to the DNI was a doomsday scenario for Secretary Rumsfeld and his USDI, Steve Cambone. And because of the volatile pre-election political environment, there was some cause for concern that support could build for this approach. As noted, there was some support for a "Department of Intelligence" approach in the Senate.

Public disclosure that General Hayden and General Clapper dissented from Secretary Rumsfeld's view and favored removing their agencies from the Department of Defense would have made huge news and given additional momentum to efforts to maximize the authorities of the new DNI.

Finally, word got back to Rumsfeld. Clapper and Hayden were at the Wye River Plantation in Maryland speaking to a group of newly promoted senior intelligence officers. They repeated their support for movement of their agencies to a DNI. Someone in the audience called back to the Pentagon to relay Clapper and Hayden's remarks, and before they were back in the car they got word that the secretary wanted to see them. "You need to tell the secretary this," Cambone told General Hayden.

The generals were invited to the secretary's office in the E Ring of the Pentagon for lunch. A joke went around later that "Rumsfeld asked Clapper and Hayden to lunch and there were only two plates at the table and they both had crow."[12] Rumsfeld frequently hosted meetings in his office on intelligence matters. A participant in these meetings remembered Rumsfeld's frequently indirect approach in formal meetings; sometimes, in regularly scheduled meetings with Director Tenet, he would get up from the conference table and walk to his standing desk while Tenet, McLaughlin, and Rumsfeld's deputy, Paul Wolfowitz, fought it out. Today, Rumsfeld would favor a more direct approach. General Hayden recalled the lunch looked like peace talks between warring nations. "We were arrayed opposite the secretary; the only thing missing were the flags."[13] Over a lunch of Mexican food, Hayden and Clapper stated their views. Hayden recalls,

> In essence we argued that there was a real danger of Congress creating a leader of the IC who truly had less power than DCIs had historically been able to wield. We both agreed that this could be disastrous and argued for legislative language that would codify a robust role for the DNI—even over those big national collection agencies inside the Defense Department, namely, the NSA, the NGA, and the NRO. We even allowed ourselves to imagine a future where those agencies could be outside the Pentagon and directly under the DNI.[14]

Rumsfeld slammed his fork into his plate.[15] "It is a terrible idea; I can't support it."[16] He spoke of the Department's "fundamental need" for intelligence and insisted the Department could not rely on someone else to supply it. To Rumsfeld, the uniformed military should understand this more than most; he said he could not believe he was hearing such arguments from two generals. It was "one of those things where the secretary said, 'How could you be recommending that?'"[17] Rumsfeld's point of view was that he had a "responsibility to provide combat support to the president for troops in battle, the DNI doesn't, and you can go on about support and all the rest—he does not have the responsibility and I need to be able to direct those assets."[18] The meeting ended on a bad note. Hayden remembered commenting to the group that "we could be headed for a disaster unless the Pentagon could find it in its heart to be 'generous.'"[19]

Rumsfeld thought the White House was being too generous by even countenancing these matters. At a NSC meeting, Secretary Rumsfeld picked at his fingernails with a pocketknife, said to be a signal of his annoyance.[20] In the dead middle of August, he was in the White House Situation Room, listening to a discussion about how much new authority a DNI should have to manage the Intelligence Community. Secretary Rumsfeld recalled his discomfort: "The president got guidance from Legislative Affairs and Public Affairs and was taken by their guidance. They wanted to put a scalp on the wall that shows we've done something. [The White House] was enamored with it. . . . They had to worry about the president's image, and I didn't. The White House had a different set of pressures than one person running one department would have." Citing his long experience in Washington and his age, Rumsfeld said, "For Christ's sake . . . I am beyond surprised about what a White House will do; they are influenced by media and political desirability of action."[21]

With Congress set to return to Washington and consider legislation to restructure intelligence, the national security advisor had called Rumsfeld and the other national security principals to the White House Situation Room to force agreement on the options for a DNI and an NCTC to put before the president for decision. Secretary Rumsfeld scoffed at the suggestion that the principals needed to make decisions *today* to accommodate the return of Congress. "The *idea* that they could *possibly* take up something this complicated is just . . ." was Rumsfeld's profession of disbelief that Congress would consider an issue of such complexity so rapidly. That reaction would soon be echoed by a prominent group of national security experts led by Henry Kissinger. "It's true, Don," someone interrupted Rumsfeld. "Senator Frist has announced the Senate will take up the measure in September."

President Bush's Proposal for an NCTC

The TTIC would be renamed the National Counterterrorism Center. It would continue to fuse intelligence collected by whatever source. Since Bush had said in his August 2 endorsement that "the new center will coordinate and monitor counterterrorism plans and activities of all government agencies and departments to ensure effective joint action, and that our efforts are unified in priority and purpose," the issue was how to shape the NCTC's "action" role, *how much* authority the NCTC would have to direct elements such as the FBI's Counterterrorism Division or the CIA's Counterterrorism Center within other cabinet departments or agencies, and, specifically, would it accept the 9/11 Commission's vision of an attending physician conducting "joint operations planning?" Despite the Commission's proviso that the NCTC should not direct the actual execution of operations, the idea engendered opposition from across the cabinet departments.

The Department of Justice strongly objected to giving the NCTC authority to direct FBI agents, and the Defense Department balked at the thought of Special Operations Forces acting at the NCTC's behest. When a Pentagon general participating in the discussions suggested that some troops might best be directed by the NCTC in support of counterterrorism missions, Steve Cambone pulled the president's homeland security advisor aside. Ordering troops into battle was the sole prerogative of the president acting through the secretary of defense; any other arrangements were non-starters.

The cabinet and agency officials had a common interest in shielding their departments and agencies from NCTC direction. In August 2004, during negotiations over the president's executive order to create the NCTC, the Justice Department suggested attaching the modifier *strategic* to the NCTC's proposed operational planning, as in, the new center's role would be *strategic operational planning*. At a minimum, the added descriptor would remove the NCTC from the tactical realm envisioned by the 9/11 Commission. *Strategic* signaled that the NCTC would be a step back from devising *plans*, viewed as a term of art. Plans could mean battle plans, or plans for a CIA operation, whereas to the policymakers at the NSC, *planning* was different. For instance, the staff of the Joint Chiefs of Staff had a *planning* function, providing strategic direction and integration of forces, but did not generally write operational war plans per se.

As the NSC grappled with the question, Fran Townsend stepped in to allay the confusion. As President Bush's top White House counterterrorism official, Townsend chaired a daily meeting with all the top terrorism officials in the Intelligence Community and across the cabinet departments. She visualized the NCTC assuming the operational functions currently residing within the NSC's Counterterrorism Strategy Group (CSG). The CSG reviewed all the terrorist threats, assigned action items, and de-conflicted roles and missions. The group had evolved over time, but under Richard Clarke in the Clinton White House, the CSG assumed a highly operational role. After 9/11, this practice had been augmented by daily sessions in the Oval Office so that the directors of the FBI and CIA could directly interface with the president.

In Townsend's view, the review of the 9/11 recommendations was an opportunity to adjust the level of operational matters managed directly by the White House. The CSG had become too involved in the hour-to-hour tactical operations of counterterrorism, at the expense of its historic role as a counterterrorism *policymaking* body. Townsend intervened in the NSC discussion and offered a formulation: "NCTC will be TTIC plus the CSG." The participants accepted Townsend's formulation.

To demonstrate that the administration was implementing the recommendations of the 9/11 Commission to the fullest extent short of congressional action, the president issued an executive order creating the NCTC in late August 2004. Replacing TTIC, the NCTC would "serve as the primary organization in the United States Government for analyzing and integrating all intelligence possessed or acquired by the United States Government pertaining to terrorism and counterterrorism." The NCTC would also "conduct strategic operational planning for counterterrorism activities, integrating all instruments of national power, including diplomatic, financial, military, intelligence, homeland security, and law enforcement activities within and among agencies, [and] assign operational responsibilities to lead agencies for counterterrorism activities that are consistent with applicable law and that support strategic plans to counter terrorism." The president's legislative submission two weeks later mirrored this approach.[22]

The President's Proposal for a DNI

Much of the debate in the August 2004 NSC meetings concerned the language for an executive order to strengthen the power of the DCI,[23] at least until Congress created a DNI. To demonstrate his support of intelligence reform until Congress acted further, the president issued an executive order that "strain[ed] the limits of his executive authority"[24] to strengthen management of the Intelligence Community. The White House did not want to create the impression that the executive orders enhancing the authority of the DCI and creating an NCTC preempted the need to legislate the 9/11 Commission recommendations. So it stressed they were a "down payment on the president's enduring commitment to work with the Congress" to establish a DNI in statute.[25] The order's central feature augmented the DCI's budget authority. The DCI could now "develop, determine, and present" a unified intelligence budget for the purpose of "the actual development of an integrated, comprehensive budget against a unified set of priorities."[26] The order also increased the DCI's powers to transfer appropriated dollars within the executive branch and "makes clear the president's intention that the DCI has the authority to move and cause assets to be tasked." Many of the authorities in the executive order on the DCI "really underscore what the DCI's authorities are and how the president expects them to be executed."[27]

As the executive order was issued in late August 2004, debate continued within the NSC on what the president would propose to Congress to create a DNI. Would the intelligence agencies embedded in cabinet departments merely report to the DNI on certain matters, such as collection priorities and resource management, or would the major intelligence agencies in the Department of Defense be removed directly into the DNI's chain of command?[28]

The National Security Council principals rejected moving all the intelligence agencies under the DNI because it "would be too disruptive particularly during a time of war, [would] undermine existing chains of command, and [would] potentially weaken intelligence support to key government departments and missions."[29] On the same grounds, the principals vetoed a softer approach that would have moved only the Defense Department's national intelligence agencies under the DNI. On the other end of the spectrum, the Defense Department also advanced an option that would maintain the existing confederation but give the DNI the authority to direct agencies through an Intelligence Community Council consisting of all the heads of the intelligence agencies.[30] This, too, was nixed because the DNI would be too weak.

So as far as Bush's legislative proposal went, what would the DNI control? The president decided that the CIA would no longer be an autonomous agency. His bill provided that the director of the CIA would be under the "authority, direction, and control" of the DNI.[31] The CIA would report to the president through the DNI. This gave the DNI an oversight role into the CIA and interposed the new office between the White House and "the president's agency."[32] This was significant because as far as the White House was concerned, the DNI would have troops in the CIA.

However, the central issue was how much new authority, if any, the DNI would have over DoD intelligence budgets. Defense thought that efforts to increase the DNI's authority could upset finely tuned power-sharing relationships between intelligence and the Defense Department, a construct that ensured meeting national and war-fighting intelligence requirements. "Current structures developed over forty years [into] a working set of relationships. . . . [It was] not clear what the value was in upsetting them in return for something that in the end did not address"[33] the heart of the issues of 9/11.

The secretary of defense and his undersecretary of defense for intelligence, Stephen Cambone, peppered the White House with letters and memos. Noting the 9/11 Commission's "rush to reform intelligence," Rumsfeld warned of the "grave danger of serious error."[34] Some of the options before the NSC, Rumsfeld believed, would cut the military out of the intelligence process.[35] "It is the responsibility of the DoD to see that forces have the intelligence they need, and they cannot do so if, as the result of budget arrangements shifting to [the] DNI; it must be done in a way that the military is not cut out."[36] Rumsfeld wrote, "Members of Congress, the press, and Kerry can say what they want and afford to be wrong, and there is no penalty. The president of the United States has to be right on something of this importance."[37] The memorandum ended with a single word: "Caution."

By September 11, 2004, the third anniversary of the attacks, Andy Card and Condoleezza Rice were at Camp David with the president. They put before him several intelligence reform-related issues. That same day, Secretary Rumsfeld sent another memorandum over to the White House. Addressed to the president, its subject line put the word *Reform* in quotes to signal Rumsfeld's displeasure with the draft legislation. The secretary wrote that the relationship between the DNI and the secretary of defense "has the potential to result in a useful tension" if the cabinet secretaries were to maintain the ability to develop their own budgets. But the formulation offered by the White House staff "could harm U.S. intelligence capabilities." If the DNI were given expansive budget authority, "the result would be a train wreck, or you and your successors will have to spend a great deal of time acting as a referee."[38]

Despite Rumsfeld's protestations, the president decided that he would recommend to Congress that the DNI would have near absolute authority over the movement of national intelligence funds to agencies embedded in other departments. Although his own opposition to declassifying the top line intelligence appropriation prevented a direct, clean appropriation to the DNI, the president's proposal included language to allow the DNI authority over the funding once appropriated by Congress "without reference to the accounts appropriated" and to ensure that the actual expenditure of funds would occur "only as authorized or directed" by the DNI.[39] This budget-execution power meant that the DNI would control the national intelligence dollars even though they might be in the Defense Department's bank accounts. This formulation allowed the president to claim full budget authority for the DNI despite not favoring the 9/11 Commission's arrangement of declassification with a direct grant to the DNI. To address Secretary Rumsfeld's concern about managing the Defense Department, the DNI would be required to give prior notice to the cabinet secretaries before transferring the money.[40]

The secretary of defense was not giving up. He fired off another memorandum to the White House wondering how he could be held accountable for managing the Defense Department if the DNI had the power to send money directly to his subordinates without any say whatsoever from him.[41] To address the Defense Department's concern, a provision was inserted into the legislation to institutionalize a process by which cabinet officers could register their views with the DNI via a Joint Intelligence Community Council (JICC).

As the NSC debated the particulars, the secretary of defense and the vice president underscored the president's previous emphasis on not upsetting the chain of command between the president and his "line operators." The vice president's chief counsel, David Addington, frequently repeated that the president had made three overarching decisions with regard to intelligence reform. First, the DNI would have full budget authority. Second, the top line of the intelligence budget would remain classified. And finally, the chain of command would remain intact. The chain of command was critical for Vice President Cheney.

Addington developed language (later to become known as the "chain-of-command language") that was inserted into the president's bill. Its purpose was to preserve the ability of cabinet secretaries, especially the secretary of defense, to manage their own departments. Some called it a savings clause, language that would help settle future disputes about where the cabinet secretaries' authorities ended and the DNI's began. The language read:

> Nothing in this Act or amendments made by this Act shall be construed to impair or otherwise affect the authority of (1) the Director of the Office of Management and Budget; or (2) the principal officers of the executive departments as heads of their respective departments.

It was inserted with little debate as the NSC participants concerned themselves with the DNI's budget authority. Its import was unclear to many of the lawyers working on the legislation and would take weeks to decipher and appreciate. The mysterious chain-of-command language would become a talisman, a necessity for some and a poison pill for others. Its insertion would go largely unnoticed at first, but it would emerge to bedevil the legislation and later the DNI himself.

CHAPTER NINE

Cabinet Room

In early September 2004, with Congress returning to session, the president invited the congressional leaders to the West Wing. The setting was the Cabinet Room, just steps from the Oval Office. There, Harry S. Truman had been sworn in as president after rushing back from a card game in the Senate upon getting the word that President Roosevelt had died. The room is perhaps most recognized as the setting for President Kennedy's meetings with the ExCom, his national security officials, during the Cuban Missile Crisis.

Five weeks earlier, the president endorsed the creation of a DNI and NCTC from the Rose Garden. Today, he was meeting with congressional leaders to provide more details. It was also an opportunity to demonstrate that the president was leading on the issue. Members of Congress arrived at the White House in full view of the White House press corps, who would report that the president was "convening congressional leaders to discuss the 9/11 Commission's recommendations." Collins and Lieberman were there; after a month of hearings they had now adopted the 9/11 Commission's language and plan.[1] The president's legislative affairs staff scurried about counting heads to make sure all the invited members were present in the Cabinet Room. The president entered, shaking hands, back-slapping, clasping, and joking his way through as the White House legislative affairs specials and other staff stood at attention, the backs of their legs against their leather seats to make maximum way for the entourage working the circumference of the table. Following the president were his chief of staff, his national security advisor, his chief legislative affairs representative, and the vice president. Each one dropped off from the gaggle as he passed his seat at the table, which was decoratively marked by a heavy card with calligraphy and an embossed gold presidential seal.

Collins, the moderate Republican Senator from Maine, was known as an extremely hard worker. She had cleared her calendar for the summer and fall to work on nothing but intelligence reform. For her, a committee staffer remembered, it was "all hands on deck."[2] She had already chaired five committee hearings in August and spent the month studying the Intelligence Community. She had a reputation as a centrist with an independent streak. As a moderate in a closely divided Senate, she was often among the most highly sought-after Senators, as she could just as easily vote with the Democrats as with her Republican colleagues. Although she was the "shortest-tenured committee chairman,"[3] she had plenty of experience in the halls of Congress, having served as a legislative aide to then senator William Cohen of Maine before she began her electoral career. Both of her parents had served terms as mayor of Caribou, Maine. She and Senator Lieberman, who had been Al Gore's vice presidential nominee and who also had an independent mind, had forged a bond with the Commission in their intention to enact a DNI and an NCTC with sweeping powers. Senator Lieberman had unreservedly adopted the 9/11 Commission's recommendations on the day they were announced. And Senator Collins by July 30 had announced, "I support the concept of the national intelligence director."[4]

Also present was Representative Jane Harman who had begun a campaign for a DNI months previously. Her father was a refugee from Nazi Germany, and she attended Smith College and Harvard Law School. Afterward, she became chief counsel and staff director of a Senate Judiciary subcommittee. She left Congress to run for governor of California, and after she lost ran again to reclaim her seat representing Venice Beach in Los Angles. She loved her nickname, GI Jane. As a member of Congress, she was relentless, working her way up to become the ranking Democrat on the House Intelligence Committee. The other House leaders around the table were not fans of the 9/11 Commission. Hastert and DeLay had both fought its creation and, later, an extension of its deadline, fearing that it had turned into an instrument of the Democrats. The Speaker of the House was a former wrestling coach and history teacher from Illinois. Hastert explained his style as a "coaching philosophy: if the coach is in the headlines every week, the team is in trouble; if the team is in the headlines every week, you are doing all right."[5] According to a former staffer, DeLay "genuinely believed the American people could not care less about the 9/11 Commission's recommendations."[6]

Making his way to his seat, the president shook hands with Duncan Hunter who was eager to tell the president the damage the 9/11 Commission recommendations would cause the warfighter. Jim Sensenbrenner of Wisconsin, chairman of the House Judiciary Committee, also joined the House team. Sensenbrenner seemed to relish sticking to his guns under barrages of scorn and condemnation. An heir to the Kimberly Clark fortune in Wisconsin, he was a Green Bay Packers fan; he has a picture in his office of himself at the North Pole in a Packers cheese head hat. Sensenbrenner claimed 115 provisions that he had helped get signed into law during his six years as chairman. His staff compared his legislative prowess to Senator Edward Kennedy's. As chairman of the congressional committee with jurisdiction over the FBI, Sensenbrenner had a prodigious list of legislative accomplishments after the attacks of September 11, including strengthened immigration-enforcement legislation and the enhanced law-enforcement capabilities known as the PATRIOT Act. During negotiations over these landmarks bills, Sensenbrenner knew how to press an issue to squeeze out maximum advantage. His negotiating motto was "Know when to hold 'em, know when to fold 'em." Until it was time to fold 'em, Sensenbrenner would fight tooth and nail.

As the president neared his seat, he warmly embraced the Speaker. They were close. President Bush and Speaker Hastert decided shortly after Bush took office that their fates were intertwined. The president knew that strategically he could ask the House to advance the bulk of his agenda in an expeditious manner. He needed a strong alliance with the Speaker to negotiate from a position of strength on major legislation with the Senate. Hastert similarly perceived his legislative success as tied to President Bush. He worked early in the process to identify issues that could divide or separate the White House and House leaders, and tried to resolve them. The Speaker decided early in 2001 that he would not allow major items with veto threats to emerge from a conference committee, and split the Republican caucus on the floor. One of the underappreciated reasons for why President Bush had so few vetoes in office is due to this tremendous cooperation and collaboration.[7] Managing the intricacies of this relationship often fell to Scott Palmer, the Speaker's chief of staff, who sat in a chair against the wall roughly opposite the president's seat.

The president sat down with his back to the glass doors leading to the Rose Garden. The back of the seat was several inches higher than the others, and before the president on the table was a wooden box with a button to signal the White House Mess to send a waiter. Next to the box sat two peppermints, a white legal pad with a thick black marker, and a coke in a tall, clear glass. At the president's knee, a phone was fastened onto a table leg.

President Bush held dozens of these meetings when Congress was in session to press for action on legislation. From his home turf in the majesty of the White House, they showed that he was on top of his congressional agenda. Each of these meetings would begin with a visit from the press. A pool spray, a representative selection of the press corps—one print reporter, one TV reporter, and several photographers and camera men—were ushered into the room by the White House Press Office's "press wranglers," typically young press aides who devoted their time to the care and feeding of the media.

The president called the meeting to order and gave the signal: the two doors opposite him on his left and right flung open and in charged the press. Two men with portable klieg lights sprinted to either side of the room, dropping to their knees to find an electrical plug. A dozen men with cameras hoisted on their shoulders jockeyed for position for a shot of the president and the assembled legislators. Next, a mob of photographers, flashbulbs firing just as the klieg lights illuminated the table, bathed the president and his guests in a brilliant, made-for-TV aura. A sound man with a boom mic, a microphone at the end of a long pole, hovered, dangling the microphone about two feet above the president. Finally, the reporters with notepads in hand arrived and tried to figure out which members of Congress and which cabinet officers were at the table.

The president opened, "I want to thank the members who are here. Thank—thank you all for coming today. We are going to discuss intelligence reform. I will be submitting a plan to the Congress that strengthens intelligence reform—strengthens the intelligence services."[8] Since the president had first endorsed the DNI, there had been many hearings in Congress on the 9/11 Commission recommendations. His endorsement had been criticized because the president's chief of staff said the DNI would only "coordinate" budgets. This sounded weak; Senator Lieberman worried it meant creating a "kind of Potemkin national intelligence director, where you see the façade but there's no real authority behind it."[9] Full budget authority was the magic phrase: if you were in favor of it, then you supported the 9/11 Commission's vision of a strong DNI. President Bush stepped up to the plate: "We believe that there ought to be a national intelligence director who has *full* budgetary authority. We'll talk to members of Congress about how to implement that. I look forward to working with the members to get a bill to my desk as quickly as possible."

To usher the media from the room, the press wrangler's favorite technique was to repeatedly shout: "Thank you. . . . Thank you everybody." The president sat smiling, not wanting to appear reluctant to answer questions. He said nothing as the klieg lights were extinguished and unplugged and the press receded from the room. Ready to get down to business, the president kicked off the meeting.

At 9:22 a.m. Bloomberg News flashed an all caps bulletin: "BUSH SAYS INTELLIGENCE DIRECTOR NEEDS FULL BUDGET AUTHORITY." A White House legislative affairs aide forwarded it to a colleague in the meeting with the note, "Perfect Headline."[10]

In the Cabinet Room, Rice detailed the president's plan for the DNI.[11] The president mentioned that he would have to leave early for a trip to Florida to tour damage from Hurricane Frances but that Rice would remain to answer questions. The Senate leaders applauded the president's plan, agreeing, "Let's get this done." Senator Lieberman thanked the president. "You've crossed a bridge with real budget authority."[12] But the House Republicans expressed misgivings. Tom DeLay spoke up. "Even the 9/11 Commission members admitted they did not do all [the recommendations] right, [we would do] devastating harm if we took their suggestions straight up. [Congress should also legislate on] immigration, money laundering, and law enforcement—take it slowly and do the right thing." Chairman Hunter called for protecting the Department of Defense: "DoD is the big user of intelligence; we cannot have a break in the hardwire between intelligence assets and their primary users." The president said, "That's right." Hunter continued, "DoD must have a seat at the table, the Commission did not talk to the warfighters. Our national intelligence assets are hardwired to the warfighters."[13]

Soon the trees and bushes shook and strained as chopper blades sent a rush of air into the Rose Garden. Marine One was coming in for a landing and its decoys spread over the city to draw any fire before rejoining the formation for the trip to Andrews Air Force Base. Marine One landed just beyond the Rose Garden, visible through the window over the president's shoulder. Moments later, Bush strode out of the Rose Garden across the South Lawn, waving to an assembled crowd of well-wishers and under the gaze of the press before boarding.

CHAPTER TEN

Attackers

The Senate's secret chamber, S-407, is high in the dome of the Capitol. The most sensitive classified matters of state, at least those briefed to the full Senate, are discussed there. It is a small hearing room with a horseshoe-shaped dais. Behind the dais is the seal of the U.S. Senate, festooned with an image of fasces, symbolizing freedom and authority.[1] It is a cocoon, soundproofed to thwart eavesdropping. Guards protect its sole entrance and a closet of safes containing the senators' classified notes.

Today, the Senate was recessing to its hidden meeting space for a briefing from the nation's top military brass on the ongoing military operations in Iraq and Afghanistan. A polite Senate official gathered the phones of the arriving senators. If properly manipulated by a foreign intelligence service, they could become microphones relaying conversations within the room to a listening post. Some senators occasionally doubted whether the precautions of surrendering their electronics were necessary; they griped that Secretary Rumsfeld hardly shared sensitive information with them. "I get more from the *Washington Post* than I do from these briefings," was a familiar refrain.

With the attacks of September 11, military action in Afghanistan and Iraq, and frequent spikes of intelligence suggesting a coming terrorist attack, the senators were making the climb to S-407 frequently. As the senators arrived, they passed a crowd of administration briefers, including the chairman of the Joint Chiefs of Staff and his entourage of decorated officers. And, of course, Secretary of Defense Donald Rumsfeld was there. The senators ambled in and, if the leather seats behind the horseshoe dais were full, sat in ordinary folding chairs set up to accommodate the hundred. A leadership staffer recorded the order in which the senators arrived; the earliest were listed first on the roll of questioners. Now that the room was full, the briefing could begin. A lighting scheme, not unlike the "Vacancy" sign at a roadside motel, reminded the audience that their discussions were sensitive. Today, the system was illuminated as "Top Secret."

After the brass briefed the Senate, Senator Frist called the order of questioners—"Brownback, Durbin, Warner. . . ." Senator John Warner of Virginia was known to have misgivings about the DNI's impact on the equities of the Department of Defense. At a hearing he had held the previous month, Warner offered that reformers ought first to "do nothing to undermine the confidence the battlefield commanders have in the intelligence support on which they must depend."[2]

A fellow senator remembered Warner rising and posing a question to Secretary Rumsfeld in his grand style.[3] "What effect would the Commission's proposal have, what would be the impact on the warfighter on our ability to provide battlefield intelligence at a critical time?"[4] Senator Collins saw this as a setup that had been rehearsed in advance. Rumsfeld's response likely reflected what he said in public. There was nothing more important than to preserve the ability of the warfighter to fight and win wars. Intelligence failures were more likely if in haste the chain of command became duplicative or confused.[5] In testimony before the 9/11 Commission months prior, Rumsfeld had sought to preempt a DNI recommendation, calling ideas to put all agencies under a single intelligence czar a "great disservice." He told the Commission of the benefits of a decentralized approach: "There may be ways we can strengthen intelligence, but centralization is most certainly not one of them."[6]

At a similar classified briefing for House members, Rumsfeld was more dismissive of the 9/11 Commission's recommendations. Dan Keniry, the deputy assistant to the president for legislative affairs responsible for the House, was in the audience and viewed Secretary Rumsfeld's remarks as a direct contradiction of the president's position. "Emphasizing his point, he gestured to the uniformed officers in the room" to explain the intelligence needs of the warfighters.[7] Rumsfeld's commentary was brazen enough that a Republican Congressman friendly with the president approached Keniry and said, "*You need to do something!*" Keniry exited the room and called the West Wing. He got his boss, David Hobbs, and the White House Chief of Staff on speaker phone and relayed Rumsfeld's remarks. Congressman Chris Shays, Republican of Connecticut, told the media at the time that Rumsfeld was "blatant" in his opposition.[8]

But with Collins and Lieberman firmly in the lead, Rumsfeld would have a hard time sowing dissent in the Senate. Collins and Lieberman were increasingly taking the view that the problems on 9/11 spoke for themselves; it was obvious that the intelligence system was broken and the only reason nothing had been done was that bureaucracies in the executive branch and their allies in Congress were protecting their turf. Collins and Lieberman had given the report "considerable weight,"[9] calling it a "stinging indictment of the Intelligence Community's organizational structure."[10] The SHSGAC aligned closely with the 9/11 Commission, taking three of their former staff aboard. They adopted the rhetoric of the 9/11 Commission, concluding that "transformational intelligence reform is urgently needed" and "structural reform is necessary to unlock the potential in the U.S. intelligence apparatus to counter twenty-first-century threats." Their rationale was in many respects indistinguishable from the reasoning and arguments in the 9/11 Commission Report. The current system would not protect U.S. national security in the twenty-first century; the intelligence agencies needed to become a more "agile and flexible network."[11] The committee "took the 9/11 report and said let's start there."[12] The committee and the 9/11 Commission worked hand in glove, swapping language back and forth. "We worked very closely, ran language by them constantly," remembered Michael Bopp, the majority staff director.[13] Embracing the Commission completely, they believed their bill represented "the culmination of years of the most thorough and extensive review of the Intelligence Community in history."[14]

As Collins and Lieberman charged ahead, opponents lashed out in hopes of derailing the Commission's recommendations. Attackers would appear from the ranks of the disenfranchised Senate committees, a coalition of Washington statesmen, a former director of Central Intelligence, and, most significantly, the Senate's old bulls. There were two opportunities in the legislative process for the attackers to stage an ambush.

Senator Stevens was no fan of the 9/11 Commission. Senator Ted Stevens was the "old bull" of the U.S. Senate, most often described as "gruff."[15] He had joined the U.S. Army Air Corps in World War II, and at age twenty-one flew military transports over the Himalayas to supply Chinese nationalist troops fighting the Japanese. His was the first plane to land in Beijing after the war had ended.[16] He earned the Distinguished Flying Cross for bravery.[17] After the war, he worked his way through law school, tending bar and selling his own blood.[18]

Stevens was chairman of the most powerful committee in Congress, the Appropriations Committee. Institutionally, the most powerful congressional committees are those that pass bills that are eventually enacted into law—a law proves that a committee can implement its will, that it cannot be ignored. *Any* committee can pass a bill and nominate it for action in the U.S. Senate. But the Appropriations Committee's bills *must* become law. This committee is the manifestation of the most potent congressional power, found in the Constitution's Article I, Section 9: "No money shall be drawn from the Treasury but in consequence of appropriations made by law."[19] This was a constitutional grant of authority to direct billions in federal dollars. The committee's members occupied their own stately offices behind muraled walls in the Capitol. An Appropriations Committee seat was among the most coveted in Congress not only because of the ability it conferred to affect public policy. It also allowed senators to direct federal spending to benefit home-state constituents through what were called earmarks. With over forty years in Congress, Stevens was among the most powerful senators ever. Known as the emperor of earmarks, one study determined that he had written into legislation mandates for 1,452 projects for Alaska, with a value totaling $3.4 billion.[20] One of his colleagues said of him, "There is no senator in the history of the United States who has ever done more for his state than Senator Ted Stevens."[21] For the money he delivered to his home state, he was named "Alaskan of the Century."[22]

Apart from his institutional power, Stevens, known for having a "short fuse and a long memory,"[23] used his temper as a tool in the legislative process. He loved the comic-book figure the Incredible Hulk and used this character for inspiration in legislative fights. Like Dr. Banner, who transformed himself when he needed supernatural powers, Stevens wore an Incredible Hulk tie on days "when I know I'm going to get into a terrible fight."[24] When other senators saw he was wearing the tie, they knew to look out.[25] The *New York Times* called Stevens "a senator whom colleagues are hesitant to cross." He once said of himself, "I'm a mean, miserable S.O.B."[26]

As the report gained steam, Stevens got angry and directed his famous temper at the Commission's recommendations. When Secretary Lehman briefed a meeting of all the Republican senators on the Commission's conclusion that the Intelligence Community was in need of dramatically increased oversight, Senator Stevens stood up. "This is all bullshit, a lot of crap, John, you don't know what you are talking about, we have very strong oversight of the Intelligence Community, I'm the oversight and we are not making any changes in that because it is working just fine."[27] Stevens blasted the Commission's transformation into a private entity that lobbied Congress and the White House, called the 9/11 Public Discourse Project (PDP). He also strongly opposed the Commission's effort to declassify the top line of the intelligence budget, citing concerns about showing our hand to our adversaries and the potential erosion of authority for the Defense Department.

Senator Robert Byrd of West Virginia, also an appropriator, faulted the Senate's "rush pell-mell into making sweeping intelligence changes simply for the sake of change."[28] He and his cohorts favorably cited an op-ed faulting the 9/11 Commission's insistence on unanimity as representative of the kind of "herd thinking now being blamed for that other recent intelligence failure—the belief that Saddam Hussein possessed weapons of mass destruction."[29]

He and Stevens allied with Henry Kissinger and a band of national security greybeards who warned that "racing to implement reforms on an election timetable is precisely the wrong thing to do. Intelligence reform is too complex and too important to undertake at a campaign's breakneck speed."[30] Kissinger testified before Stevens and Byrd at the Appropriations Committee of concern that "the reforms of the magnitudes that are being talked about and with the impact that they will have on the conduct of intelligence and on the national security machinery . . . will inevitably produce months and maybe years of turmoil as the adjustments are made in the operating procedures of the national security apparatus and of the intelligence machinery." Kissinger argued for "coordination, but not centralization." Concentration of power in one individual might perpetuate groupthink, the chief flaw in the Iraq WMD analysis. Senator Byrd, a fierce advocate of the Senate as the world's greatest deliberative body, encouraged a delay. "Congress should look at a far broader canvas, including the intelligence failures that contributed both to the war and to the continuing insurgency in Iraq."[31] Byrd lamented that the Senate had shirked its duty by rushing legislation, from the creation of the Department of Homeland Security to the Iraq Use of Force Resolution; now the Senate was threatening to repeat those mistakes.

Former DCI Gates, from his post as president of Texas A&M, had warned that summer that creating a DNI separate from the CIA would result in a "eunuch." Now Gates launched a broadside against the Commission's recommendations, warning that the Commission had "diluted" the authority of the position they urged Congress to create.[32] Gates faulted the Commission for its "erroneous assumption" that because Goldwater-Nichols worked to unify the Department of Defense under a secretary, the Intelligence Community could be similarly unified under a DNI. "Goldwater-Nichols worked at Defense in large measure because the changes were limited to one cabinet department." While Goldwater-Nichols vested authority in a secretary of defense, the DNI had to share power with other cabinet secretaries. In particular, Gates saw the Commission's grants of authority to the DNI to hire and fire and to draw intelligence officers from across the IC into intelligence centers as faulty. Instead of ceding power to a DNI, cabinet secretaries "realistically will demand significant influence" in naming positions within their departments and in how intelligence centers would operate. He underscored that the DNI would not "directly control any part of the Intelligence Community." "Held up against the harsh light of bureaucratic politics and practice, the role of the DNI as recommended by the Commission could, in fact, potentially be weaker than the present DCI." Nowhere would the DNI be "unambiguously in charge." Gates warned the SHSGAC: "the danger will be in the temptation to find a middle road, a compromise, that mitigates controversy and unhappiness both in the executive and legislative branches, and that pretends to solve the problems the Commission has identified."[33]

The former and current chairmen of the Senate Intelligence Committee ("the SSCI Senators") shared Gates' view that the Commission approach was faulty. Senators Specter, Shelby, and Roberts advocated for what many described as a "Department of Intelligence" approach and criticized the 9/11 Report and the SHSGAC for timidity. "We feel strongly that the [DNI] must have day-to-day operational control of all elements on the Intelligence Community performing national missions." Senator Bond argued that the Commission had overemphasized budget authority, "Arm twisting that is largely limited to budgetary problems and powers will not solve the problem. ... Budget authority alone is not going to get them to turn over the cards."[34] "Clear lines of authority between the DNI and our national intelligence agencies, extending beyond budgetary control, are critical."[35] Real reform would give the DNI the express authority to supervise, direct, and control the CIA and the national intelligence agencies in the Defense Department.[36]

As noted, leaders of the SASC, Senators Warner and Levin ("the SASC

Senators") questioned the 9/11 Commission's rationale for a DNI. They saw the concentration of power in a DNI, be it the Commission's approach or the SSCI Senators, as unduly intrusive on the Defense Department. They made a run at "whittling away at what would be under the DNI's purview."[37] Since Collins and Lieberman were seen as enhancing centralized management of the *national* intelligence budget, the SASC Senators supported moving some of the Defense Department's intelligence assets out from under the purview of the DNI.[38] Senator Levin, the ranking Democrat on the Armed Services Committee, strongly opposed the notion that the NCTC should be able to devise operational plans for the Defense Department.[39] He stated, "We should not be providing the power or responsibility, primary or otherwise, for operational plans to the NCTC." Like the arguments DoD made at the NSC, Levin argued again that *operational plans* was a term of art signifying plans for the conduct of military operations.[40] He expressed "grave reservations" about giving the NCTC the ability "to assign a component part" of the CIA or the Defense Department with a task.[41] Seeking to protect the flow of intelligence to tactical commanders, Senator Warner also sought to insert into the bill President Bush's chain-of-command language.[42]

In the face of these attacks, Collins and Lieberman sought to maximize the power of the DNI and the NCTC, but within the structure advanced by the Commission (i.e., not creating a Department of Intelligence).[43] Transferring the national intelligence agencies out of the Defense Department would be a "bridge too far" politically;[44] it would "sever the connection between those essential combat-support agencies ... and the secretary of defense."[45] Bopp remembers, "They thought the best chance of actually passing something was what we were doing ... so they were trying to balance the need for a strong DNI against what was possible."[46]

The Collins-Lieberman bill provided that the DNI, like the DCI, would serve as head of the Intelligence Community, act as principal intelligence advisor to the president, and direct and oversee the national intelligence budget.[47] Their bill gave the DNI new budgetary authority. Like the president's executive order, the DNI would "determine" the budget of the National Intelligence Program.[48] The Senate bill adopted the 9/11 Commission's recommendation that the DNI receive an appropriation from Congress.[49] For the DNI to receive its money directly from Congress, the top line of the intelligence budget would have to be declassified.[50] A second key part of the bill was a muscular NCTC. Its primary mission would be to unify the civilian and military counterterrorism efforts by developing interagency plans.[51] Planning would also be "at a more tactical level, such as hunting for Bin Ladin."[52] It would also "assign counterterrorism responsibilities for counterterrorism operations to departments and agencies."[53]

Collins and Lieberman would not surrender the Commission view that "we need a Goldwater-Nichols for intelligence." They maintained that it was highly instructive to their effort "because of the principles that underlay Goldwater-Nichols: that good people cannot overcome bad structure on a consistent basis, and that the aim of structural reform is to clarify responsibility, authority, and accountability."[54] They believed their bill was "transformational reform" of the Intelligence Community.[55] The Iraq intelligence failure also animated their efforts. The Collins-Lieberman bill required an Office of Alternative Analysis to subject future NIEs to "a thorough examination of all facts, assumptions, analytic methods, and judgments utilized in or underlying any analysis, estimation, plan, evaluation, or recommendation contained in such estimate."[56] To combat groupthink, they encouraged the DNI to set up alternative analysis teams in each element of the Intelligence Community.[57]

The first avenue in the Senate to attack the Collins-Lieberman bill was the process by which a committee considers changes to a piece of legislation called a mark-up; any Senator on the committee is able to change the bill, in this case drafted by Collins and Lieberman, if they have the votes. Prevailing at mark-up against a united chairman and ranking is unlikely as the senators generally defer to their committee leadership unless something vital to them is at stake. The real danger for Collins and Lieberman would be the floor of the Senate. The Senate's rules allow *any* senator to offer *almost any* amendment to legislation. The Senate was designed to be the more deliberative chamber, the saucer to cool down the hot tea that might be served in the House. One of a senator's most vital powers was the ability to influence any piece of legislation. In the House, a Committee on Rules could declare amendments "out of order." This check was necessary with the House's 435 members; unrestricted rights to offer amendments would overwhelm the legislative process. But in the Senate, there were only one hundred members. They saw it as their duty to take more time and deliberate. The floor of the Senate would be dangerous territory. The committees that felt disenfranchised by the process, the intelligence and defense committees, could attack the bill. It was also an opportunity for the Senate's old bulls to use delaying tactics to halt its consideration. As the Senate opened its consideration of the intelligence reform measure, Collins and Lieberman were immediately deluged with hundreds of amendments. Navigating the Senate floor was a test; it was a gauntlet through which Collins and Lieberman needed to pass to protect their approach from the onslaught from other Senate factions.

Riding the momentum of the 9/11 Commission, Collins and Lieberman were able to parry the efforts of the SASC Senators to trim the authorities of the DNI. The 9/11 PDP considered the Levin amendments "killers or poison pills."[58] Arguing that under the SASC approach "only twenty percent"[59] of what had been within the purview of the DCI would transfer to the DNI, the SASC's attempts were defeated. Collins and Lieberman were able to fend off Senator Levin's efforts to limit the NCTC to "strategic planning," on the grounds that doing so would "frustrate" the goal of the NCTC by limiting it to only "big policy questions."[60] The duo also defeated efforts to limit the scope of the DNI's budget authority and deterred Senator Warner from offering an amendment to insert the administration's chain-of-command provision into the bill.[61]

The efforts by the SSCI Senators to create a Department of Intelligence flopped. A plan advanced by Senator Roberts would combine the other intelligence agencies with the CIA but gave the impression that the senators "would have wiped the initials 'CIA' off the government's organization chart."[62] The vice chairman of the SSCI called the Roberts plan "overly simplistic" and "disbanding and scattering" the CIA "overkill."[63] George Tenet came out of retirement to equate the Roberts plan with driving "the security of the American people off a cliff."[64] Senator Specter's plan drew similar attacks from the 9/11 PDP who argued privately to the Senate that they opposed building another "giant governmental pyramid" and that stripping the intelligence agencies out of Defense "could hurt combat support."[65] President Bush also opposed it because it would separate him from his line operators. The 9/11 PDP fought these efforts as a bridge too far that would require transferring the combat-support agencies out of the Defense Department in the midst of two wars. Senators Collins and Lieberman, like the Commission, calculated that an approach that preserved the dual-masters system was the only one with a chance of enactment. The SSCI Senators' approach, with too many assailants, failed on the floor of the Senate, garnering only nineteen votes.[66]

As Collins and Lieberman surged ahead, Senators Stevens and Byrd were "appalled" by the Senate's rapid movement and made a last-ditch stand. Senator Byrd, famous for passionate Senate floor speeches incorporating historical analogies, usually from the Roman Senate of ancient times, in the service of furthering congressional power, led an effort to roll back the DNI's power to transfer money as he saw fit.[67] He likened his efforts to the struggles of the English Parliament to assert dominance over the kings and queens of England. He said he was acting in the tradition of the "Englishmen who spilled their blood to wrest the power of the purse away from monarchs."[68] Collins and Lieberman and the 9/11 PDP saw Byrd's efforts as "constraints . . . on the ability of the DNI to transfer funds and personnel within the intelligence community."[69] Seen as an attempt to weaken the DNI, his effort went down, garnering only twenty-nine votes.

The best ground to strike a blow to Collins and Lieberman would be on whether to declassify the top line of the intelligence budget. Declassification was opposed by the White House, the old bulls, and the defense faction. Their message was simple: we should not declassify information that might benefit our enemies. Stevens offered an amendment to strike the section of the Collins bill that mandated the declassification of the intelligence budget.[70] Collins and Lieberman were able to muster an argument that the Stevens amendment would limit the authority of the DNI to receive a congressional appropriation directly. The 9/11 PDP weighed in against it on the grounds that classification would "enshrine principles of excessive secrecy."[71] The Senate voted the amendment down 55-37, causing Stevens to erupt and threaten to delay the bill.[72] The 9/11 PDP marveled at the "mighty courageous act" in opposing the chairman of the Appropriations Committee.[73]

In the end, sentiment for "reform" was too great. Lieberman defended their pace: "The rush is we were attacked on September 11. It is more than three years later, and Congress has not acted to adequately reorganize our Intelligence Community."[74] Capitalizing on the strength of the 9/11 Commission, Collins and Lieberman cruised to victory. On final passage, their bill passed the Senate by a 96-2 vote. Collins and Lieberman had been faulted for their lack of experience but had triumphed nonetheless. Giving the helm to the SHSGAC now seemed inspired. While others considered them to be unversed in national security law, the committee was "comfortable with the notion of being . . . objective . . . with no political stake in how the community would be affected by their bureaucratic changes."[75] Unlike would-be leadership by a committee with a parochial interest, their bipartisan, honest approach had yielded an outcome that supporters saw as best for the country.

The experience of fending off all comers on the Senate floor heightened their resolve to have their way in coming negotiations with the House. A unanimous bipartisan commission of statesmen entrusted the Senate with enacting their recommendations. The president supported them. The Democratic nominee for president supported them. The victims' family groups were behind them. The media and editorials were encouraging. The House Democrats embraced the Senate's bill and joined the coalition. Even some of the Republicans on the House Intelligence Committee were known to be sympathetic to their approach. After the trauma of two intelligence failures, they had been given the honor of remaking the national security infrastructure for a new era in American history. They had taken the mantle of the 9/11 Commission.

For Senator Collins, this was a personal triumph. She outmaneuvered the Senate bulls by mastering the details. She "artfully deflected most attackers simply by insisting that their concerns stem largely from their ignorance of [the bill's] contents."[76] Chairman Roberts conceded that "she's already been able to hold her own here against four other committee chairmen, including me."[77] Harman said, "This fight will separate the men from the boys, and she is very much a man."[78]

CHAPTER ELEVEN

High Ransom

"Denny Hastert hated this idea from the beginning," said one former congressional staffer. The Speaker himself recalled his feeling at the time was that the Commission was just "going to create a bigger bureaucracy."[1] Although pressed by the White House to move a bill, Speaker Hastert saw Rumsfeld's hesitation and knew something wasn't right. Hastert remembered telling the White House, "If there is no unanimity on your side, why should we walk the plank on this thing?"[2] Tom DeLay's view was that "no one cares about this bill except the 9/11 Commission, the Democrats, and the *New York Times.*" But in the months before the 2004 election, it was dangerous to be seen as dismissive of the Commission and its recommendations. While they considered the Commission to be dominated by Democrats and the family groups to be partisan, scuttling legislation to enact the Commission's recommendations was not politically feasible. "Never declare a corpse before an election," said one staffer.

With a decision to initiate a legislative process for the sake of electoral prudence, DeLay's attitude became: "Take everything remotely related to security we've ever wanted and stuff it in the bill, either to kill the bill or to get it all; the sky's the limit."[3] The House committees welcomed this view, rejecting suggestions that their legislative approach should be limited to the four corners of the 9/11 Commission Report. They would not roll over and rubber-stamp the Commission's ideas. The House considered Senator Frist's decision to "disenfranchise" the committees with national security expertise to be irresponsible and charged all its committees with national security within their purview to produce legislation. They called it a "comprehensive approach" to terrorism. The leadership called their committees back to Washington from the August recess to hold hearings. Thereafter, the leadership staff would orchestrate the simultaneous production of legislation from thirteen different committees and meld it into a comprehensive bill to be put before the House for a vote as soon as possible.

Some saw this as a rope-a-dope strategy. The House would pass a bill creating a DNI and an NCTC before the elections to fend off charges they had ignored the recommendations of the popular 9/11 Commission, but it would be on their terms. The bill would be made more palatable by marrying it with other legislative priorities, especially the toughening of immigration restrictions that terrorists might exploit, and specifically a provision to make legal status in the United States a prerequisite to getting a driver's license. In negotiations with the Senate, the House would hold out the prospect of a deal, but only at the high price of Senate acceptance of House provisions to restrict immigration, and only if Duncan Hunter was satisfied that the equities of the Defense Department were protected. The Speaker thought the process needed to play out; if the Senate could not meet its price, the House would be content to run a four-corners offense and run out the clock.

Still, there was resistance to acting at all. "Why are we even doing this?" said one. Some within the House perceived the White House as reaching into the House leadership to appeal for action on the grounds that the Commission had made Republicans politically vulnerable and to deny Senator Kerry an issue against the president. These skeptics believed their leadership and the White House were fundamentally misreading the electoral import of the issue. Citing the virtues of a rigorous congressional committee process that produces legislation only after exhaustive and thorough analysis, they resented what they thought was the general Bush White House congressional strategy, aided and abetted by the House leadership: ram through legislation with speed. The House Republicans had similarly grumbled about having to pass President Bush's education-reform proposal when they saw the Department of Education as a hindrance to the local control of schools. But to them, the most egregious example of legislative haste was the passage of the Homeland Security Act in 2002. The president's staff, from a series of meetings in the bunker of the White House, had devised a legislative proposal to create a Department of Homeland Security in absolute secrecy. The legislation was then sprung on Congress in a presidential address to the nation, and the House was force-marched into passage seven weeks later.

The intelligence reform legislation, coming at the end of Bush's first term, was controversial among House Republicans precisely because it was preceded by numerous legislative victories in President Bush's first term. President Bush and his ally Speaker Hastert had spent a tremendous amount of capital over four years and were now asking for *another* major piece of legislation that a significant number of their members were not excited about. Dan Keniry, President Bush's legislative affairs deputy for the House, noted that

> [t]o fully appreciate the mood of the participants in the negotiations over the Intelligence Reform legislation it is important to recognize the principal players were working on many controversial issues simultaneously. They all brought the baggage of many issues that had come before, and those experiences colored their attitudes as they came into the room to work out the final version of the intelligence bill. This dynamic increased the likelihood that the negotiators may have been trying to leverage one item for another. Among the rank and file, different factions or caucuses were still chafing from the last fight and sought to take it out on the new business at hand.[4]

Against this background, the doubters were aghast that "all of a sudden" they should drop everything and overnight rewrite the 1947 National Security Act, whose intelligence provisions had not been amended wholesale in over fifty years. The Armed Services Committee cited the legislative process in the 1980s to reorganize the Department of Defense as an ideal model. Back then, the committees with the appropriate expertise took four years to conduct hundreds of hearings, briefings, and meetings to arrive at the Goldwater-Nichols Act. Chairman Duncan Hunter debated whether to withdraw from the process but ultimately decided to embrace leadership's plan to pass a bill creating a DNI and an NCTC and "be as involved as possible to try and steer it in the best substantive direction."

Hunter would play an outsized role in devising the House bill's treatment of a DNI and an NCTC. The House's respected veteran expert on intelligence and chairman of the House Intelligence Committee, Porter Goss, who supported simply strengthening the DCI's position,[5] had just been nominated by President Bush to be DCI. With Goss now out of the game, Duncan Hunter would largely have the field to himself. A new chairman of the House Intelligence Committee was installed, Congressman Peter Hoekstra, but he called himself the "new kid on the block," whereas Hunter had been active on national security from his post as chairman of the Armed Services Committee for the last two years. Although the staff of the House Intelligence Committee was involved in the drafting of the provision, a participant recalled there was a "glass ceiling" on including more potent authorities for the DNI. A staffer recalls, "We were handed a script . . . that we shall not affect anything on DoD."[6]

The HASC, HPSCI, and staff from the Appropriations' Subcommittee on Defense drafted a bill that created a DNI that contained many of the authorities and titles enjoyed by the DCI. It made the DNI the head of the Intelligence Community and the principal advisor to the president on intelligence matters.[7] It also maintained the status quo with regard to the DNI's ability to build the budget. But Hunter ensured that the prerogatives of the cabinet secretaries could not be trumped by the DNI. For example, the heart of the 9/11 Commission's recommendation was budget authority, and its chief feature was that the money from Congress would flow through the DNI for disbursement to the intelligence agencies. Hunter rejected this and instead suggested that the money for the defense intelligence agencies travel through the secretary of defense for his disbursement to the intelligence agencies in the Department of Defense. Specifically, Hunter enshrined this arrangement in his legislation by including text dictating that the money from Congress would travel "through the *heads* of departments."[8] As Hunter explained, "The person who passes out the money has the real interest and the real responsiveness from the bureaucracy."[9]

The House bill, like the president's bill, rejected the 9/11 Commission's recommendation to declassify the top line of the intelligence budget. And the House bill rejected the 9/11 Commission's recommendation that the DNI have unfettered authority to transfer intelligence personnel across agencies to meet new or emerging needs without the concurrence of the head of their department.[10] The House bill limited the power of the DNI to transfer dollars appropriated by Congress for other purposes,[11] although the limitations were largely consistent with limits placed on other cabinet secretaries. The House bill, like the president's bill, limited the NCTC to conducting strategic operational planning rather than planning actual operations.[12]

In all, the House bill was taken to be weak on DNI authorities. The White House, while supporting passage, announced its concern that the House bill "does not provide the DNI sufficient authorities to manage the Intelligence Community effectively." In contrast to the House bill, the White House noted that the president's bill contained full budget authority for the DNI, "including clear authority to determine the national intelligence budget, strong transfer and reprogramming authority, [and] explicit authorities to allocate appropriations."[13] Senator Lieberman dismissed the House bill as not giving the DNI "the strength it needs to really run our national Intelligence Community."[14] Some 9/11 Commissioners fretted that the Republicans had drafted the bill without consulting the Democrats.[15] The commissioners debated whether to bash the House Republican bill. Former Commissioner Richard Ben-Veniste said to his fellow commissioners, "I do not believe we have the luxury of silence when faced with a naked attempt to politicize the process."[16] John Lehman advocated a measured tone and was against "needlessly provok[ing] Sensenbrenner and his supporters."[17] Seizing the issue of their exclusion from drafting the House bill, the House Democrats praised the Senate for being "100 percent bipartisan."[18] The House Democrats favored the Senate bill because it was a "clean bill"; it did not include "extraneous" matters not in the 9/11 Commission Report.[19]

The House Republican leadership's "comprehensive approach" also gave a prominent role to Jim Sensenbrenner as the chief advocate for immigration provisions. To Sensenbrenner, the 9/11 Commission's silence on immigration restrictions was a glaring omission, particularly since the 9/11 hijackers had exploited loopholes to gain entry into the United States.

A House Democratic and 9/11 PDP effort to pass the Collins-Lieberman bill through the House failed on a vote of 213-203. The Republican Leadership bill passed the House by a vote of 282-134 on October 8, 2004, less than one month before election day. Including dozens of provisions on foreign affairs, transportation security, money-laundering, border security, and a whole raft of other policy matters, the bill totaled 542 pages.

Kean and Hamilton ultimately did not criticize the House bill as strongly as some of the Democratic commissioners would have liked. "Tom and Lee have deliberately refrained from criticism of the House leadership, for the very reason that the situation remains dynamic and we still seek to move them—and believe they will move—in the Conference committee. How much they move is the question. The role of the White House will be very important here as well."[20]

• • • • • • • • • • • •

For now, the House faction favoring passage of an intelligence bill had won out. The election was still a month away and the Senate, basking in acclaim for their bipartisan bill, was eager to resolve their differences with the House to produce a final bill to send to the president for signature. Management of the House committees' interaction with the Senate, and especially the settling of disputes among House committees, would be overseen by the Speaker's chief of staff, Scott Palmer. Generally such a high-ranking leadership staffer would not become directly involved in a legislative negotiation with the Senate; that work fell to the committees with legislative expertise on the subject matter at hand. But this was an extraordinary situation. The House had thirteen committees of jurisdiction who would need to interface with the SHSGAC to negotiate a final bill.

The task before Scott Palmer was exceedingly complex. The chief of staff has to manage the Speaker's relations with the White House, the Senate, and his party's caucus. To his colleagues who elected him Speaker, he is their representative in negotiations with the White House and the Senate. But as a leader, the Speaker also has a duty to the president to help enact his legislative agenda for the good of party and nation. Finally, as the leader of the party in the House, the Speaker must safeguard against electoral defeat by reconciling the strategic interests of the party with the preferences of its individual members.

Executing these duties when the House was in session, Scott Palmer spent much of his day at his desk, working his way through crises brought to him by breathless aides and complaining congressmen. Because of his close friendship with the Speaker, Palmer carried tremendous authority. He was a thirty-year friend of Denny Hastert's, since their days in Illinois politics. They shared a Capitol Hill townhouse in Washington. Palmer had accompanied the improbable rise of the former history teacher to Speaker of the House.

For the coming negotiations with the Senate on the intelligence bill, Palmer would need to mute the hostility of the House Republicans toward the Commission. At the same time, he needed to demonstrate to the public that the House Republicans were serious about responding to the popular Commission and acting responsibly to secure the nation from terrorist attack. Specifically, Palmer's job would be to corral Chairmen Hunter and Sensenbrenner and their staffs into sincere negotiations with the Senate, at least until after the 2004 elections. The White House's interest was in getting a deal and took a public approach of supporting the "best of both bills." Seeing the power of the Speaker as the only means to induce compromise from Sensenbrenner and Hunter, the White House sought to elevate Palmer's stewardship of the process. Complicating this task was a commitment that the Speaker and DeLay had made to Sensenbrenner and Hunter that a final deal with the Senate would only be agreed to if the chairmen were satisfied.

Despite these assurances, Hunter and Sensenbrenner, seeing that enthusiasm for the 9/11 Commission's recommendations had infused pre-election Washington, began to make calculations to maximize their leverage in negotiations with the Senate and prevent being forced to compromise by their leadership. The two chairmen and their top staffers—Robert Rangel, the staff director of the HASC, and Phil Kiko, the staff director for the Judiciary Committee—met for a secret dinner at the Capitol Hill Club, catty-corner from the Cannon House Office Building. The House Armed Services Committee was one of the largest committees in Congress, with thirty-three Republicans. Additionally, given his personal popularity and the Republicans' natural inclination to support the Defense Department, Hunter would have sway over many more. Sensenbrenner had a substantial following, too. That the immigration system was broken was an article of faith among many House Republicans. Given the opportunity to stand up for tightening immigration law, many House Republicans would get behind Sensenbrenner. Recognizing that together they controlled a substantial bloc, over slabs of steak, the two struck a secret side deal. To buttress their positions against Senate momentum, their pact was to stick together: until both were satisfied with the work product, nothing was final.

CHAPTER TWELVE

Touching Gloves

With only sixteen days until the election, the Senate could feel its leverage slipping away. Late on a Sunday afternoon, a pack of Senate staffers fumbled around southwest Washington, DC, looking for an obscure congressional building. Although only a few hundred yards from the Capitol, this patch of low-rise governmental offices was considered the boondocks. The Senate staff was looking for the auxiliary offices sometimes used by the House Intelligence Committee in the Ford House Office Building. The Senate was working on Sunday because with the elections looming there was barely enough time to reconcile all their differences with a reluctant House and pass a final bill for the president's signature.

So the Senate staff came in overwhelming force, toting books, bills, position papers, graphs, statutes, statements, and charts—one staffer even had a roller suitcase packed with documents. These twenty flooded into the office space temporarily occupied by the House staffers. It resembled a college fraternity house: there were pizza boxes strewn about and a muted TV showed an NFL game. The House staffers, casually dressed, seemed bemused by the invasion. With an air of detachment, the House staff called the meeting to order. Tweaking the Senate for showing up with a platoon of negotiators, the staff director of the House Intelligence Committee addressed the Senate throng: "The four of us you see here today are the only four staffers you'll ever see in these negotiations." He introduced the staff directors of the Judiciary, the Armed Services Committees, and the clerk of the Defense Appropriations Subcommittee and explained that they had been empowered to negotiate on behalf of the House Republican majority.

While the Senate was eager to expedite negotiations, the House dashed their hopes. Negotiations were impossible tonight—"No one has read the

Senate bill." The House gently mocked the Senate for the delay in sending over a complete bill, which had been held up for eleven days as the Senate's clerks tackled the laborious task of incorporating amendments accepted on the Senate floor into the final product. Two of the 9/11 families were so angered at the delay that they went to the Office of the Senate Clerk to press them to hurry up.[1]

Careful not to cede the moral high ground, the House negotiators named a strong DNI and NCTC as two of their prerequisites to a deal. They also insisted that there would be no declassification of the aggregate budget total for the Intelligence Community, and adding, "We can't break something that works today."[2]

The Senate asked one its staffers, Gordon Lederman, imported from the 9/11 Commission, to state their case: they wanted community-level leadership of the Intelligence Community and integration modeled on the law that had unified the armed services under a combatant commander reporting to the secretary of defense. The Intelligence Community had to be flexible and agile to fight networks of international terrorists—the DNI needed to be able to move people and money quickly without interference from other cabinet secretaries or from Congress. It needed to set standards and have the ability to manage the community. Above all, the DNI had to have institutional clout, and that would come through power of the purse, by receiving the intelligence appropriation directly from Congress. The DCI had "no idea" where the intelligence dollars were going. The DNI needed more authority.

The House staff dismissed these arguments as "folklore" and demanded the Senate cite one example where the secretary of defense had unjustly thwarted the DCI by withholding intelligence dollars. If anything, the DCI's role needed a check; institutional tension could be a good thing. After declaring that negotiations would be made difficult by this critical "factual disagreement," the group agreed to reconvene the next morning.

This exchange was the opening act in an opaque congressional process called "conference"—a process designed to allow the House and the Senate to reconcile their bills through negotiations. This conference would be a clash of world views; the Senate saw the Intelligence Community as one whole in need of a powerful manager, while the House sought to preserve a careful balancing of authorities between the DNI and the departments. It was an article of faith to the Senate that intelligence was already broken, whereas the House feared a solution in search of a problem might break what already worked. The House leadership saw the SHSGAC as national-security neophytes tapped to rubber-stamp the 9/11 Commission's will with the House Democrats as their co-pilots. The Senate saw the House's paeans to "the war-fighters" as a mask for their blindly pro-military parochialism at the expense of a larger good.

Where the House saw the Senate bill as "full of deadly mistakes, deadly mistakes that the author does not even know about because he simply copied what somebody else put down,"[3] the Senate saw conservative Republican zealots seeking to hijack a bill to enact punitive anti-immigrant measures. A House leadership staffer worried that the Senate's zeal was Congress at its worst, "messing around with intelligence because of a bunch of families who don't know anything," and added that the House's members were "offended at the idea that national security was being driven by a bunch of families and commissioners."[4] The SHSGAC saw themselves as the triumphant victors who had vanquished the Senate's old bulls. They transcended partisanship and united the Senate behind a dramatic new national-security blueprint for a new era while the House tried to score political points by advancing its narrow agenda. The Senate was transcendent; a House negotiator remembers being seen as "knuckle-dragging Neanderthals."[5]

The Senate's and the House Democrats' strategy was that, with everyone behind them, they should bludgeon the House Republicans until they gave in. For the Democrats in the Collins-Lieberman camp, it was a win-win. If, before the election, the Republicans would not budge, the Democrats would highlight their recalcitrance. If they caved to the Democrats and the Senate, all the better: their policy preference would prevail. Their substantive and political interests were in alignment, so they would turn up the heat. (However, some Democrats supported delaying agreement on the intelligence reform bill until after the election. They preferred not to give President Bush an opportunity to be presidential in a Rose Garden bill-signing ceremony just as Americans stepped into the ballot box.) A House negotiator sized up the Senate's attitude: "The Senate thought they had all the cards, started off thinking this has to pass, you'd have to be insane not to pass it, we can pretty much get them to swallow the Senate bill and not have to do much."[6]

The White House trod gently. As the final arbiter, the president could veto whatever the conference devised. But wielding a presidential veto was not the best way to do business with members of his own party, especially when the president needed them for an ambitious second-term agenda. But on the substance of the full budget authority issue, the president had embraced the Senate's formulation for a DNI and had described the House bill as weak.[7] The White House had expressed concern that the House bill did not provide "sufficient authorities to manage the Intelligence Community effectively"[8] and explicitly expressed its preference for the Senate's "strong budget authority."[9] But it also favored numerous aspects of the House-passed bill, including its simplicity, believing that the Senate had larded its bill with too much bureaucracy. The White House came out in favor of the "best of each" bill and called for expeditious completion.

• • • • • • • • • • • •

As the staff skirmished, the new chairman of the House Intelligence Committee became assertive. With Goss leaving Congress to become DCI, Hoekstra was now thrust into the intelligence overhaul. The chairmanship of the Intelligence Committee was a prestigious post. The appointment of Intelligence Committee members was reserved exclusively to the Speaker. This was no ordinary ascension into a chairmanship; he would be taking over in the middle of the biggest reorganization of the Intelligence Community since World War II, and his fellow members were irritated at being passed over. Hoekstra felt he had stepped into the "line of fire with your own people shooting at you."[10]

Not only was he chairman of the House Intelligence Committee but Hoekstra also became chairman of the Conference Committee, a special body composed of senators and congressmen charged with the specific task of reconciling the differences on the intelligence reform bill before Congress. Formal conference meetings are one of the rare occasions when members of the House and Senate of both parties sit together in public and discuss legislation. As public meetings, formal conference gatherings are often opportunities to set out views and jockey for position. Because of the unusual scrutiny on the intelligence reform legislation and because the election was only weeks away, this time it was also an opportunity to posture before an audience of press, staff, and family members of the victims of the September 11 attacks.

Chairman Hoekstra gaveled the public Conference Committee to order. The 9/11 Families sat in the audience in silent support of the Senate bill. Former commissioner Tim Roemer lurked. The meeting began smoothly;

a succession of speakers, including the Democratic members of the House, extolled the Senate bill. Congressman Skelton explained that since ninety-six senators plus all the Democrats in the House equaled a majority of Congress, the Senate bill should be adopted—and doubly so, given the support from the White House, the victims' families, and the 9/11 PDP.

By now, Jane Harman and Susan Collins had become fast friends. To signal their new friendship, and the House Democrats' alliance with the Senate, at the conference committee meeting Harman turned to the audience and declared, "Susan Collins rocks." Together with Senator Lieberman, they would be the three strongest advocates for the 9/11 Commission's vision of a strong DNI. The 9/11 PDP supported the trio and reiterated its support for the Senate's bill.[11] They warned that if the DNI wasn't going to be given strong authority to determine the intelligence budget and flexibility to move people and money around to meet new threats, to hire and fire heads of the agencies, and to force information-sharing across the government, Congress should not bother. In a letter to Collins, Kean and Hamilton wrote, "Half-hearted reform would leave us worse off than we are today."[12]

With his turn to speak, Hunter warned, "[There is a] very careful balance. Let's not sever the lifeline between these troops and the platforms, the people who are shooting the bullets."[13]

Sensenbrenner also laid down markers. His immigration provisions were not "extraneous," they were vital to fill important gaps in national security.[14]

Hoekstra began to wrap up the meeting and casually mentioned that the House Republicans would soon present what he called a "good-faith global product," an offer from the House to the Senate. Harman seized the opportunity to highlight that the House Democrats had not been party to the House Republican offer and were firmly aligned with Collins and Lieberman. They protested against the method by which the House Republicans had assembled the "good-faith global product" and dismissed the Republican attitude as "take it or leave it." The Senate Democrats jumped in to needle the House on the virtues of bipartisanship and not staining the Senate's transcendent methods by presenting a "one-sided approach," especially "in front of the families of the victims."[15] Senator Collins stepped forward to throw Hoekstra a lifeline. "It's really important that we not overreact." She and Senator Lieberman would sit down with Chairman Hoekstra and his counterpart, Congresswoman Jane Harman, to start talking about the House offer.

The get-together by these four to discuss the bill began a variant of the conference process that they nicknamed the "Big Four." Congressman Hoekstra would later compare the partnership that he developed with Collins, Lieberman, and Harman to the bond forged in combat. The four of them were a "band of brothers and sisters"[16] allied against an array of hostile forces. But Hoekstra was in a terribly uncomfortable position. As the Speaker's man on the Intelligence Committee, he owed his seat to Denny Hastert. Hastert and DeLay, in turn, had pledged to Chairmen Hunter and Sensenbrenner that they would not make a move without them. On the one hand, Hoekstra was personally an advocate for a strong DNI. But as the House's top representative on the conference committee with the Senate, Hoekstra owed a duty to advocate the House position as expressed in the "comprehensive approach" that had passed just days before. Regarding his predicament, Hoekstra recalled that the Speaker and DeLay's commitment to Hunter and Sensenbrenner "made life really hard."[17]

These opening skirmishes marked the first serious obstacle to the 9/11 Commission juggernaut. Negotiations between the House and the Senate were proving difficult; both sides took a step back to assess strategy. If the House was going to rope-a-dope past the election, the Senate needed to activate its allies to pressure the House—and, further, pressure the White House to make the House negotiate in good faith. The Senate would deploy the 9/11 Commissioners and appeal to the Families and paint the House as recalcitrant in the face of a national security imperative. Tim Roemer was eager to get in the fight. "We need to keep the bipartisan pressure on the White House and the Congress to pass a strong bill. This may all quickly evaporate after the election. Now is the time to call Andy Card, House and Senate leadership, and the conferees and urge them to complete a bill in the next 48 hours."[18] They would maintain a line that this bill should be confined to just matters arising from the 9/11 Commission Report. Sensenbrenner's immigration concerns were extraneous and should be considered in another forum.

The White House developed its own conference strategy, which was to frequently reiterate that the president supported a strong DNI with a robust complement of authorities to manage the Intelligence Community. Andy Card would stay in close contact with Senator Collins to assure her of their common cause. But the White House also privately appealed directly to Duncan Hunter, orchestrating a series of calls from the Defense Department and the vice president underscoring the president's position and his confidence that the Defense Department would not suffer under any new arrangements. The president, on the campaign trail fighting John Kerry for reelection, was held in reserve. The White House's inside game would be to support an expansion of Scott Palmer's role in managing the process for the House. Hoekstra alone could not induce Hunter to compromise. The White House would work on Hunter, but they also recognized that they needed the power of the Speaker to broker an agreement with the Senate. If Palmer played a hands-on role in the conference negotiations with the Senate, maybe he could cajole cooperation, since he implicitly wielded the Speaker's cudgel. Inducing compromise from Hunter would require close cooperation between the White House and the Speaker. Meanwhile, the White House would work to convince the Senate that a deal was impossible without their accepting some of Sensenbrenner's immigration provisions. The Senate should find something in the House bill they could support, with which they could buy off Sensenbrenner. That would have the possible effect of inducing more cooperation from Hunter if he was left standing alone against the Senate. Palmer remembers,

> It took a while to educate [the Senate] to the fact that there was another point of view, that there was a more comprehensive view and that there were people in the House who were bloody serious about getting it. . . . But part of my job was to try and explain . . . just how . . . willing the people on our side were to blow the thing up if they did not get what they wanted.[19]

CHAPTER THIRTEEN

Dirty Bombs

Duncan Hunter conducted his business in the Member's Dining Room, a small enclave downstairs from the floor of the House of Representatives. The room had been constructed in the late 1950s; a fresco by Constantino Brumidi, originally located in the House Chamber, peered down from the wall, and there were majestic columns and beautiful curtains flanking the room. Hunter was a regular in the dining room and had his own table. His daily dish was a medium-rare rib-eye steak, and with a knife in his left hand, he oversaw a parade of staff that rotated through to receive tasks.

A veteran of many conferences with the Senate, he had a simple congressional strategy: pursue everything he cared about with unrelenting gusto. This tenacity had allowed him to rise in the House and into the position of chairmanship of the House Armed Services Committee. Hunter understood how to maximize leverage in congressional negotiations. Seeing that the greatest vulnerability for the House was the Senate's and White House's refrain that the House plan's budget authority was weak, Hunter sought to introduce a new argument: the Senate's budget language would be harmful to troops in the field.

The House budget-authority language most important to Hunter and most disliked by the Senate and White House was the requirement that money appropriated by Congress travel "through the heads of departments" on its way to the intelligence agencies in the Defense Department. By seeming to bypass the DNI, the House's arrangement would hurt the DNI's ability to assert any measure of control over defense intelligence agencies. Advocates of a strong DNI believed that if the DNI were "writing the checks," the intelligence agencies would have to be responsive. This was exactly Hunter's argument: the defense intelligence agencies' first duty was to assist the troops in the field, and that was placed at risk by a DNI who enjoyed primacy over the secretary of defense. Early in the conference negotiations, Collins, Lieberman, Harman, and Hoekstra appealed directly to Hunter. "The Big Four Spoke with Duncan Hunter but failed to move him."[1] "Hunter sees himself as the last defender of the common soldier's ability to get adequate and timely intelligence." Reportedly, "Senator Collins characterized the discussions as 'extremely frustrating.'"[2]

To bolster his case, Hunter needed someone from the Pentagon to speak out against the Senate's budget language. This would be a difficult proposition; the Defense Department worked for the president, who was their commander in chief, and Defense was under strict orders from the White House not to contradict the president's strong DNI position.

Hunter was not much for formal process. "His style was just to pick up the phone and call a sergeant or the vice president" when he needed something done.[3] Hunter hit the phones. He first tried Secretary Rumsfeld, asking Rumsfeld to go public in his opposition to the Senate's budget approach and endorse Hunter's formulation.

Rumsfeld had been under fire because of reports that his intelligence lieutenant, Steve Cambone, had been making the rounds on the Hill to lobby against the Commission's recommendations. The exchange at the military operations briefing with Senator Warner—where the secretary seemed to confirm his misgivings about the 9/11 recommendations—had gotten around. The White House suspected that the Defense Department was quietly working against the president's strong-DNI position.

A public endorsement of the House budget position was a bridge too far for the secretary. "I cannot and will not contradict the president on this thing," Rumsfeld told Hunter.[4] Hunter accepted his answer. "He was the president's guy [and] needed to be a loyal trooper."[5]

Hunter then decided to go after the next best thing—the chairman of the Joint Chiefs of Staff, Richard Myers, the principal military advisor to the president, the National Security Council, and the secretary of defense. The chairman's duties included strategic plans for the armed forces, and, as the top uniformed official in the Defense Department, he represented the service branches in meetings of the National Security Council. Weekly, he and Secretary Rumsfeld met with the president privately in the Oval Office. Hunter would remind him that the law gave the chairman of the Joint Chiefs an obligation to render his professional military judgment when asked. About nine in the evening, Duncan Hunter picked up the phone again and called for General Myers.

At Bolling Air Force Base in Washington, DC, General Myers was enjoying a special dinner with other top military brass and their wives. The purpose of the dinner was to give enlisted aides enrolled in a course in food service the opportunity to practice their trade for VIPs. In keeping with the event, General Myers and his compatriots were in full military regalia. Toward the end of the dinner, General Myers was pulled from the table to take an urgent phone call.

"Dick, Duncan Hunter here." Hunter explained that he was in serious conference negotiations with the Senate and needed him to state in writing his opposition to the budget formulation for the DNI posited by the Senate.[6] Given Hunter's assertiveness, General Myers had had plenty of contact with him through the years. Hunter was a man of action and hard to say no to, but standing outside his black sport utility vehicle on the phone while the dinner continued inside, Myers told Hunter that he had to be loyal to the president.

Undeterred, Hunter asked Myers whether the Senate approach would limit the "effectiveness" of the armed forces. Hunter reminded Myers that he had what Hunter believed was "a statutory duty, an obligation to answer, [to] give your personal views on these—on these important security matters."[7]

Myers relented. "Okay, I owe you that," Hunter recalled him saying. Myers responded that in his opinion it would [limit the effectiveness] of the armed forces.[8] General Myers called back to the office and directed the drafting of a letter overnight. Myers informed Rumsfeld of Hunter's request and that he would respond.[9] Secretary Rumsfeld understood that "of course" General Myers had an obligation to write the letter. No one called the White House.

Myers faxed the letter to Hunter and then sent it along to Secretary Rumsfeld. It read in part:

> In this regard the budgets of the combat support agencies should come up from the agencies through the secretary of defense to the national intelligence director, ensuring that required warfighting capabilities are accommodated and rationalized and ensuring that the secretary meets his obligations. For appropriations, it is likewise important that the appropriations are passed from the National Intelligence Director *through the Department* to the combat support agencies. It is my understanding

that the House bill maintains this vital flow through the secretary of defense to the combat support agencies. It is my recommendation that this critical provision be preserved in the conference.[10]

Hunter waited for a propitious moment to spring the letter. The White House had been working on Hunter to allow for more powers for the DNI. To combat the perception left by Secretary Rumsfeld's appearances on Capitol Hill where he appeared to dissent from the president's position, Card had orchestrated a call from Steve Cambone to Hunter to make it clear that the Defense Department supported the budget formulation in the bill that President Bush had sent to Congress. Hunter replied, "Message received," and hung up. Next, Steve Hadley was sent to the Hill to try to make progress with Hunter. If *the commander in chief* in a time of war was comfortable with giving the DNI more budget authority, Hadley would argue, then Chairman Hunter should not worry how the Defense Department would fare under the new law. The president was in the best position to make the judgment on what was best for the troops.

Hadley, diligent and earnest, had mastered the intricacies of the intelligence budgeting process during six weeks of laborious negotiations with the Defense Department over the budget language in the president's submission to Congress. Hadley and a few aides went to Capitol Hill and set up camp in a small conference room in Speaker Hastert's office, the locus of conference negotiations activity, ready to meet with Hunter and work out a compromise. As the meeting began underneath the bronze and crystal chandelier, Chairman Hunter pulled the Myers letter from his pocket and slid it across the table to Hadley. Hunter calmly explained that given the position of the chairman of the Joint Chiefs, he certainly could not be expected to agree to alternative arrangements. The nation's top military official saw harm in the Senate's and White House's approaches; Hunter was duty-bound to hold firm with the House's language. Hadley studied the letter, "I have not seen this." Unflappable, Hadley said he would discuss the matter with Chairman Myers, but he added that he had been sent to the Capitol on behalf of the president and that the commander in chief was confident that the budget language would not harm the effectiveness of the armed forces. The meeting was over.

The persistent view in the Senate was that President Bush was not *really* in favor of creating a DNI.[11] Andy Card remembered that this "really did bother me, and it bothered the president; the president took the heat for making the decision to support it, but once he makes the decision he wants everyone to be on the team."[12] To combat this perception, Andy Card had spent time one afternoon personally calling Senate staff to reassure them that the president was committed to getting a deal. The Myers letter would upset these efforts. Upon receiving the news of the Myers letter on a tarmac in Iowa where he was campaigning for the president, Card was furious. "I was hot, angry."[13] "I didn't want the president to be perceived as against the reforms, if he was a status quo president after 9/11, it was not going to work."[14]

General Myers recalls receiving a phone call from "one of the president's inner circle" with a stern message. "I hope you know, General, you just cost the president the election."[15] Myers recalls answering, "What are you talking about?" Card told him that the letter showed a split between the military and the commander in chief. Myers replied that he was under a statutory obligation to give his military assessment.[16]

Andy Card called Secretary Rumsfeld with the same message. Rumsfeld remembers replying, "Come on, Card, that's utter nonsense. This has nothing to do with politics. General Myers had to do what he did."[17] Rumsfeld's view of the negotiations was that Andy Card was working with Susan Collins, "making compromises." Rumsfeld sent over a note that afternoon with press guidance for how the White House might reply to press inquiries about Myers's apparent break with the president. In the cover note, Rumsfeld wrote, "Again, Andy, my apologies that I did not give you a heads-up this morning."[18] The letter made it into the papers, but its real impact was on the conference negotiations. The White House efforts to move Hunter were dead in the water. The letter was a shield against any entreaties for a stronger DNI. The media would use the letter against President Bush as evidence that the Pentagon was trying to scuttle the reforms of the 9/11 Commission. Senator Collins saw the Myers letter as a shot from Rumsfeld. "I was totally convinced [Myers] did not do that on his own, Myers did not do anything without Secretary Rumsfeld telling him to, and I am convinced that it was Rumsfeld undermining [the bill] and pretending he has clean hands."[19]

• • • • • • • • • • •

The House negotiators boasted that the Myers letter had hit "like a nuclear bomb."[20] Bolstered by the Myers letter, the House devised a new offer to the Senate. It contained minor concessions: the DNI would "determine and develop" the budget rather than merely "developing it." At the behest of the White House, the House now for the first time adopted the chain-of-command provision as its position. Congresswoman Carolyn Maloney and a group of 9/11 Families held a press conference to declare, "Mr. President, do everything in your power [to force the House to compromise]. Act now. Only then will Americans heading to the voting booth in November be able to judge whether you did everything you could to protect them."[21] Privately, Commissioner Gorelick worried that they had lost their momentum. Citing her travels around the country, Gorelick reported to her colleagues that "the perception is that the House Republicans are 'implementing the 9-11 recommendations.'"[22] Recognizing that the congressional battle was not "penetrating into the campaign news cycles," the 9/11 PDP proposed an "escalation plan" to ramp up public pressure. Again the commissioners sought to put out Kean and Hamilton to call for action and to ask Senator McCain to warn the president that "the ship is almost on the rocks" but that it will not "sink silently."[23]

The House, seeking cover, appealed to the White House to say something nice about their forthcoming offer. The White House demurred. Next, the House sought to induce support from Philip Zelikow, the former executive director of the 9/11 Commission. Watching closely from his post back at the University of Virginia in Charlottesville, Zelikow was very worried that the Commission's momentum was nearly gone. The 9/11 Commission's rollout strategy was predicated on the election as the driving force for their recommendations. Without this impetus, their recommendations, like those of a dozen commissions preceding them, would be lost. Zelikow recalled, "If we did not break impasse, we might well lose the bill . . . I thought we were right on the edge."[24]

So when Scott Palmer called seeking support, Zelikow was open to his appeal. Palmer explained the dynamics in the House Republican Conference. Palmer believed that Hunter would not just give up and agree with the Commission's language. Since Duncan Hunter could bring over many members, the Speaker would not roll over Hunter and vote a bill that a majority of his conference would not support. A House leadership staffer remembers it "took hours of walking through and convincing" Zelikow that the DNI authorities in the House bill were sufficient. "Scott Palmer was on the phone with him saying, 'Does this do it, does that do it?'"[25] Zelikow remembers consulting General Hayden on whether the House formula would work. It could, if the wind was blowing in the right direction. In other words, the House bill's authorities were weak, but congressional and presidential support for the DNI's efforts could compensate for the deficiencies. Zelikow, a historian, took a long view. The House bill was better than nothing at all, and over time the DNI could accumulate more authority, as the secretary of defense had done from 1947 until finally in 1986 the Department of Defense was truly unified under the secretary by the Goldwater-Nichols Act. Zelikow trusted Palmer as sincere and an honest broker and made what he considered a pragmatic judgment. At Palmer's request and believing he was acting to break the logjam, Zelikow wrote an e-mail to the Senate on behalf of the House position.

Soon thereafter, a fax rolled off the machine at the vice president's West Wing office. The fax was from Chairman Hunter's office. A note on the cover page directed the vice president to read the startling commentary from Philip Zelikow on the new House language on budget authority offered to the Senate. In an e-mail to Senate negotiators, Zelikow called the new House bill "a significant improvement." And he dismissed a Senate critique of the House's bill: it was a "useful list" of the differences in approach but not a "substantive policy analysis that weighs the significance of the differences, many of which do not seem important."[26] Zelikow lamented that under the House approach, the aggregate intelligence budget total would remain classified, thereby maintaining the status quo necessity that the money travel through the office of the secretary of defense before reaching the defense intelligence agencies. But if it were a mere "pass through" from the DNI and the funding could not be withheld, skimmed, conditioned, or obstructed by the secretary of defense, then, given that the House bill had strong budget and personnel provisions, the House's approach "seems a relatively reasonable way to do the job." Even without a "pass through arrangement," this "should not be a reason for bringing down the whole bill." To the Senate negotiators, Zelikow offered some advice in the hope that they would declare victory and accept the House offer. Zelikow concluded, "You are in the midst of the fight and may have trouble seeing beyond all the smoke hanging over the battlefield. But you have achieved much, including the core of a good bill on these key points. Well done."[27]

For the House, this was a coup. The 9/11 Commission's own guy was endorsing the House bill. The House Republicans were jubilant. The Zelikow e-mail threatened to change the narrative. It was the Senate that was unreasonable. Hunter pressed the advantage. "We now have a bill that is acceptable to the staff director of the 9/11 Commission. The question is: Why can't [the Senate] take yes for an answer."[28] The Senate negotiators were zealots; the Zelikow e-mail proved it.

But the Zelikow e-mail backfired. While Zelikow beckoned them away from the smoke-filled battlefield, the Senate was not ready to surrender the fight. In their minds, the whole battle had been about "fighting Rumsfeld"[29] on behalf of the 9/11 Commission, and now, coming down the pre-election stretch in the heat of battle, Zelikow had betrayed them, like Brutus turning on Caesar. Senator Collins was furious, citing the Zelikow e-mail as "basically disowning the report that he had written."[30] Harman called Zelikow. "Harman was like, 'Who are you to make political judgments about the Congress?'"[31] It was especially galling since Zelikow had not informed Kean and Hamilton of his intentions and the e-mail appeared only days after a Kean-Hamilton public letter had warned that without full authorities for the DNI, "we do not believe such a position should be created."[32] Bearing the condemnation from the Senate, Zelikow e-mailed his colleagues that he was a "seriously unpopular person right now" and defended his actions. "[Collins, Lieberman, and Harman] are so caught up in the fight, and in their frustrated (and understandable) anger toward Rumsfeld, Hunter, Cambone, Myers, etc. that they don't have a strategy to win, and have trouble seeing that the House offer is a way forward."[33] Privately, Commissioners Bob Kerrey and John Lehman agreed with Zelikow that the House was moving toward the Senate[34] and that the core ingredients for the success of the DNI were now in the House bill.[35] Still, Kean and Hamilton promptly disavowed the Zelikow e-mail. "The commissioners speak for the commissioners. . . . Dr. Zelikow speaks for himself."[36]

Senator Collins and Congresswoman Harman called the Zelikow e-mail and the Myers letter "dirty bombs" that undermined the Senate's negotiating position.[37] "The Zelikow e-mail hurt a lot. It was widely perceived by the supporters of intelligence reform on the Hill as the single thing that really killed us."[38] Meanwhile, having successfully drafted the chairman of the Joint Chiefs of Staff and the former executive director of the 9/11 Commission into their camp, the House was emboldened.[39] The Zelikow e-mail and the Myers letter did indeed deal serious setbacks to the Senate's position and made White House efforts to induce the House to compromise impossible.[40] "We have gone about as far as we can go without jeopardizing the troops in the field," one House aide told a publication.[41] Most Republicans doubted that the 9/11 Commission bill was an issue in their reelection campaigns, but in any event,[42] the Zelikow e-mail and the Myers letter inoculated them from charges that they were obstructing a landmark national security measure.

Sensing an imminent collapse, Governor Kean and Congressman Hamilton reemerged to throw a Hail Mary pass. "Al Qa'ida wants to hit us again and we cannot wait [any longer]. . . . Dramatic reform of our institutions is necessary. . . . Come together and complete action . . . the hour is late . . . [the parties must] redouble their efforts." To try to repair the damage of the Zelikow e-mail and spin Zelikow's apparent defection, Kean and Hamilton said, "The Senate bill is preferable, but we believe that the House has made a genuine effort to come forward over the weekend and that . . . the difference is clearly narrowing."[43] Now just days before the election, the Senate, the 9/11 PDP, and the 9/11 Families were in a panic. The Senate sent a message to the 9/11 PDP that the negotiations were "on the verge of break-up" and that their "urgent attention" was required.[44]

• • • • • • • • • • • •

In those days before the election, only Capitol Police Department officers stalked the halls of the Capitol, save for the stray staffer traveling to a meeting. The officers stood like sentries outside important offices, on top of padded "welcome mats" to make the hours standing post on marble easier on their joints. Occasionally, a few reporters hung around outside the Speaker's office just off the Capitol Rotunda, hoping to catch a glimpse into what was going on inside. The Speaker of the House controlled a suite of ornate rooms on the west face of the Capitol. They had been created in the early 1900s from space previously occupied by the Library of Congress. Many of the windows provided a view of the National Mall. As the members of Congress campaigned for reelection, Scott Palmer and his staff were some of the few left behind to deal with the House's legislative business. In this vacuum, empowered by the Speaker to organize the House's efforts,[45] Palmer gradually became the House's chief negotiator with the Senate. "He is calling the shots for the house in conference," Zelikow reported to his colleagues.[46] In these efforts, Palmer was joined by Chairman Hoekstra, who, assured of reelection, could afford to stay behind in Washington.

Palmer's overriding motivation was to protect the Speaker's and the

House's position. Believing there was electoral vulnerability even beyond the 2004 election for the House in being seen as obstructionist, Palmer saw his role as maneuvering the House into good-faith negotiations with the Senate. The White House had actively promoted an increased management role for Palmer, seeing that the power of the Speaker would be necessary to induce compromise from Hunter—to say nothing of Sensenbrenner, whose provisions the Senate ignored, hoping they would just go away.

In frequently unstructured discussions lasting late into the night, Palmer listened to the senators and then summoned the staff from the Armed Services Committee to explain themselves, either privately or in impromptu appearances before the Big Four. This process engendered resentment. Some staff saw Palmer as running out well ahead of the Speaker and the position of the Republican Conference. The committees griped that they were not sure whom to negotiate with—the Senate or Palmer. Having a few members of Congress and staff sitting around trying to figure out how to proceed on the "basis of over-simplifications and hyperbolic characterizations"[47] was not the way to produce a good result. Palmer was very close to the president's chief lobbyist, David Hobbs. Speaker Hastert remembered that "sometimes I was not sure whether Palmer was working for me or for the White House."[48] Ironically, Palmer and Hobbs often worked so closely together that Hobbs frequently took similar criticism at the White House: as he passionately explained the point of view from the Speaker's office, Hobbs was reminded that he worked for the president, not for Denny Hastert.

Gradually, through hours of meetings hunkered down with the Big Four, often with dinner ordered in and beers pilfered out of the Speaker's refrigerator, Palmer became enmeshed in the details of legislation. The Speaker recalled that Palmer was "very cerebral, a very smart guy but once he buys into something he is 180 percent into it and it is hard to get him to focus on anything else."[49] Palmer's staff remembered he was moved by a meeting with the 9/11 Families. "He came out shaken and more committed" to getting a deal.[50] Scott was "looking through a different prism than the way most House Republicans were, he looked at it through the prism of . . . the White House, the 9/11 Families, and through the Senate."[51] Palmer's original motivation for good-faith negotiations with the Senate had been born from his analysis of the politics. He strongly disagreed with the point of view expressed by the majority leader that there was no political risk in playing hardball on the Commission recommendations. Palmer recalled,

"I think I figured out pretty early that this was a political nightmare if we didn't deal with it. But as I got more into the weeds, I came to appreciate from a substantive level how important it was to get this done."[52]

In the hours and hours of meetings and discussions in the deserted pre-election Capitol, Scott Palmer won the trust of Collins and Lieberman. Collins recalled Palmer "over and over again whipping people back into shape."[53] David Hobbs remembered Palmer was seen as an "honest broker."[54] Senator Collins remembered the Families had a profound influence on Palmer: "They truly touched him and he felt we had to produce."[55] Jane Harman called him a "lovely man."[56]

Hastert and DeLay may have left town in August believing that the strategy was to run out the clock, but over time Scott Palmer, their chief negotiator back in Washington, had come to believe that the Senate's position was not as bad as the House had originally thought. As Palmer gradually moved toward the Senate–White House view on the authorities of the DNI and NCTC, Collins and Lieberman, in turn, began to see that maybe they needed to come up with something to assuage Sensenbrenner. Insisting that they were not on the committees of jurisdiction over immigration provisions, they invited their fellow conferee, Senator Richard Durbin, who also served on the Judiciary Committee, to meet with Sensenbrenner.

As the window narrowed before the election, Palmer engineered a meeting between the Speaker and Senator Collins in Bangor, Maine, where the Speaker was campaigning. The Senate saw this meeting as important because they heard for the first time and directly from the Speaker that he wanted to get a deal. The Bangor meeting inspired a brief surge of optimism that the bill might get done before the election. Hadley returned to the Capitol to try his hand again with Duncan Hunter, while the White House's top national security budget official, Robin Cleveland, was brought in to work with Hunter's staff. Andy Card called Kean and Hamilton to assure them that the White House was working hard to get the bill done. But there was no progress.

Seeing his efforts at sincere negotiations frustrated, Palmer advised that it was time to start thinking about how to explain the collapse to the media. Hoekstra announced that the members should head home for the election but that staff would keep working. Frustrated, Hoekstra called the White House and directed them to expend their energy on inducing compromise from the Senate; the House had nothing more to give.

With prospects for an agreement near dead on October 27, some of the 9/11 Family members held another press conference to blame President Bush for allowing members of his own party to "derail the legislative process." Because the president had not "taken the time from his campaign to come to Washington himself to see this through" with the election approaching, they warned, "Now it's our turn."[57] These statements, coupled with the news that some of the 9/11 Families were traveling around the country on John Kerry's campaign plane,[58] reaffirmed for some Republicans that many of the 9/11 Families, or at least those who received media attention, were political and in league with the Democrats.[59]

On October 29, the Big Four held a conference call with the media and explained that they were suspending negotiations until after the election. Lieberman professed deep personal disappointment.[60] Chairman Hoekstra left town. While the 9/11 PDP and the Senate worried that the election meant the end of their effort to enact their recommendations, they had won over a powerful ally. Over the long term, the Bangor meeting was significant because the dynamics of the conference began to shift. Instead of a fight between the House and the Senate, the Speaker's affirmative support empowered Chairman Hoekstra to play a more active role in reaching an agreement. The new dynamic was that Hoekstra became aligned with Collins, Lieberman, and Harman against Hunter and Sensenbrenner.

Despite fears that the legislation was dead, the chief of staff to the Speaker of the House had changed the posture of the House. Instead of burying the legislation after the election, Palmer would fight to revive it.

CHAPTER FOURTEEN

Time for a New Approach

The president closed the red folder and, bothered by its contents, tossed it on his desk. It skimmed across the polished surface, gliding into a paper tray bearing a folded sports page and small blue boxes containing presidential gifts—key chains, tie clips, and cufflinks—souvenirs the president could bestow upon visitors to the Oval Office. The tray occupied the front right-hand corner of his otherwise unadorned desk, closest to his secretary, who would later retrieve the folder and stamp "President Has Seen" across the document's first page. As the folder came to rest, the president's chief of staff, Andy Card, took the seat next to the president's desk while the president's legislative affairs chief, David Hobbs, stood before the desk. One of Hobbs's staff hovered at the corner, standing over the paper tray.

The red folder was stamped Top Secret. Its contents, now visible to the hovering staffer, were the morning's casualty reports from the Second Battle of Fallujah. In a joint U.S.-British operation, the U.S. Marines had begun an offensive on November 8. It would be some of the hardest urban combat since Vietnam. Fallujah had become an insurgent stronghold, wired with booby traps and improvised explosive devices (IEDs).

The visitors came bearing an assignment for the newly reelected president. "Mr. President, we need you to call Chairman Duncan Hunter," announced Andy Card. After resounding electoral victories for the Republicans, a House leadership aide had told the press that "the wind has been taken out of the sails for Collins and Lieberman."[1] A typical House view was that what "kept this thing on artificial life support was this notion that we absolutely had to produce something or there was going to be hell to pay on the election campaign trail . . . so election comes and goes, life goes on, the world did not end."[2] Hunter's determined opposition had prevented a preelection deal, and with the election passed, an agreement would be harder than ever. To rebuild momentum, the president's team needed the president to weigh in and call Hunter.

The president had spoken out the day Senator Kerry conceded defeat. There was "something refreshing about coming off an election. . . . I earned capital in the campaign, political capital, and now I intend to spend it."[3] President Bush had in mind reforming the tax code and Social Security. However, to get to his second-term agenda, he needed to clear the decks of old business: "Congress will return later this month to finish this current session. . . . Our government needs the very best intelligence, especially in a time of war. So I urge the Congress to pass an effective intelligence reform bill that I can sign into law."

But calling Duncan Hunter was too much. "What? Are you kidding me? I don't want to talk to Duncan Hunter." Accustomed to the president's feigned outrage, Card answered calmly, "We need you to call him, Mr. President." The president must have been recalling previous occasions when he had been enlisted to induce flexibility from Hunter. In 2001, before September 11, the president had requested a massive increase in defense spending but still had had to cajole Hunter into voting for it, because Hunter wanted more.

The president told the would-be recruiters that he liked Duncan but that the congressman was just going to talk and talk and talk and run on about details no one had ever heard about, and at the end of the call they would all wonder what had been accomplished. Card and Hobbs pushed ahead and explained that Hunter had rejected all efforts at compromise in budget language with the Senate and the White House. The Speaker's office had been engaged with him for weeks and they, too, had failed. A presidential call was the only hope of nailing down some increased budgetary powers for the DNI.

The president relented, setting off a scramble in the anteroom of the Oval Office to find Duncan Hunter. Congress was out of session and Hunter was somewhere in his district near San Diego. The staff handed over a page of talking points explaining why the DNI should at least have the same powers over intelligence spending as the current DCI. The president wouldn't get to finish all that.

As his anteroom staff frantically dialed every number in the White House database for Duncan Hunter, the president needled, "Is this call going to happen?" Apparently accustomed to the teasing, the president's secretary calmly answered, "Yes, just a minute." The trio of staff in the Oval Office shifted back and forth while the anteroom staff left voice-mails at every known listing. The president playfully hectored them, "Can this happen *today?*" Unable to produce Hunter, Hobbs announced, "We'll come back once Hunter calls in."

"I'll be here," the president replied drolly.

Hobbs had retired to his office when his silver Motorola flip phone vibrated. It was the president's secretary; the president was on the phone with Hunter. Hobbs and his staffer raced through the West Wing, through the anteroom, and into the Oval Office. Hobbs went for the spare phone near the fireplace to listen in on the conversation. This was his customary post to listen in on presidential phone calls to members of Congress. By pressing mute, he could relay commentary to the president in real-time. When Hobbs tuned in, an unbridled Hunter was giving an impassioned oratory that the combatant commander in the theater whose men's lives are in danger have to have control of intelligence assets.[4] "I just repeated that over and over," recalled Hunter.[5]

The president was trying to interrupt Hunter's oration. "Dunc . . . Dunc . . . I gotcha, Dunc . . ." Unable to get a word in, the president put the phone on the desk and glared across the room. "Hobbs! I told you this was a bad idea!"

Returning the phone to his ear, the president tried again to interrupt Hunter. "Dunc. Dunc. I know, I know, listen." The president placed the phone on his chest and glowered at Hobbs. "I told you this would happen! He's just talking and talking!"

The president interjected more forcefully. "Dunc! Dunc!" Back in command of the call, the president made his points: "First, Duncan, this has to get done, it is going to come back and get worse for everybody. Second, we have come a long way, my way, toward your way, for example, classifying the top line, making sure the money runs through DoD, gives DoD the amount of flexibility they need. You need to take this language. . . . Duncan, at this point my staff tells me I need a couple of extra words" to ensure that while DoD would play a role in the budget process, the defense secretary would not have the ability to veto the DNI's budgetary decisions.[6] "I know Hastert's office has been trying to get you what you need and they've been holding out to get you what you need. Duncan, I appreciate what you are doing and why you are doing it, but you've got to take your language but with one tweak, it is how things work now, coordination is what happens now and it is sufficient."[7]

Hunter agreed to take a look at the new language. He had received the message from the commander in chief: We need to get this done, and you need to give.

. . . .

After the election, the House Republicans gathered in the caucus room named after Speaker "Fighting" Joe Cannon, who had ruled the House with an iron fist in the early 1900s. They had kept their majority despite a lot of baggage, including that the war in Iraq looked to be going badly. They had risked not enacting an intelligence reform bill and had not been punished. "We won, we won this thing, we got through the election without passing a bill and having won the election, we did what we set out to do."[8] Now safely through to the other side, they were surprised to hear the Speaker announce that the House needed to finish up the intelligence reform bill in the pre-Thanksgiving wrap-up session in three weeks. A staffer for Tom DeLay felt the air go out of the room when the assembled members heard the news. Those opposed to acting on the Commission's recommendations at all found this irritating. "Having just taken all the pain from people saying it would cost them the election not to do this . . . and they win . . . the first thing you want them to do is say now that you've suffered, you suffered because you stood on principle," but now you are expected to take up something you disagree with and pass it?[9] But from the Speaker's point of view, given the campaign by the 9/11 Families, this issue would not go away. Palmer insisted that not acting would be a political nightmare. It was a "political macro issue, not in the town halls, but we were taking on water with it."[10]

Members rose to criticize the Senate and the idea of revisiting the recommendations. In at least one leadership staffer's mind, this was the first time that the Speaker was being personally faulted. "The perception was that our leadership is doing the White House's bidding and not ours." "Denny always saw himself as the president's guy and DeLay saw his responsibility to the members, and when DeLay saw how this thing was going he was not going to get in front of the members."[11] DeLay would not help get a deal and pass the measure. It was going too far. "My job was the eyes and ears of the conference, to let the Speaker know where he stood at any particular moment."[12] Another senior staffer saw the resistance as part of the "rawness on the part of House Republicans of dealing with the Bush administration."

On a host of legislative items in Bush's first term, the White House legislative affairs strategy was to "work through leadership . . . have leadership basically muscle the process to short-circuit the regular-order legislative cycle and the congressional committees. . . . You just try to ram through with speed an outcome."[13] DeLay recalled leaving the conference thinking that they needed to rethink moving the bill forward; the leadership had "underestimated how much the rank-and-file members did not want to do this." A DeLay staffer recalled, "This is how you end up in a Speaker's race, because you're not listening."[14]

Hastert was in a position familiar to all congressional leaders when the president is of the same party. He had to balance the occasionally conflicting imperatives to support the president but also to advocate and fight for the views of the members of his conference, the votes on which he relied to be elected Speaker. From the vantage point of a rank-and-file member of the House, worse would be his selling out to the Senate. There was truth in the old joke that, in the House, regardless of party, the real enemy was the Senate.

The 9/11 Families continued to berate the House Republicans. As Roemer pushed for still more press conferences, Hamilton's top staffer worried that this tactic had outlived its utility. "First, they are just making the people they need to persuade mad, if the Republicans are even listening. Second, I don't think anyone is listening."[15]

After the election, Governor Kean reported on a conversation he had with Senator Collins. Believing "we will not get as good a bill in the next Congress," Collins "has decided to make one more serious try at a bill. The bill 'may not be exactly the bill we were fighting for, but it will still be a big step forward."[16] The negotiations resumed. Senators Collins and Lieberman were playing a weak hand; the House felt less pressure to compromise. Senator Collins began to think about giving up and told her staff, "I am beginning to think this isn't worth it, we've made so many compromises and watered things down so far I am not sure it is worth it to pursue this."[17] "We're at the point now of what's the absolute, most stinky thing we have to do to get a deal," explained one Senate Republican aide. "It depends on how far [Senate conferees] are willing to come to the House position."[18] On the other hand, Collins and Lieberman were under pressure not to completely capitulate to the House. Collins and Lieberman's colleagues pressured them to stand firm. "Just to get the DNI is not enough. It's like getting the ark without any animals on board."[19]

Striking the Deal on Budget Authority

In the face of determined House opposition from Hunter, the White House revisited its strategy. The White House pre-election objective was a decisive statutory win for the new DNI, a textual basis that would signal that the balance of budget authority formerly residing in cabinet departments now had shifted to the DNI. The House language that the money flow "through the heads of the departments" seemed to go in the opposite direction, a savings clause for cabinet secretaries, indicating that the balance of power remained in their favor. The Senate's goals were more expansive: to push the DNI's authorities to the outer limits short of creating a Department of Intelligence. But looking at the landscape—a House barely willing to consider the legislation at all—the White House took a hard look at the language on the table.

Now the president's Office of Management and Budget (OMB) director posed a question to his staff: given the vast authorities of the OMB director over the mechanics of the budget process, couldn't OMB ensure that the secretary of defense could not withhold, skim, obstruct, or condition intelligence funding? The House language did stipulate that OMB would only apportion funds to the intelligence agencies "at the exclusive direction of the director of national intelligence." This language could enable OMB to build an arrangement that guaranteed that the routing through the secretary of defense was truly a pass-through. The White House devised an argument for the Senate that the House language, with assistance from OMB, could constitute full budget authority: though the money would be traveling through the Defense Department, the White House could interpret the House budget language, once law, to the benefit of the DNI. The money, once directed toward an intelligence agency by the DNI, would be in an armored car to protect it from malign influence.

The question was whether the Senate could accept it. To convince the Senate that the House budget language could be made to work, the White House deployed in force. Arriving at Senator Collins's office in the Russell Senate Office Building early the morning of November 9 were Steve Hadley and OMB director Josh Bolten, along with his top national security budget chief, Robin Cleveland, and the requisite legislative affairs representative. Bolten and Cleveland had good relations with Senator Collins. Cleveland had traveled with Congresswoman Harman previously, who had vouched for her with Collins. Throughout the prolonged engagements with Duncan Hunter, Collins and Lieberman had come to trust Cleveland as an authority. "She was a wonderful ally to have," the senators recalled.[20]

Bolten and Cleveland made the case that the president was committed to a strong DNI and would make every effort during implementation of the law to ensure their shared intent was carried out. The statutory language used in conjunction with a helpful OMB would give the DNI the authority he needed.

"What do you think, Susan?" Lieberman asked, signaling that *he* was satisfied.

Senator Collins repeated the concern that by having the money traveling through the office of the secretary of defense, they might allow the secretary to tax, skim, withhold, or condition the funding directed by the DNI to thwart the DNI's influence over the intelligence agencies in Defense. Cleveland offered that this concern could be addressed through insertion of language ensuring that funds directed by the DNI would be executed "in an expeditious manner."[21] Collins could accept the House language with this addition. Still the Senate's acceptance was a major compromise to the House position.[22] Senator Lieberman recalled that "Robin Cleveland assured us it would work. That was absolutely key."[23]

There was in general the realization that the House simply did not want a deal as badly as the Senate, leaving the burden of negotiating flexibility with the eager party. Although there were still the matters of the NCTC, and what to do about Sensenbrenner's immigration provisions, and how to nail down the tricky issue of the White House's chain-of-command language, the biggest obstacle to an agreement had been cleared: the budget language was final. A Democratic congressional aide was later quoted describing the negotiations:

> Reality set in . . . we've run out of time, and the Republicans and the Pentagon just weren't going to budge. I think our best hope is that the national intelligence director is a person of such stature that he can assert his authority even if he doesn't have explicit control over the appropriations.[24]

The 9/11 PDP was cautiously optimistic. "The conference lives. The House is re-engaging. The House recognizes that the Senate has moved. Palmer has committed to resolving the budget authority questions in a manner that works for the Senate, and was apparently open-minded about the rest. What remains to be seen is how much the House, in turn, will move in response to the Senate."[25]

Striking the Deal on the National Counterterrorism Center

"Well, let's just get Phil Zelikow on the phone then and ask him what the Commission meant." Palmer's rump group of negotiators had spent Saturday painstakingly delineating the differences among the House, Senate, and White House. At issue tonight was the National Counterterrorism Center. Palmer called for Zelikow's number and pulled a group of staff into the Speaker's office and dialed Zelikow.

Weeks before, the 9/11 PDP had faulted the House's version of the NCTC, calling the Senate bill "preferable" and the House bill only "part of the way there."[26] The Senate had railed against the House approach, charging that the House's "proposal weakens the NCTC . . . by limiting the Center to 'strategic operational planning' rather than the more granular planning of operations such as the hunt for Bin Ladin."[27] The Senate, strictly adhering to the vision of the 9/11 Commission, cited the Kean-Hamilton letter in opposing the House approach. "'Clear assignment of responsibility' for net assessment for 'operational planning' (not just 'strategic' planning), and a direct relationship for the NCTC director to the president as well as the DNI—these are the essential ingredients for a different and better way to manage counterterrorism efforts across the U.S. government."[28] The House countered that their "intent is to have an organization that can do strategic operational planning and the assignment of governmental-wide roles and missions . . . such an organization is *not* capable, nor should it be, to do planning of specific operations (as an example, a 'snatch and grab')."

Zelikow clarified that the Commission had not intended the NCTC to actually direct operations; instead it would assign roles and mission responsibilities as part of its "strategic operational planning duties to lead departments or agencies, as appropriate for counterterrorism activities that are consistent with applicable laws . . . but shall not direct the execution of any resulting operations."[29] While Zelikow recognized that opponents of an operational planning function sought to limit it to "strategic" planning because to some "strategic was code for you don't do real work," its insertion into the law was "unfortunate but not fatal." There was enough positive language in the statute to ensure that the success of the planning mission "would turn on the way it would be implemented."[30] Since a planning function for the NCTC had been Zelikow's idea, since he thought it could work despite being limited to "strategic" planning, the Senate conceded. If Zelikow was okay, the Senate was okay.[31]

· · · · · · · · · · · ·

Sensing momentum, the conference picked up its pace. "Scott Palmer has the conferees locked up. They have been meeting all day, and will meet again today, as they did yesterday, well into the night."[32] Sensenbrenner was on hand, seeking earnest negotiations. "Sensenbrenner pops in and out of the room. Twenty-five staff outside the room are called in from time to time, but it is mostly the conferees by themselves, trying to cut deals."[33] Over the previous weeks, the White House, the Senate, and Chairman Hoekstra lobbied Sensenbrenner to be flexible. Collins and Lieberman had Sensenbrenner's chief lieutenant, Phil Kiko, the staff director of the Judiciary Committee, over to the Senate for dinner. At a White House meeting on another topic, President Bush grabbed Kiko's arm, "I really need some help here [with your boss]." Kiko said he would try and the president moved on. After a few paces, the president turned and said again with emphasis, "I *really* need your help here."[34]

During conference negotiations, the Senate mustered up a few immigration provisions they could live with in an attempt to placate Sensenbrenner. Sensenbrenner pocketed the concessions but was not satisfied. He viewed the Senate as having accepted only noncontroversial provisions. The Senate had given him "the easy ones," he would later say. Noting that the nineteen 9/11 hijackers had obtained driver's licenses, Sensenbrenner insisted on language making legal presence in the U.S. a prerequisite for getting a valid license.[35]

· · · · · · · · · · · ·

Despite the acceptance of the House budget authority and NCTC language, Hunter upped his ask. Claiming that because the House had made some important concessions to the Senate, Hunter now needed the White House's chain-of-command language inserted into the bill. The provision, authored by David Addington and inserted into President Bush's legislative submission in September, had been designed to preserve the ability of cabinet secretaries, especially the secretary of defense, to manage their own departments. The Senate saw it as a poison pill, a blank check for cabinet secretaries to ignore the DNI. Anyone could thwart a directive from the DNI by claiming the order contravened the powers of the cabinet secretary in whose department the intelligence agency resided.

Amidst confusion over the provision, a White House legislative affairs officer arranged for the author of the chain-of-command provision to make a rare appearance on the Hill. Arriving in a suit and tie after church on a Sunday morning, Addington entered the Speaker's office to meet with the bedraggled Senate and House negotiators. After discussions with the Senate and House staffers, and to their surprise given his reputation as "the vice president's most effective warrior,"[36] Addington suggested a compromise that was consistent with the president's policy of maintaining a unified chain of command. If the Senate was worried about the president's original language being written into statute, the negotiators could instead call upon the president to issue guidelines to protect the chain of command. Addington penned the new approach on an index card he produced from the breast pocket of his suit jacket and handed it the negotiators. Addington was known to support a view of presidential power that critics considered expansive. Surprisingly, the Senate accepted the Addington guidelines approach on the spot. They trusted that the president would write guidelines favorable to the DNI. But they also saw a quick resolution to a thorny issue; they could volley the issue back to the executive branch. Surely if the author of the provision, Vice President Cheney's general counsel of all people, was okay, Duncan Hunter would not have a leg to stand on. The Senate glimpsed the goal line; they could finally be done with Duncan Hunter.

However, to the shock of the White House and the Senate, Hunter rejected the Addington compromise. He could not accept a guidelines approach that could be revised by the next president. He needed the chain-of-command assurances in statute, which would be beyond the whim of a future president who might favor a strong DNI at the expense of the secretary of defense. Hunter insisted on the president's original formulation from September. To the Senate and the 9/11 PDP, Hunter was "representing DOD positions with zeal, and of course would like to bring the whole bill down. Some on the Senate side, egged on by some CIA officials, are responding in kind."[37]

As the negotiators worked furiously to reach a deal before Congress returned to Washington, Zelikow saw two sides again at loggerheads. "Hunter's unreasonableness mixes so combustibly with the Senate's stubbornness. Both sides of course feel they've given away too much."[38] Unable to bring Sensenbrenner and Hunter aboard, Palmer foresaw a legislative train wreck. "Palmer was so desperate for someone to lean on Hunter" that he asked Zelikow whether Lee Hamilton had any influence over him.[39] Under pressure from the Speaker's allies to get the Senate to agree to tightening immigration, and from the Senate to get the House to accept a stronger DNI, and from the White House to deliver its preferences from both, after fifteen days of negotiations lasting past midnight,[40] Palmer pulled aside a White House staffer and warned, "DeLay is working against me. Down at the White House, the president is too protected. He does not know this is dead. I am going to Illinois tonight to try and light up the Speaker but I should have made this clear yesterday. It is too late, the Senate is stupid not to give us what we need to buy off Sensenbrenner and isolate Hunter, wake up the president and let him know this is dead."[41]

CHAPTER FIFTEEN

Black Saturday

With the prospects for a compromise slipping, less than twenty-four hours before the House would come into session, the White House deployed reinforcements. Palmer's longtime friend and President Bush's legislative affairs chief, David Hobbs, a product of the House as a former longtime aide to Majority Leader Dick Armey, personally knew the committee chairmen whose support Palmer needed. Now Palmer was out on a limb and had had it. Neither Sensenbrenner nor Hunter would budge. Passing through some reporters near the Rotunda of the Capitol, Hobbs arrived in the suite of ornate rooms surrounding the Speaker's office, where about twenty congressional staffers loaded down with binders were hoping to negotiate and hammer out the final legislative text of the bill. Other aides moved swiftly to and from an interior room where Sensenbrenner cursed the Senate.

After hours of fruitless shuttle diplomacy, Palmer grabbed his keys and walked out. He made it as far as Statuary Hall when Hobbs caught up with him and pulled him back. After coaxing Palmer onto the Speaker's Balcony, overlooking the National Mall, they discussed how far they had come to be in a place of such grandeur. Soon they returned to the problem at hand and discussed an almost unthinkable maneuver: steamroll over the opposition of two committee barons and bring a bill to the floor they did not support.

If the gamble failed, Hastert could lose his job. Calling a vote on the compromise would effectively be a vote of confidence; the Speaker would be exhorting his Republican colleagues to trust and follow him, despite the misgivings of his lieutenants. If the gambit failed, it could betray weakness that might persuade his troops to select a new leader when they met in coming weeks to organize for the new Congress. He would be standing before his colleagues and putting his credibility on the line against two powerful allies, effectively daring them to oppose him.

Legislative histories are replete with examples of powerful congressional leaders strong-arming their colleagues for votes, such as Lyndon Johnson leaning into and jawboning a tentative senator into his corner, but Speaker Hastert would be in an especially precarious position. Hastert would be asking the rank-and-file members of the House Republican caucus to look past the concerns of two respected chairmen in favor of two institutions they regarded with eye-rolling disdain: the United States Senate and the 9/11 PDP.

This was a terrible option. They had to try again. Hobbs needed to keep Sensenbrenner at the table and cajole him into a compromise. But they had to get him something on immigration. His negotiations with the Senate negotiators were deteriorating into shouting matches, and Sensenbrenner was threatening to walk out. Could the president bail Palmer and Hobbs out? The problem was Bush was en route to Latin America for a summit of the Asia-Pacific Economic Cooperation. But desperate to forestall a Sensenbrenner walkout, Hobbs escaped from the room and dialed the White House "signal," the Situation Room's operator, who could track down the president, the vice president, the cabinet, and the White House staff in minutes. Hobbs reached the president's chief of staff in a motorcade in Chile. Hobbs and Card agreed that President Bush should call Sensenbrenner.

Within minutes, the president, now aboard Air Force One, was calling. Hobbs called Sensenbrenner into the Speaker's conference room and handed him the phone, and then he stepped to the other side of the room and hoped for the best. The president expressed sympathy for what Sensenbrenner was trying to do with immigration generally, but he asked him to be flexible and narrow his demands. The president stressed the importance of getting a deal because of the ambitious legislative agenda for next year.[1] "Out of respect"[2] for the president, Sensenbrenner dropped his insistence on the driver's license provisions (though he had a price which he would soon demand of the Senate).[3] It was an efficient deployment of presidential power.

"Sorry to have to do that to you, Jim," said Hobbs. Surprisingly, the irascible Sensenbrenner was not annoyed that Hobbs had called in a presidential air strike, a favorite tactic of last resort for a legislative affairs staffer who could no longer make progress with a member of Congress.

After the phone call, Hobbs grabbed the lead Senate staffer, Michael Bopp. "The president softened him up; now go negotiate with him."[4] But the period of good feelings engendered by the president's call to Sensenbrenner was short-lived. In exchange for dropping the driver's license provisions, Sensenbrenner asked the Senate to adopt other immigration provisions, including giving immigration judges new discretion on whether to grant political asylum to immigrants.[5] While Collins and Lieberman contemplated the new offer, Palmer, Phil Kiko (the staff director of Sensenbrenner's Judiciary Committee), and Sensenbrenner retired to Scott Palmer's office. Word soon arrived that the Senate rejected his new proposals. Kiko looked at Sensenbrenner and said, "Jim, it's time to go."[6] Sensenbrenner pulled his staff and his visiting son together and marched out of the Capitol. Palmer and Hobbs wondered if he would go quietly or wage a guerrilla war to encourage his colleagues to vote against the bill.

Without Sensenbrenner, the scramble to keep the bill alive focused back on Duncan Hunter. If the negotiators could bring Hunter aboard, maybe the Speaker could go ahead without Sensenbrenner. But to proceed with a vote over the opposition of *two* committee chairmen would be dangerous.

The Speaker had just arrived back in Washington early Friday evening, not long after Sensenbrenner had walked out. His presence was a relief; having done all they could do, his staff and allies hoped that now maybe the Speaker could knock some heads together. Palmer and Chairman Hoekstra joined the Speaker in his office. Collins, Lieberman, and the White House staff remained in an adjoining room and comforted themselves with the thought that the bill was just too big to fail; there had been a sense of inevitability to it for months that they hoped would bring it across the finish line. And if even half the Republicans joined the unanimous Democrats in voting yes, the compromise bill had a majority.

Inside the Speaker's office, Palmer laid down the case for moving forward. Hunter did not want a bill. He had refused every concession. He had even rejected language Vice President Cheney supported to ensure the chain of command would be preserved. His arguments were not substantiated. To not pass the compromise would be crazy: You mean to tell me we're not going to pass the bill that the president and the Commission say is necessary to protect the country? At the very least, the politics would be horrendous; they would hand the Democrats a gun to shoot them with. Hoekstra also played a key role in encouraging the Speaker to call a vote.

Palmer remembered the Speaker had been noncommittal on moving ahead without Hunter. He directed Palmer to try again with a new offer. Senators Collins and Lieberman were wary. Hunter had doggedly fought them for weeks; at this point the Senate and White House believed he did not want to reach agreement. But it made sense to Collins and Lieberman to give it one last shot. They felt they owed it to Scott Palmer, whose sponsorship of sincere negotiations in the face of opposition from House chairmen had kept the bill alive for weeks. And Palmer needed it badly. He had lost Sensenbrenner and he did not need his boss to take a stand against two of his allies plus Tom DeLay. Regardless, the White House and Senate negotiators had the impression that despite the Speaker's direction to try again with Hunter, he was ready to put the bill up for a vote with or without Hunter.

They took one last action; they ratified a previous discussion that the name of the new position should be changed to DNI. It had been previously called a NID, short for national intelligence director, as the 9/11 Commission had named it. The Big Four agreed "NID" sounded weak and reminded them of a bug.[7]

When the Speaker departed for the night, a bottle of wine was opened, wine glasses were produced, and Palmer, Hoekstra, Lieberman, Collins, and staff sipped cautiously, not sure where to go as they contemplated their next move. The senators allowed themselves to reminisce and trade old war stories. An end to a four-month, epic battle seemed at hand. They were on the verge of something historic, revamping an intelligence structure that had been largely untouched for over fifty years. The group grew reflective and shared a few laughs.

The House team and Senate staff remained in the Capitol. With the Speaker considering muscling aside the opposition, it felt like they had new leverage to reach a last-minute agreement with Hunter. Now, fifteen hours before the House was to come into session, the group came up with a new plan. Would Hunter accept language ensuring that the president issued DNI guidelines that would "take into account" the importance of the secretary of defense in managing the intelligence agencies in his department? Because it paid homage to the interests of the secretary, it seemed to be a compromise Hunter could accept. By 10 p.m., Hunter countered with language that guaranteed the primacy of the secretary over the DNI. The Senate tried again, this time with a variation designed to protect the prerogatives of the DNI, and with that, at 11:19 p.m., Hunter came by the Speaker's office to inform Palmer he could not support the compromise.

Palmer disappeared into the adjoining office to phone the Speaker at home. He would explain that he had gone the extra mile to get Hunter's support but that they had to go forward. Palmer emerged some time later, ashen. His boss was angry at being put in this position, though Palmer did not say that at the time. Palmer told the group to assemble the text of a final bill for passage. It was not clear whether the Speaker would intervene with Hunter or go forward without him, or both.

Palmer recalled, "When I came out of that room and reported to the senators, they were jubilant, they were very relieved, very happy. I was happy, too, but I knew it could be undone."[8] Senator Collins and Lieberman were elated and sent word to their fellow senators to convene at ten the next morning, that a compromise was set to be voted on the next day. The White House was relieved, and word was sent to the presidential party in Latin America that the Speaker had finally realized the hopelessness of trying to bring Chairman Hunter aboard. Bush was told to expect passage of the compromise tomorrow. Collins and Lieberman left the Capitol around midnight in a drizzle. Before they left, Lieberman turned to Collins and hugged her.[9]

To check on the Senate, the White House's and Speaker's staff set out across the Capitol after midnight. Crossing the darkened Rotunda, they spotted a DeLay staffer on a cell phone. It was an awkward encounter. The Speaker's staff shrugged and kept walking. Through the underground tunnels across the Capitol grounds in the Dirksen Senate Office Building, staff frenetically worked through the night to assemble the bill for passage.

• • • • • • • • • • • •

The next morning, as some of the Senate staff awoke from a night's rest atop tables in their offices, Duncan Hunter was at his usual seat in the Member's Dining Room, having his regular breakfast of steak and eggs. The Speaker had asked to see him, and Hunter called his staff director, Robert Rangel, into the dining room for an update. His staff director reported that the Speaker intended to go forward without accommodating Hunter's concerns. Hunter replied, "I can't go along with that." Rangel pressed, "You are going to tell the Speaker you are not going along?" "That's what I am telling you, Rangel, I can't go along with this." Hunter got up from the table and said, "Here goes nothing."[10]

The Speaker gave Hunter the soft touch. "He did not threaten him, [but] the Speaker did put the arm on him and ask him for his support." "I understand you've got misgivings but we need this, I need this, the president needs this."[11] The Speaker's office scrambled for last-minute help. Could Vice President Cheney, known to have been uncomfortable with the recommendations, reassure Hunter that the Department of Defense would fare well under the compromise? The vice president called Hunter that morning to seek his support. After all, it was known to be Cheney's "chain-of-command" language that Hunter was holding out over; if it was all right with the vice president, it should be fine with Hunter. "Can't you make a deal?" the vice president asked.[12] Hunter said that during the call Cheney "wanted to have a compromise and wanted to have a bill,"[13] but Hunter would not give in. "I owed my colleagues my best judgment. Was it good for people who wear the uniform of the United States? My answer was no."[14]

One Republican congressman called the revolt led by Hunter a "war" in the Republican ranks.[15] Hunter's resistance resonated with many in the House GOP conference. Hunter came to personify a growing anti-leadership sentiment that had been building through President Bush's first term.

As the Speaker remembered, he had to move forward that Saturday morning:

> I know we are trying to work with Hunter and Sensenbrenner, but in the long term when you give and give and you give sometimes you've just got to get it done . . . I thought we had negotiated everything we could possibly get out of it and Sensenbrenner and Hunter got a lot of what they wanted, not everything, but Vice President Cheney was satisfied and he was the guy who was the defense guy and if the White House is satisfied and can live with it, they helped bake the cake. We did not have anywhere else to go.[16]

The word that the Speaker was putting the bill on the floor had electrified the Senate. The Senate conferees gathered at 10:00 a.m. to hear about the compromise measure that Collins and Lieberman had struck. The two were given a round of applause; they had won over the Speaker and were about to vanquish two powerful chairmen in the House. Senator Collins had a press "victory statement" in hand, ready to celebrate the bill's passage, which was only "minutes away."[17] Emerging from the meeting, the chairman of the Senate Intelligence Committee flashed a victory sign and

The 9/11 Commission meets with President Bush on April 29, 2004. *Courtesy of the Office of George W. Bush*

The 9/11 Commission report sits on the Resolute desk. *Courtesy of the Office of George W. Bush*

President Bush shaking hands with Congressman Duncan Hunter. *Courtesy of the Office of George W. Bush*

President Bush reading the 9/11 Commission Report. *Courtesy of the Office of George W. Bush*

President Bush meets with congressional leaders in the Cabinet Room on September 8, 2004, and endorses "full budget authority" for the director of national intelligence. *Courtesy of the Office of George W. Bush*

The president sits with Condoleezza Rice on a secure video teleconference on the 9/11 Commission recommendations from his Crawford ranch in late July 2004. *Courtesy of the Office of George W. Bush*

President Bush stands with members of his national security team in the Rose Garden on August 2, 2004, calling for the establishment of a national intelligence director. *Courtesy of the Office of George W. Bush*

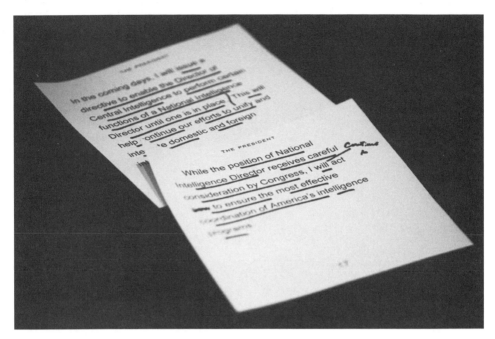

President Bush's notes. *Courtesy of the Office of George W. Bush*

President Bush calling Duncan Hunter to ask for support on the intelligence reform legislation. *Courtesy of the Office of George W. Bush*

President Bush signing the Intelligence Reform and Terrorism Prevention Act on December 17, 2004, at the Carnegie Mellon Auditorium with Senators Collins and Lieberman and Representatives Harman and Hoekstra, among others, behind him. *Courtesy of the Office of George W. Bush*

asked for a cigar.[18] Lee Hamilton met with the Democratic Leadership and reported their strong support.[19] The former 9/11 Commissioners and staff celebrated expectantly. "The moment of truth is upon us," e-mailed one.[20] Zelikow e-mailed a congratulatory note to his colleagues: "Great changes in government do not happen in a single stroke. They are evolutionary. But even in evolution there are moments—natural historians refer to them as 'punctuated equilibrium'—when evolutionary pathways shift suddenly and dramatically in new directions. We may be on the edge of such a moment."[21]

But earlier that morning, Jim Sensenbrenner had called Tom DeLay. The Speaker was trying to roll him. Sensenbrenner was going to activate a special clause in the rules of the House Republican Conference. If he could get the necessary signatures, an emergency meeting of the conference would be immediately convened. The provision exists as a check on the leadership by giving an avenue to disgruntled members to force a debate about a specific piece of legislation, or, in the most dramatic way, to remove one of the elected leaders (except the Speaker, who is elected by the full House). For a chairman to activate the provision was an extraordinary event; chairmen address their grievances in private, with the Speaker and the majority leader, not in front their colleagues. One former House leadership staffer described it as "the equivalent of saying we don't trust you and therefore want an airing."[22] DeLay gave Sensenbrenner the green light. Sensenbrenner knew he would, but even if he had not, Sensenbrenner would have done it anyway. Phil Kiko already had the fifty signatures in hand.

DeLay went to the Speaker that morning. He held Palmer in high regard and considered him to be "one of the best chiefs of staff anywhere, anytime." DeLay respected Palmer's "uncanny political acumen." "Most of the time he was right . . . this was the only time Scott broke away from everybody, I don't know why, it just wasn't Scott."[23] His staff remembered that DeLay had been telling the Speaker all along that the situation among the rank and file was bad, "but [Hastert] did not believe it; Palmer would always say it is not that bad. The Speaker was blissfully ignorant, Palmer had it, the Speaker did not have his hands on it."[24] Palmer recalled, "But the Speaker saying going forward did not mean trouble was not on the horizon the next morning; he was surprised but disappointed to learn the opposition was going to crank up as much as they had; we underestimated the reaction."[25]

At the news that the emergency-conference provision had been activated, panic set in. At 10:00 a.m., the White House staff was urgently summoned to the Speaker's office. A rebellion was in motion. Hunter would soon announce his opposition, and Sensenbrenner was circulating a document explaining the immigration provisions the Senate had rejected.

In the two weeks since the election, the Speaker had come a long way. Campaigning across the country for Republican candidates, he had led the House Republicans to a triumphal reelection. Now, on a Saturday morning, instead of accepting plaudits, the Speaker was managing a revolt.

Typical weekly conference meetings brought the 227 rank-and-file members into a huddle. The majority leader would call the plays with the silent nod from the Speaker, who had approved the game plan in advance. A member of the leadership presided over the gathering, choreographing committee chairmen to stand before their colleagues and explain whatever bill they would soon vote on. The majority leader usually then complimented the chairman's work and seconded that the plan put forward was the right thing to do. This was the way marching orders were delivered by a united leadership. Members occasionally stood up and expressed misgivings, but never the committee chairmen. They owed their seats to the Speaker; they were on his leadership team and were obligated to help corral wayward rank-and-file members. And doing so was in their best interest: the strength of the majority was in its unity. Of course, this time it would be different.

Sensenbrenner recalled that he "got up and said, 'Hey, wait a minute.'"[26]

As noted, with two committee chairmen leading an uprising, the Speaker reversed course and pulled the intelligence reform bill off the agenda.[27]

His spokesman would later recall that Hastert "wanted to have a family discussion about this bill." "We support the president. We think it's great that he wants the bill, but at the end of the day the Speaker listens to his members. We never like to rely on Democrats," the Speaker's spokesman explained.[28] Hastert said, "We are going to keep working on this."[29] Hastert's maneuver to delay consideration of the bill was one of conference management colored by the experience to pass a Medicare prescription drug bill in 2003. While the House Republican leadership supported the bill, many of the rank-and-file members did not believe in creating a new entitlement program. Vote counts declined steadily throughout 2003, and on the law's final passage the vote was held open for hours in the middle of the night to corral enough votes. The leadership worried about their continuing ability to push through legislation that did not have broad support across their conference. With more Republicans holding out on the intelligence reform bill than the Medicare prescription drug bill, David Hobbs saw the intelligence reform delay as part of the process of maintaining conference unity:

> We had an ongoing debate through the years on "majority of the majority"; there were several examples where you would get less than half of the Republicans but 75 percent of the Democrats and you will have a three-hundred-person win, but the 120 who voted no are all going to be Republicans and they are half [of] your conference and you are Speaker, but you are not going to stay Speaker very long if you do that very often.[30]

The Senate's elation the previous night reflected a misapprehension of the way the House works. "Their attitude was 'Speaker says we're going to do it, he's got absolute power, it is done.'"[31]

Hastert saw the disagreement with DeLay as "part of the process."

> DeLay and I got along but we did not always agree and I think we had a pretty honest exchange of views and Tom was pretty reactionary sometimes. I was more pragmatic than Tom was, sometimes I won and sometimes he won. But we also worked together and did not take disputes public.[32]

Hastert recalled that his attitude on the conference was "sometimes you just have to pull the plug on some things and step back, and clearly the conference was not happy because we had chairmen who were influential, so we had to step back, and we re-did, renegotiated. . . ."[33] DeLay explained that his remark, "the Speaker has a tough decision to make," was intended to pose a dilemma. "I was trying to tell the conference without slapping the Speaker upside the head that this isn't ripe."[34]

Palmer stated, "I think Denny got it right, listening to his troops, and, gauging the fact that Tom was not helpful and the others came on as strong as they did, a strategic retreat and regrouping was necessary."[35] Robert Rangel, staff director of the House Armed Services Committee, noted, "There was a substantive component to it, but it also reflected great umbrage not just on this issue but in how the leadership and the White House chose to operate and impose their will on the House and the Congress."[36]

President Bush commented, "I thought it was going to pass up to the last minute."[37] Senator Collins recalled that "it never occurred to us that with Hastert's support Hoekstra wouldn't be able to deliver, never occurred to us; we were absolutely shocked."[38] When they got word that the deal had collapsed, Commissioner Gorelick deployed to the Hill and issued an "urgent plea" to her colleagues for help in rescuing the deal,[39] but it was too late. "[T]he strength of the entrenched status quo has been enormous, beyond the experience of practically everyone we know," Zelikow believed.[40]

Rumsfeld continued to loom over any discussion of the bill, this time regarding its demise. "It's well known that the secretary of defense wasn't enthusiastic about this loss of budget authority."[41] "The president should come forward and tell us the truth as to how he feels about" a forty-billion-dollar intelligence budget in the hands of Rumsfeld.[42] Some in the press took as incontrovertible that the Pentagon was behind the takedown. The *New York Times* stated as fact that "senior Pentagon officials" had "quietly lobbied for months to block the creation of the job of a powerful national intelligence director,"[43] and the press peppered the White House with questions about whether the president would "lean on" Rumsfeld to make public statements to get the bill done.[44] Hunter hinted that Rumsfeld was opposed: "It's become very clear to the conference that he is not in support of some of the things the Senate wanted to do."[45] However, Senator Warner stated, "I'd also like to be on the record. Rumsfeld did not lobby me in any sense on this."[46] Secretary Rumsfeld, traveling in Europe for a NATO summit, protested: "I am supporting the president's position. I am part of his administration." However, at a subsequent press conference, his lack of command of the details seemed to devalue the president's own endorsement. "I am not knowledgeable enough to agree or disagree [that the bill doesn't support tactical intelligence]." Rumsfeld's comments resurfaced the issue of whether Bush *really* wanted the 9/11 Commission's recommendations to be enacted. Rumsfeld reported that "the president's position is evolving." His performance reinforced the perception that the Defense Department was not *really* in favor of the bill, but only the president's position, and that only because they had to be. One commentator called the comments "slippery."[47]

The letter from General Myers took on new significance and became the symbol of Pentagon opposition to the president's position. "Do you believe that General Myers . . . would send such a letter without the knowledge or authority of the secretary of defense?"[48] The drumbeat continued about the Pentagon's role. Had they "sabotaged" the president?[49] Harman waved around the Addington language on *Fox News Sunday*: "This is the handwritten language . . . drafted by the counsel to the vice president of the United States, somehow [this] wasn't enough."[50] The 9/11 PDP repeated its charge for action. Tim Roemer said, "More body bags may have to happen before we get change. . . . [A]l Qa'ida is metastasizing around the world in 60 different countries."[51] Kean stated, "This bill will pass. The question is whether it will pass now or after a second attack."[52]

Hunter was influenced by his son, who asked, "Don't give this one up for us, Dad."[53] Reveling in his takedown of the bill, Hunter invoked the almighty:

> A non-responsive chain of command or having a lack of a chain of command translates into combat casualties . . . thank God for the House Republicans. They're listening to the Joint Chiefs of Staff and decided that we needed to make sure the Senate came across the finish line on this important lifeline between the troops in the field and the people that run the satellites.[54]

Senator Rockefeller claimed to be so upset at the collapse that he was going to go back to his office "and start throwing some chairs around."[55] He added, "Americans ought to remember the name Duncan Hunter, and also Jim Sensenbrenner, because they brought the bill down, the most important national security bill in the last generation."[56] Kean agreed that not passing the bill was a risk to American lives.[57] Chairman Sensenbrenner, lambasted by the Senate in the aftermath of the blowup, was embittered. "It will be tougher now because the well got even more poisoned by the senators and their supporters thoroughly criticizing Duncan Hunter and myself by name on the talking-head shows yesterday."[58] Sensenbrenner only got angrier. A few days later, the Senators antagonized Sensenbrenner further by calling his immigration provisions "unnecessary or . . . irrelevant."[59]

The 9/11 Families had been devastated by the collapse of the reform bill and redoubled their efforts with the 9/11 PDP. While the chairman and the vice chairman "tip-toed" around questions from reporters inviting them to blame President Bush, the Families were more direct and would take on "anyone who stood in the way of the intelligence reform bill."[60] Kean said, "The president has got to go to work."[61]

So with the Defense Department off-message, the Democrats in full attack mode, and the House Republicans complimenting each other, the White House needed a new plan. As the president relished the political capital supplied by the election victory and in the midst of the Second Battle of Fallujah in Iraq, in what the *New York Times* called a "stunning lack of respect for the wishes of their newly re-elected chief executive,"[62] a new media narrative emerged: could the president control his own Defense Department, which in the eyes of many had spiked the intelligence compromise? Could the president lead a newly emboldened House Republican majority? Was their defiance a harbinger of what President Bush's second term would bring? Passing intelligence reform became a "key test for Bush" and a "crucial test of President's Bush clout and his approach to governing in a second term."[63] Shocked from its post-election euphoria, the Bush White House was now challenged.

CHAPTER SIXTEEN

Win at All Costs

One of the gems of Virginia is the Tides Inn, a Chesapeake Bay hotel on its own peninsula with a clear view of the Rappahannock River. The hotel had been cleared of other guests, and the Republican leadership in the House and Senate had come to town for a summit to plan the next Congress. The attire was casual; Speaker Hastert was wearing a sleeveless sweater vest over a white shirt and khaki pants.

The congressional leadership settled into their seats in the hotel's conference room. Out of the bay windows, U.S. Coast Guard boats bobbed on the waters of Carter's Creek. The Coast Guard was there because the Speaker of the House of Representatives and the president pro tempore of the U.S. Senate—the second and third in the presidential line of succession—were in attendance. The White House brought a team down to the retreat to lobby for an ambitious second-term agenda. Josh Bolten, the president's OMB director, and Karl Rove, the architect of the president's reelection, were on hand. But a familiar issue intruded. Before moving on to new business, the agenda showed one item under "old business": what to do about the intelligence reform measure they had left smoldering in a heap the week before.

The president pro tempore, Ted Stevens, an ardent opponent to the 9/11 Commission's approach, addressed the group. Since the collapse of the bill, the president had been excoriated. Despite his misgivings, Stevens said Congress had to pass the bill next week to help the president.

Next, David Hobbs spoke. The compromise had failed because "people's positions are changing from what they had previously agreed to."[1] The president's lobbyist lifted his hands in the air, "Hold to the light the language Hunter says he supports and the language he had objected to—there's absolutely no difference." Hobbs suggested that the only explanation for

Hunter's opposition was that he simply did not want a bill.[2] But this was just what Tom DeLay's staff was worried about: beware of a "get-it-done-at-any-cost attitude," a leadership staffer later warned the White House; "if you force us to vote without Hunter, it will cause serious damage and burn a lot of capital; DeLay is not in buckle mode, he is getting madder and madder. Don't raise the stakes because the result [the collapse of the intelligence reform bill] could be the same."[3]

DeLay was angry because in his mind the White House and the Senate had cooked up the plan to put the bill on the floor despite the opposition from Hunter and Sensenbrenner. Hobbs's tone irked DeLay further and he got aggressive. "That is bullshit, David, that is *bullshit*."[4] "It was an octave higher than normal talk," according to one witness.[5] "That's a *chairman* you're talking about," DeLay added, glowering at Hobbs. A DeLay staffer later said that it was a "remember-you're-a-staffer moment." Hobbs handled it well, according to two witnesses; essentially, he apologized and gracefully made the point that the bill had to get done because it was time to move on to new issues in a new Congress. DeLay told the White House the only way to get through this was to deal with Hunter.[6] Throughout the argument, Hastert had sat quietly, "steaming," a former leadership aide recalled.[7] Once the discussion ended, the Speaker walked out.

The White House gave up trying to cajole the leadership into simply disregarding Hunter and putting the bill up for a vote; Hunter's concerns would have to be addressed. The Speaker asked Chairman Hunter to put in writing his "bottom line." Two days later on December 2, Hunter produced a letter to the Speaker with the "minimum necessary to ensure that our combat troops now and in the future are well served by our Intelligence Community."[8] The letter reiterated that Hunter could support the original "chain-of-command" language offered by the White House or a slightly modified version. But Hunter could not work off the language Hastert had tried to roll past him. If the language Hunter had opposed became law, "the record and history would show that there was an explicit and conscious decision to shift critical authorities to the national Intelligence Community at the expense of the defense."[9] The Senate had previously rejected both formulations that Hunter now called his bottom line. But just bringing Hunter aboard would probably be enough to force a compromise through; Sensenbrenner was lost.

The White House would have to squeeze the Senate and Hunter toward a compromise. The president spoke loudly and forcefully in public for a bill. Behind the scenes, the White House had been working on rolling back the Pentagon. Bush and Cheney worked the phones: the president called the Speaker and the majority leader to press for a resolution; the vice president dealt with Hunter. For his part, Steve Hadley tried to work with Senator Collins for new flexibility on the chain-of-command approach.

It got off on a bad note. In a private conference call with the White House, Senator Collins reacted angrily to the suggestion that she agree to an alternative formulation of the chain-of-command language. "The letter from the president says that I'm never going to break the chain of command. We've given to Hunter. I've given things I would not have given had I known he would block the bill." The Senate was sensitive to the charge that they had already given too much to Hunter. "If you reopen, the perception will be that Collins got rolled. I worked hard, did a lot for the White House; [this went down] because the White House would not take on Hunter even though they knew we were right."[10]

On December 2, General Myers, during questions at a Christian Science Monitor breakfast, stated that "the issue that I specifically addressed in a letter to Chairman Hunter has been accommodated, I'm told, in the bill."[11] The White House put out the word that the chairman of the Joint Chiefs was comfortable with the compromise bill.

Also on December 2 the president checked in with the Speaker, who asked the president to ask Collins to be flexible. Angry at Hunter, she and Lieberman "refused to return to the negotiating table, telling reporters . . . they expect a letter from the White House firmly endorsing the existing bill."[12] The president hung up and called Senator Frist, asking him to exert some influence to win some flexibility for the Speaker, who was desperate to get out of the situation. Karl Rove called Collins to ask for flexibility.[13] Hobbs went back to Collins the next day. The bill was "best and final. It is grossly unfair to ask me to compromise. I am easier to roll because I care about the bill, and the Speaker is in a box."[14]

Most commentators blamed the president for not muscling Hunter into submission. Wisely, however, Kean and Hamilton did not join in the public castigation of the White House. Former 9/11 Commissioners changed their message and argued that a DNI would be better for the war fighter.[15] While he called on Congress to pass a bill, Kean and Hamilton were not goaded by the press into criticizing the president.

The president knows best how to deal with Congress. He's had a lot of success with them. . . . I wouldn't be the one to advise him how to deal with it. What we do want is to join with the president in a full-court press to see if we can get this enacted by this Congress. I wouldn't presume to tell the president how to do his job, but we do believe that the president is totally committed to this bill.[16]

On the afternoon of their press conference, Kean and Hamilton went to the White House to press for action. The president was in Canada and insisted from afar that "I want a bill, let's see if I can say it as plainly as I can: I am for the intelligence bill."[17]

Kean and Hamilton met with Vice President Cheney in his West Wing office about thirty feet from the Oval Office.[18] Unlike the Oval, which was shorn of papers and personal effects for official visits, the vice president's desk was always stacked with documents and intelligence products. On the floor next to his desk was a carrying bag sprouting with newspapers. The vice president played a very important role in congressional relations for the White House. Speaker Hastert had given him an office just off the floor of the House, and Cheney employed three legislative affairs representatives to keep him apprised. Hastert had a good relationship with Cheney, going back to their days in the House together, and he commented that when it came to the president, "Sometimes I saw him three times per week then I would not see him for three weeks, but Cheney, you could always get a hold of him, back channel into the White House, you go through him."[19] "I always said if there was good news the president would call you, if there was bad news Cheney would call you. If there was a heavy ask it would come from Cheney."[20] The vice president always held his cards close to his vest and only gave his counsel to the president in private, rarely speaking in large meetings. He agreed to help Kean and Hamilton, adding, "You won't always see what I am doing, but I will be helping you."[21] One White House senior staff member recalled: "I don't think the vice president ever supported the policy. It was a struggle between his policy concerns and loyalty, and loyalty won out over his own views."[22]

As the vice president prepared to reengage Chairman Hunter to break the logjam, Robert Rangel reached out to Senator Collins's staff director, Michael Bopp. The staff saw it as part of their duty to come up with legislative solutions that finessed tough issues. "I thought, 'What if magically I could get Susan Collins and Duncan Hunter to a common view and meet in the middle on this handful of sticking points."[23] Rangel and Bopp "had a pretty good exchange; we did not get there, but out of that came some ideas: maybe there is a way to get there and finesse this" by kicking the chain-of-command question to a different mechanism for later implementation. "It was a lengthy, iterative conversation; Michael Bopp and I were doing what-ifs, exploring the art of the possible ... we began to look creatively at some formulations."[24]

Finally, Hobbs reached Rangel on a Saturday night. "After a discussion, I agreed to take back to Chairman Hunter the following formulation: 'the president shall issue guidelines to ensure the effective implementation and execution within the executive branch of the authorities granted to the director of national intelligence in a manner that *respects* the chain of command.'"[25] The language suited Collins and Lieberman, who believed that since the president was for a strong DNI, his guidelines would ensure that the DNI's powers extended to the fullest. The next day, Hunter expressed interest in the new formulation, but he wanted it tweaked to ensure a future president would not unduly disadvantage the interest of the secretary of defense. Hobbs, Rangel, and Bopp experimented with a new verb that would give Hunter the assurance that the chain of command would be preserved while not violating Senator Collins's insistence that the DNI not be hamstrung. The staff looked at an online thesaurus for a new verb. How about *abrogate*? As in, the guidelines "shall not abrogate the chain of command." It worked for Bopp, and he undertook to sell it to Collins. Collins sought out Lieberman, who was at the Kennedy Center Honors, in the same hall as Vice President Cheney, who was also on hand with the president for Washington's annual awkward night with the Hollywood elite.

The Kennedy Center Honors are an annual ritual in Washington, DC. In 2004 Warren Beatty and Elton John, among others, were on hand to receive awards for Lifetime Contributions to American Culture through the Performing Arts. Always held the first weekend in December, a week of events culminates in a Sunday-night performance in the Opera House of the Kennedy Center. The honorees, adorned with their medals on rainbow ribbons, sat in a special box on the balcony, a few feet away from the presidential box, where President Bush and Vice President Cheney and their wives were seated. On stage, Kid Rock sang Elton John's "Saturday Night's Alright (For Fighting)." The black-tie, mostly staid Washington crowd behaved robotically at first, calmly viewing until Kid Rock exhorted them to "make some noise." This provoked an uneven distribution of revelers getting to their feet for obligatory rhythmic clapping and the finger-snapping. Jack Nicholson overcompensated for the Washington crowd by dancing in the aisle, clapping his hands above his head.

As Lieberman listened to the Elton John tribute, he checked his BlackBerry. A message from Senator Collins asked whether they could accept the change to "shall not *abrogate* the chain of command." Lieberman quickly replied at 11:20 p.m. that *abrogate* worked for him.[26] At the news, Rangel would try to sell it to Hunter but he was on a plane back to Washington from the West Coast. Collins thought that if Hunter thought the new language came from her, he would surely reject it. She wanted the White House to float the language to Hunter. By now, Hunter had landed back in Washington and learned of the new language from his staff, and he was looking to speak with the vice president. But first Hobbs needed to get the vice president behind the new language and ask him to nail down Hunter. Hobbs called the White House signal looking for Cheney. Hobbs knew the vice president would leave that night for Afghanistan to attend the inauguration of Hamid Karzai. But the vice president was still at the Kennedy Center. Hobbs reached someone on the vice president's Secret Service detail outside the presidential box. "When the VP steps out of the box, he will have two messages. One message will be from Duncan Hunter and one from me. *Make sure he calls me back first!*" When the vice president called Hobbs, he said he could not agree to *abrogate* off the cuff without talking to his lawyer. Hobbs said, "This is all bullshit, Mr. Vice President," and explained that he had just turned to an internet thesaurus for a new word that said the same thing as the compromise of November 20. The vice president decided *abrogate* was fine and reached out to Duncan Hunter.[27] Hunter agreed on the condition that the vice president commit to letting the House and Senate Armed Services Committees be consulted before the president issued the chain-of-command guidelines. Duncan Hunter recalled, "I did it because I trusted Vice President Cheney. I knew he would see that the guidelines were written the right way."[28] Rangel recalled that this was Hunter's attempt to

> beef up this framework to get a commitment from him as VP when the time came around to basically implement this, [since the formulation would be] kicking back to the Executive Branch the responsibility for

fleshing out this . . . balancing of authorities, . . . that it would be done properly in terms of SecDef authorities.[29]

The vice president agreed and the deal was done. Seeing that a compromise would be better to accept if it came from the president, the next morning Hobbs inserted "shall not abrogate the chain of command" into a letter to the Congress and rushed down to the Oval Office to get the president's signature. Shortly thereafter, the White House released the president's letter to the press. It read,

> Accordingly, in developing implementing guidelines and regulations for this bill, it is my intention to ensure that the principles of unity of command and authority are fully protected. It remains essential to preserve in the heads of the executive departments the unity of authority over, and accountability for the performance of those departments. In particular, as we continue to prosecute the global war on terrorism, the integrity of the military chain of command and the principle of battlefield unity of command must continue to be respected and in no way abrogated.

The big question was why would Hunter, with the bill seemingly dead, agree to this new formulation?

> The why is that by this point the objectives and conditions had changed. The issue had now taken on a huge public and political significance and most of the key concerns had been largely addressed. So while he stood tall in the saddle at the right time, Hunter is essentially an institutional guy and was uncomfortable with the role of being the sole obstacle standing against his president and his leadership. So as the staff guy, I felt it was my job to continue to search for options and possible outcomes that preserved the key principles but also presented opportunities for closure. I never believed he relished the role he was forced to take in parting with the Speaker in such a significant and visible way. But he felt he had to as a matter of conviction and also because the White House and Speaker's staff forced him against the wall.[30]

With the bill now back on track, the question was what to do about Sensenbrenner. The Speaker had gotten Hunter something but could not leave Sensenbrenner with nothing. From the Speaker and the president, Sensenbrenner extracted a major concession. Early the next year, the White

House would work with Sensenbrenner to come up with a mutually accept-able provision on his idea to make legal residence a prerequisite to a driver's license. The Speaker committed to putting the language on the first "must-pass" bill in the next Congress. Because Sensenbrenner knew there would be a supplemental appropriations bill to fund the wars in Iraq and Afghanistan, he recognized that there was a fast-moving vehicle that could carry his bill to the president's desk. He would also only have to negotiate with the White House; no more sessions with the Senate Democrats who had doggedly fought him. In recognition of this arrangement, the president's letter on the chain of command also contained the White House commitment.

> Measures proposed that were not incorporated into the bill . . . should not prevent the Congress from passing this historic legislation now. I look forward to working with the Congress early in the next session to address these other issues, including improving our asylum laws and standards for issuing driver's licenses.

Sensenbrenner would still vote against the bill explaining that the "Senate was hell-bent on ensuring illegal aliens can receive drivers' licenses, regardless of security concerns. This Sept. 10th mentality in a post–Sept. 11th world is unwise and among those I intend to rectify next year."[31]

• • • • • • • • • • •

The Speaker reconvened the conference, again in their basement meeting place. He addressed his troops. "We had a tough meeting seventeen days ago; I listened to a lot of you on chain of command and border enforcement. I figured this bill was not ready to move."[32] Hastert reported that Hunter had had positive experiences in getting his issue addressed, but that they could not move the Senate on all of Sensenbrenner's issues. The Speaker had talked with the president about the need to make sure driver's license standards happened, and he has now passed on assurances that it would be addressed. This time, DeLay spoke up. "The Speaker is right. The Senate only wanted the DNI and NCTC. If the Senate had done it their way, troops would have been at risk—you've never heard me comment. Senate has come to be embarrassed by their bill, but remember the Speaker put experts on the Conference Committee. The Senate gave Durbin veto power but we got law enforcement language and we will put immigration language on the next must pass bill and we will live to fight another day."[33] Hunter announced to the conference that "we've fixed chain-of-command." Sensenbrenner announced that "I am the skunk at the garden party. I am not signing on. . . . The Senate caved on the easy stuff."[34]

After the meeting with his Republican colleagues, Hunter went to the press:

> It says that the chain of command shall be respected and not abrogated and it goes straight to the Goldwater-Nichols statutes, which say that a commander in the theater, taking his command from the secretary of defense and above him from the president of the United States, has every military asset under his command, including intelligence assets. It builds a fence around the chain of command that means that in the future, if there is a question as to whether a combatant commander in Iraq has access to an intelligence aircraft, for example, if there's a question as to whether he has access to that aircraft if he needs it in battle or another agency has access to that aircraft, it's very clear now that he has access to that aircraft.[35]

The press aboard Air Force One en route to California with the president asked whether Hunter had been promised anything in exchange for support of the bill.[36] Collins said the new language

> would in no way weaken the authorities of the new director of national intelligence. All the language does is provide a little extra comfort to Congressman Hunter and others who shared his view that we were not in any way affecting the chain of command.[37]

As the House prepared to vote, aboard Air Force One from California to Andrews Air Force Base President Bush played Gin while he monitored the debate on C-SPAN.[38] As the bill passed 336-75, with sixty-seven Republicans voting no, including Sensenbrenner,[39] David Hobbs called the plane to tell the president that the bill had passed.[40] Speaker Hastert sought out Chairman Hoekstra and Congresswoman Harman on the House Floor. The Speaker gave them each gavels to signify their hard work on the intelligence legislation. Harman was touched by the gesture and considered the Speaker "very gracious."[41]

Senator Lieberman considered Speaker Hastert and President Bush critical to the passage.[42] "It wouldn't have happened unless the White House wanted it to happen." Chairman Hoekstra added,

One of the critiques of Speaker Hastert was that he saw himself as not the Speaker but as the advocate for the president's policies; this would explain why Speaker Hastert and Scott Palmer were so supportive. The president did want it. If the president did not want it, or was lukewarm about it, the Speaker would not have pushed it.[43]

The press reported,

Bush, who had come under heavy criticism for failing to get members of his party to support the bill, demonstrated that his administration still can get results when it turns up the heat on recalcitrant Republicans. "There would be no bill if it had not been for this president's forceful and very skillful involvement," said Warner.[44]

Now Bush had "reasserted himself as a force in coming battles on Capitol Hill by getting reluctant fellow Republicans to embrace a major overhaul of American spy agencies."[45] After the Senate's vote on final passage, the 9/11 Families, posted outside the Senate, cried tears of joy. Roemer saw their efforts to pass the bill as a "cathartic process." "It was like they could then begin to deal with the loss of a husband or brother or sister or wife."[46] Roemer e-mailed his colleagues: "How fitting it will be to pass 9/11 reforms on December 7, 2004—63 years after Pearl Harbor."[47] A spontaneous celebration broke out back at the offices of the SHSGAC. The staff congregated around Collins and Lieberman who thanked the staff.

Ironically, the two groups most often cited for the hostility toward the DNI—the Office of the Vice President and the House Republican Leadership—played critical roles in enabling the passage of the compromise bill. Cheney's eleventh hour intervention helped bring Duncan Hunter aboard. "I would say that without the help of the president and the vice president, we would not be here today. Their intervention at critical points throughout the debate was absolutely essential in helping us forge the compromises that were necessary to move this bill along."[48] Some observers at the CIA saw President Bush's post-election intervention as critical. "We all thought reform was dead, and indeed Bush could have buried it by simply saying nothing and letting the clock expire. Instead, he asked Congress to send him a reform bill, and jolted the process out of its coma. Some people say Bush tried to block reform—that is just not true. He could have killed it through silence, but he spoke up for it at the right moment."[49] And Scott

Palmer, acting on behalf of the speaker, was pivotal. Senator Collins noted on the floor of the Senate in thanking Speaker Hastert that "his chief of staff devoted hundreds of hours to assisting in these negotiations."[50] Scott Palmer was recognized by the 9/11 PDP, the Families, and the Senate; they would repeatedly cite his efforts as indispensable to passage of the bill.[51] Philip Zelikow, speaking at a Washington think tank in 2010, would recall that were it not for Scott Palmer and the Speaker, the Commission's reforms would have died.[52]

From his private dining room off the Oval Office, President Bush called Senator Collins to congratulate her. She called the intelligence bill "the most satisfying accomplishment of my Senate career."[53] She, Lieberman, Collins, Hoekstra, Rice, Goss, Mueller, and Frist joined the president onstage for the signing at the Mellon Auditorium, where the 9/11 Commission had announced its recommendations just under five months previously. There were about three hundred spectators seated in small gold chairs in the "gloriously ornate" setting.[54] Bush spoke for seven minutes, sat briefly at a desk labeled by a placard reading, "Protecting America," and signed the bill. He greeted the congressional leaders with handshakes and arm-grabs and then was off.[55]

CHAPTER SEVENTEEN

Bureaucratic Black Arts

A top 9/11 PDP staffer reported to the former 9/11 Commissioners his analysis of the chain-of-command language. "As you can see, it is unclear what it means: all sides can claim victory. Everything depends on guidelines from the president that have yet to be written."[1] The comment could have applied to other parts of the new statute. Throughout the legislative process, when the parties came to loggerheads, they repeatedly left the details to the executive for implementation. Seeing the importance of implementation immediately after the deal was struck, Senators Collins and Lieberman took to the floor of the Senate to expound on their intent, seeking to influence how the new statute would be interpreted.

In their floor statements, Senators Collins and Lieberman sought to pump up the authorities in the statute in line with their vision of an expansive DNI. Senator Collins stressed that with regard to the budget build, "the word 'determine' in the legislation means that the DNI is the decision maker regarding the budget and does not share this authority with any department head."[2] They sought especially to give meaning to the chain-of-command language that would benefit the DNI. "This provision does not authorize the president or department heads to override the DNI's authority as contained in this legislation."[3] Indeed, Collins and Lieberman sought to ensure that the DNI "will have the power to force the various defense and non-defense intelligence entities to work together seamlessly" and to ensure that the DNI was the direct interlocutor between the military forces and the defense intelligence agencies. "The DNI would also be a single point of contact for the military."[4]

They also sought to improve the standing of the NCTC, urging that "we need to centralize this precious resource rather than dissipate them across the intelligence community."[5] With regard to the strategic operational planning mission of the NCTC, Senator Lieberman revived the 9/11 Commission's notion that it would be involved in planning of specific operations, although he carefully noted that the NCTC has "no operational authority."[6] Senator Lieberman cited the expansive views of the 9/11 Commission that the NCTC should be like the planning staff of the Joint Chiefs of Staff "that does planning for operations conducted by the combatant commands."[7] "The NCTC must reach below [the] strategic level in order to have the impact envisioned by the Commission and this legislation."[8] Indeed, the hunt for Usama bin Ladin qualified as an issue for strategic operational planning.[9] "The NCTC would recommend to the CIA and the Defense Department's Special Operations Command . . . whether to infiltrate or raid a sanctuary."[10]

As the Senators sought to lock in their expansive vision for the DNI and the NCTC and downplay the role of the chain-of-command language, in a rejoinder, Chairman Hoekstra noted in the Congressional Record that due to "often fundamentally different philosophies and visions," the conferees agreed "to submit only a very limited Joint Explanatory Statement on the conference report, relying on the text of the legislation to represent our agreements."[11] Hoekstra insisted that "other statements by members of Congress outside the scope of the Joint Explanatory Statement . . . or commissions whose work contributed to this legislation reflect their own views and should not be construed as determinative guidance with respect to legislative intent."[12] Specifically, Hoekstra insisted on reliance of the specific text with regard to how the DNI would determine the budget, noting that beyond what was in the statute, "the legislation does not specify how budget proposals are to be developed or provided, and it is properly for the Executive Branch to determine how to execute the statute consistent with its text." "There is no specific direction to concentrate personnel holding scarce and desirable skills in the NCTC."[13] With regard to strategic operational planning, Hoekstra noted that the statute's provision for assigning roles and responsibilities "does not extend to directing the execution of any resulting operations."[14] Hoekstra sought to nullify the Collins and Lieberman statements by noting that the "nature of the authorities granted to the director of national intelligence and the relationship of the director to other federal officials were delicate and precisely negotiated issues" and are reflected solely in the text.[15]

The post-deal jockeying was necessary because the legislative process for IRTPA had not afforded the opportunity to reach a meeting of the minds.

The conferees produced only a short report, called a Joint Explanatory State-ment of the Conferees, a document that usually accompanies the passage of a law that gives additional explanation of the congressional intent. It was agreed that because settling the legislative text had been so laborious, there was not time to hash out an expansive vision of what the conferees intended.

As the legislation drafters sought to define what the law meant, President Bush's top choice for the job struggled to understand exactly what the new DNI was empowered to do. Ironically, President Bush's top pick for the job was among the 9/11 Commission's harshest critics, Robert Gates. Gates had written earlier that year that the DNI would be nothing more than an eunuch. Arriving at the White House on a Monday morning, four days before the president's second inauguration, Gates, president of Texas A&M, was seri-ously considering an offer from President Bush to be the first DNI. Over the course of several weeks, Gates had scrutinized the DNI statute. He thought the law was "strange"[16] and faulted it for vagueness on the authorities of the DNI.[17] "The president needs to make explicit publicly that the DNI is head of the intelligence community, not some budgeter or coordinator." "The posi-tion's only prayer of success is for the president to say plainly ... how he sees the job. Without his explicit mandate ... the endeavor is doomed to fail."[18]

In an e-mail to Card and Hadley, Gates outlined the weaknesses of the DNI position and asked a series of questions about whether the White House would strengthen his hand "to make the position even remotely capable."[19] Gates questioned whether the DNI could fire anyone outside of his immediate office.[20] "The DNI must be able to remove uncoopera-tive agency heads. Vision and positive leadership are necessary to change nearly 60 years of relationships and bureaucratic politics; but there must be, in the background, the possibility of sanctions."[21] Gates doubted the ability of the DNI to regulate the "essentially insatiable" desire of military commanders for intelligence.[22]

Gates' most serious concerns were about the DNI's relationship with the CIA. "Which one of you gets to tell [CIA Director Porter Goss] that his role is dramatically changed (circumscribed) with the advent of the DNI?" While the new law entitled the DNI as the "principal intelligence advisor to the president," Gates sought reassurance: would he "find himself playing musical chairs in the Oval Office?" "As they say in the movie 'The Highlander,' there can only be one." Gates insisted that the DNI would have to prepare the president's daily intelligence briefing. In a series of phone calls, Card and

Hadley had reassured Gates that the president would fill in the gaps. "I will give them credit; they were prepared to try and accommodate everything that I said needed to be done and they were very forthcoming."[23]

Now sitting in the White House Chief of Staff's office for lunch, Gates continued to press for reassurances. After four hours, Gates left the White House promising an answer the following Monday. "I think the way it was left, and I don't know about them, but I had the sense they were expecting me to say yes, and I expected to say yes; they had really bent over backward." He jokes now that "they made a mistake that a neophyte car salesman would never make. They let me off the lot without a sale."[24]

Gates returned to College Station, Texas. On Sunday night, Gates walked the campus of Texas A&M with a cigar debating whether to accept the post. Gates thought about how much he did not want to return to Washington, especially for such a "complicated" task. He also had more he wanted to accomplish at Texas A&M. Gates called Andy Card at Camp David the next morning and turned the offer down. "There was a stunned silence on the other end."[25] Despite the White House's assurances, Gates concluded that the "legislation weakened the leadership of the community, instead of a stronger person, you ended up with a weaker person because the DNI had no troops and no additional powers really on the budget, hiring, and firing."[26] Admiral Vernon E. Clark, USN, the former Chief of Naval Operations, also turned down the post.[27] Finally, Andy Card reached President Bush's ambassador in Iraq, John Negroponte. One of the nation's most distinguished diplomats, Negroponte was surprised to get a call from the White House Chief of Staff. Would he be interested in the post? "I don't know why they came to me, frankly," but he assumed it was "because there is a logic to an ambassador, [someone with] diplomatic experience, [someone who was a] customer and generator of intelligence."[28] That night, Negroponte printed the new law on his desktop computer in Baghdad and took it home to read. In his announcement of Ambassador Negroponte as the first DNI, Bush affirmed that the DNI would "lead a unified intelligence community, and will serve as the principal advisor to the president on intelligence matters" and noted that "the director of the CIA will report to John. The CIA will retain its core of responsibilities for collecting human intelligence, analyzing intelligence from all sources, and supporting American interests abroad at the direction of the president."[29]

Meanwhile, the WMD Commission, led by former senator Chuck Robb and Judge Laurence Silberman, appointed by President Bush to investigate the Intelligence Community's pre-war judgments about Iraq's weapons of mass destruction, prepared to make its recommendations. While the 9/11 Commission was high-flying, the WMD Commission worked quietly. With regard to Iraq, the WMD Commission declared that the Intelligence Community was "dead wrong in almost all" of its judgments.[30] The WMD Commission was also charged with reviewing the performance of the Intelligence Community overall and felt obligated to "ask how IC should be organized to respond to the 21st century."[31] The WMD Commission concluded: "Today's Intelligence Community [is] not so much poorly managed as unmanaged."[32] Presented with the Intelligence Reform Act just three months before it was due to report, the WMD Commission studied it closely. One senior staffer on the WMD Commission saw the DNI that emerged as flawed. "It was not weak enough to be a coordinator, not strong enough to be a Secretary of Intelligence."[33] Seen as a gesture of "do something," the new DNI was "a half-empty vessel" that the WMD Commission saw as an opportunity.[34] The WMD Commission would give the DNI a series of tasks, adding to the DNI's to-do list.

When the WMD Report was issued in March 2005, President Bush accepted their recommendations. "The central conclusion is one that I share: America's intelligence community needs fundamental change to enable us to successfully confront the threats of the 21st century." In assessing the new law, the WMD Commission called the DNI's new authorities "only relatively broader than before."[35] Citing "headstrong" agencies, the commissioners warned the president that "sooner or later, they will try to run around—or over—the DNI."[36] An "unmanaged" community manifested itself as collectors and analysts around the community working "autonomously, communicating and collaborating only episodically."[37] Too often the community was "collecting what they wanted and the analysts were making do with what was collected." "We found that really dangerous; no one answering the questions the analysts had to answer had the authority to tell the collectors what to collect, and we did not see that changing."[38]

To remedy this, the WMD Commission recommended that the DNI organize around mission. For example, "for any such target—be it a country like China, a non-state actor like al Qa'ida, or a subject like 'proliferation'—a Mission Manager would be charged with organizing and monitoring the Community's efforts, and serving as the DNI's principal advisor on the subject."[39] Mission managers should "drive" intelligence collection and identify "shortcomings in analysis."[40] The WMD Commission went on to recommend a number of other tasks for the DNI, including overhauling information sharing, creating a performance system to create jointness and build a modern workforce, and providing a variety of officers to help the DNI accomplish his work.

Ironically, the WMD Commission recommended changes in domestic intelligence, an area in which the 9/11 Commission had simply endorsed the FBI's reform plan. At the Department of Justice, the WMD Commission recommended the consolidation of the Department's "primary national security elements" under a single Assistant Attorney General for National Security to "serve as a single focal point on all national security matters."[41] The Department of Justice's primary national security elements—the Office of Intelligence Policy and Review, and the Counterterrorism and Counterespionage sections—should be placed under a new Assistant Attorney General for National Security. The WMD Commission also sought to integrate the FBI into the Intelligence Community, citing the need for "better intelligence coordination across the foreign-domestic divide."[42] It noted that the DNI would not be able to exercise any oversight over the FBI's national security mission because of fractured budgetary categories and lack of a say in the FBI director. It also found the DNI's authority over the FBI to be dependent on the authority of the Directorate of Intelligence, which the WMD Commission found to have a "pervasive" lack of authority.[43] "It has no authority to direct any of the Bureau's intelligence investigations, operations, or collections. It currently performs no analysis, commands no operational resources, and has little control over the 56 Field Intelligence Groups." The WMD Commission recommended the creation of a National Security Service within the FBI which would include the bureau's counterterrorism, counterintelligence, and intelligence functions.

In all, the WMD Commission made seventy-four recommendations. After a White House ninety-day review, forty-five recommendations were specifically assigned to the DNI to implement.[44] It significantly broadened the scope of the problems to be tackled by a DNI. The White House treated these recommendations with almost the force of law by endorsing them and forwarding them to the DNI for action. Ambassador Negroponte called them a "roadmap for launching the [Office of the DNI] ODNI."[45]

The following month, Negroponte appeared before the Senate for his confirmation hearing. Expectations were high, the chairman of the Senate Intelligence Committee, Senator Pat Roberts, declared: "Mr. Ambassador, the process of change begins with you."[46] But Chairman Roberts also lamented the outcome of IRTPA: "For now we must implement and oversee an Intelligence Reform Act that is somewhat ambiguous with respect to your authorities and responsibilities. Ambassador, this ambiguity has created justifiable concern about whether you, as the DNI, have the clear authorities you will need to meet your vast responsibilities."[47]

Awaiting confirmation by the U.S. Senate, Negroponte and General Michael Hayden, who had been nominated to be the DNI's principal deputy, sketched out the design of the new office from their temporary offices in the Old Executive Office Building at the White House. Facing the expectations set by the 9/11 Commission, the statutory mandates in IRTPA, and the presidential directives to implement the WMD Commission's recommendations, the DNI faced a gargantuan to-do list. The crush of work contributed to a sense among the embryonic DNI staff that they needed a lot of help. The White House balked at DNI Negroponte's plan for staffing the Office of the DNI. The task fell to the national security advisor to adjudicate what Negroponte thought he needed and what OMB considered excessive. Steve Hadley went over the staffing plan and pared it back considerably, but the ODNI still numbered in the high hundreds. The NSC staff believed Negroponte's staffing plan was too large but felt some deference was owed to the new DNI.

Still, by late 2005, as the DNI office was still forming, its rivals exploited the rushed circumstances of its passage, labeling it a political expediency rather than a national security necessity. Quickly, a new conventional wisdom sunk in about the DNI. Typical was an opinion article authored by former TTIC Director John Brennan. He called IRTPA a "hurried and flawed piece of legislation" rife with "ambiguous language"; it had "raised unrealistic expectations" about the prospects for the success of the DNI. There was no "overall game plan" but instead "confusion" in the IC "sown by a rush of initiatives."[48] This echoed Tenet's declaration in 2004 that IRTPA constituted a "mad rush to rearrange wiring diagrams in an attempt to be seen as doing something."[49] The DNI suffered from the perception that the defenders of the Defense Department prevailed and that the DNI was a weaker player than it might have been.

Acknowledging friction with the CIA, defenders of the DNI insist that other IC elements value the new system because they are guaranteed a seat at the table on major intelligence matters. Defenders also note that DNI Negroponte developed a national intelligence strategy to prioritize what information to collect and analyze.[50] To pursue integration, DNI Negroponte followed through on the WMD Commission's recommendation to create mission managers, choosing six to serve as "traffic cops, coordinating analysis, briefing the White House, and tasking spies on what to target."[51]

But the size of the ODNI persisted as an issue in Congress. "Little has changed—except that a new bureaucracy has been created." Hoekstra called it "large, bureaucratic, and hierarchical."[52] The size of the DNI was especially an issue in the House.[53] Jane Harman said that the DNI keeps adding "more billets, more bureaucracy, more buildings."[54] Even the former 9/11 Commissioners criticized the new Office of the DNI. Lehman faulted its "four deputy directors, three associate directors and no fewer than nineteen assistant deputy directors."[55] He asserted that the DNI had adopted the "bureaucratic model" rather than the "very straight-line . . . General Electric model."[56] Charges arose, especially in Congress, that the ODNI was a feckless meddlesome bureaucracy. Senator Feinstein expressed her "disappointment . . . I don't see the leadership. I don't hear about the leadership."[57]

The chain-of-command language proposed by President Bush and insisted on by Duncan Hunter became an obstacle for the DNI in early efforts to corral intelligence agencies residing in other departments behind ODNI initiatives. General Clapper recalled that upon assuming the post of USDI in 2007, the "prevailing atmosphere [was] . . . . "[W]e don't have to do anything we don't want to do that the DNI tees up for us."[58]

Meanwhile, the CIA reemerged as a bureaucratic rival. John Brennan, departing after twenty-five years in the Intelligence Community, wrote that the CIA was in a "year-long tailspin" and that the "despondency" of the workforce was "palpable."[59] The efforts in Congress were seen as trying to punish the agency and as attempts to loot its assets and muscle in on the chain of command. "Everything was interpreted as out to get us," remembered Goss.[60] In March 2005 President Bush visited the CIA, in part to underscore their continued centrality in national security.

While President Bush had underscored the statute's dictate that the CIA works for the DNI, the CIA advanced a new argument about its relationship to the DNI. The statute provided that the CIA "reports to" the DNI. Gordon Lederman, the former 9/11 Commission staffer who joined the

Collins-Lieberman staff, recalled that there was a conscious decision to make the CIA subordinate to the DNI but not to put it under the explicit authority, direction, and control of the DNI. The senators most feared replicating the status quo whereby the DCI did not have time to manage the IC because he was too busy being CIA director. "Reports to" was written to give the DNI some distance from the day-to-day management of the CIA. Senator Lieberman added, "The legislation has been very carefully crafted to ensure that the director of the CIA is subordinate to and reports to the new DNI only, and not directly to the president, but that the DNI does not manage the CIA's daily activities."[61]

But the "reports to" formulation gave the CIA an opening. Much later, Mike Hayden, who later moved from the ODNI to be director of the CIA, explained their argument. Congress chose "reports to" for a reason; by consciously avoiding the magic words of "authority, direction, and control," the CIA's lawyers argued, the CIA was an independent agency.[62]

Dream Team

After twenty months in the job, Ambassador Negroponte resigned as DNI to become deputy secretary of state. Many saw his departure from a cabinet-level post to a subcabinet position as revealing of the DNI's real stature and influence.[63]

With the appointment of Michael McConnell, a career intelligence professional, as the second DNI, Michael Hayden as the CIA director, Jim Clapper as USDI, and Robert Gates as secretary of defense, supporters of the DNI saw a coming golden age. Reformers hoped the "dream team," would be able to refine the roles and missions of their respective agencies and usher in a more harmonious arrangement.

In 2007 DNI McConnell and Secretary of Defense Robert Gates signed a memorandum of agreement "establishing the Undersecretary of Defense for Intelligence . . . as the director of Defense Intelligence within the office of the DNI."[64] This dual-hatting arrangement was similar to the 9/11 Commission's recommendation for a deputy DNI for defense intelligence. One commentator testified to Congress that the dual-hatting arrangement "provides the appropriate prism for this and future holders of the position to view their responsibilities. It is also symbolic of the greater cooperation between the Department of Defense and director of national intelligence in recent months."[65]

McConnell's tenure as DNI also saw the development of a groundbreaking policy to encourage information-sharing across the IC. A 2009 directive sought to encourage sharing by creating an affirmative duty on intelligence officers to share their information with other intelligence entities or otherwise make it able to be discovered by electronic means.[66] McConnell also oversaw the creation of a joint-duty program, in the spirit of Goldwater-Nichols, to facilitate rotations of IC personnel to positions outside their home agency to foster a sense of joint mission.

Even during the "Golden Age," the DNI as an institution remained an object of harsh criticism. A former CIA officer called it "an unnecessary bureaucratic contraption with an amazingly large staff" that made leadership of the community "even more muddled." He called for an "independent, bipartisan audit of the progress of intelligence reform."[67] The conventional wisdom persisted that IRTPA was "rushed," "watered down,"[68] contained "intellectual flaws,"[69] and is riddled with "weaknesses and ambiguities."[70] "Many aspects of it are a product of compromise rather than consensus."[71] "Despite the recent creation of a director of national intelligence, the U.S. intelligence community remains a dysfunctional family with no one firmly in charge."[72] The former 9/11 PDP continued to argue that the DNI that had been created was at odds with what they had proposed. "When the 9/11 Commission first recommended the creation of a director of national intelligence, we specified that the organization should consist of several hundred. Since then, I understand that the number of DNI personnel has grown substantially beyond what we envisioned."[73] Roemer argued that the ODNI was "simply not done right. The office was created in the right way, but it's too big now, and the authorities aren't appropriate for it."[74] The DNI's defenders pointed out that IRTPA mandated that several IC offices, including the Community Management Staff and the National Intelligence Council, both from the CIA, and the new NCTC, be part of the ODNI. If you took the number of staff "that has letterhead that says actual DNI on it . . . [it's] closer to 600."[75] In 2006 General Michael Hayden explained that there was "enough size that it's not dependent on the constituent parts for information."[76]

However, during this period, President Bush made some enhancements to the DNI's authorities. Secretary Gates supported this effort to update the presidential executive order often called the "foundational document" of the Intelligence Community. However, while sympathetic to a strong

DNI, Gates was now secretary of defense and could not simply "sell out his building to his old intelligence cronies," as one NSC staffer put it. "I still accepted the reality that I had believed in 2004 that the Congress will not ultimately approve handing over those authorities from the secretary of defense to the DNI, so my pitch with McConnell and Clapper and to a lesser extent Hayden, how can the four of us, we have a unique opportunity here, four heads that control the intelligence assets, who have known each other for decades and trust each other, how can we take advantage of this unique moment in time to agree [on some items] that will empower the DNI without crossing any lines on the hill."[77]

After an arduous process, the Bush administration's efforts to augment the DNI authorities via executive order were successful.[78] First, the DNI was given the ability to initiate the firing of intelligence agency heads, although the concurrence of the secretary of defense was still required.[79] Second, the DNI's budget authority was improved by adding that the DNI "shall oversee and direct the implementation . . . and execution" of the intelligence appropriation.[80]

Finally, the potential obstruction posed by the chain-of-command language was implemented sensibly. Instead of *any* intelligence official claiming violation of chain of command and thereby thwarting the initiative of the DNI, the order restricted invocation of chain of command to override DNI guidance to the cabinet official.[81] As DNI Blair later testified, "I found [stress with DoD] largely to have dissipated by the time that I had the honor of being DNI."[82]

Whatever enhancements the DNI had received, the DNI position did not fare well through the transfer of administrations. Before their confirmation hearings to be DNI and director of the CIA, Admiral Dennis Blair and Leon Panetta got off on the wrong foot. In the weeks before President Obama's inauguration, at the offices of the Presidential Transition Office, they were set to have lunch one day at 12 p.m. Blair, an admiral from a lineage of admirals, had picked up sandwiches from the nearby Subway sandwich shop and was ready to begin at noon sharp. Panetta, amiable and loquacious, was in a briefing with a variety of intelligence officials and the meeting went long. Blair waited. As 12:10 became 12:15 and then 12:20, Blair burst into the conference room: "Hey, CIA nominee, it's lunch time." The assembled crowd was surprised and it was an awkward start to a complicated relationship.[83]

In his confirmation hearing, Panetta had to be asked twice whether the

DNI was his boss.[84] His first answer paid homage to the "reports to" mandate but seemed to reflect the CIA as an independent intelligence agency model.[85]

A former four-star admiral and head of the Pacific Command, upon confirmation as DNI, Admiral Blair embarked to firmly take control of the Intelligence Community. "The one overarching driver of future intelligence greatness will be the leadership of the Office of the Director of National Intelligence."[86] Referring to the progress of the ODNI, Blair noted, "We know it hasn't gone as fast as everyone would have liked."[87] Admiral Blair focused on increasing intelligence support to combat drug gangs in Latin America, reinstituting practices to ensure a new system of satellites, and a series of reforms in counterintelligence.[88] The CIA chafed under Blair's style. The tension came to a head over the issue of whether the DNI or the director of the CIA would "select the top American spy in each country overseas."[89] Panetta had been resisting a directive from Blair that the top intelligence official, the "DNI's representative," could be someone other than the CIA Chief of Station. Admiral Blair wanted to allow for the possibility that in some countries, where perhaps an intelligence agency besides the CIA had the deepest relationship, a representative from an agency besides the CIA could be designated the lead U.S. intelligence official. At a lunch at the U.S. Supreme Court for the judges serving on the Foreign Intelligence Surveillance (FISA) Court, Blair mentioned casually that he had signed the directive and that it had been cabled to CIA stations all over the world. "*What?*" Panetta demanded. You knew I had non-concurred on the directive. Blair replied that he had to make a call and had decided the matter. Panetta returned to CIA Headquarters and sent out his own worldwide cable to stations and bases: "Ignore Mr. Blair's message."[90] Panetta argued that the matter was unsettled and that the White House would need to decide. Blair sought a ruling from the NSC, Panetta sought to make Vice President Biden the arbiter. Biden took up the issue and a separate matter on whether the CIA would have to go through the DNI on covert action matters, or continue to work directly with the White House. The CIA sought to maintain its special relationship with the White House while the DNI was seeking to become the interlocutor.[91] The DNI lost both battles. General Hayden, who agreed with the CIA's position, objected to the way the DNI was treated. "The DNI has a right to be wrong without being overruled in such a public humiliating way by the White House."[92]

After the failed bombing of an airliner over Detroit on December 25,

2009, the ODNI came under a new fusillade of criticism. Director Goss said, "What we're seeing now is that the Office of the Director of National Intelligence has not made one iota of improvement."[93] "The real problem for Blair was that he occupied a job whose powers were defined in law, but not in practice."[94] Negroponte came forward with his own misgivings. When asked about the wisdom of creating the DNI in the first place, Negroponte answered, "Yeah. I am, in fact, distancing myself somewhat from the idea ... I think you could've made the old system work."[95] Admiral Blair was later forced to resign, apparently because of friction with the White House.[96] A friend of Admiral Blair remarked in defense of his tenure that "Denny read the statute and thought it meant what it said." Of his own tenure, Blair recalled, "The greatest obstacle I faced in strengthening the role of the DNI as an IC integrator was the White House. President Obama and his closest circle of national security advisors ... had no personal commitment to a strong DNI. What they did have a commitment to was a White House micro-managed national security system.... They preferred to deal directly with intelligence agencies themselves.[97]

After the resignation of the third DNI in its first five years, many commentators asked whether the position had been set up to fail. "That reorganization was a bad idea from the start; it created unnecessary new layers of bureaucracy—the DNI now has about 1500 people, partly duplicating jobs that used to be done by the CIA. But worse, the reorganization has added to the very bureaucratic tensions it was supposed to avoid."[98]

Early in President Obama's term, Lee Hamilton testified that, "We believe the DNI has achieved a meaningful measure of success in its first years. It's been worth the inevitable turmoil. But it's a work in progress—closer to the beginning than the end of reform."[99]

Epilogue

The momentum generated by the 9/11 Commission and the 9/11 Families, paired with the intelligence failures on 9/11 and Iraq and a competitive presidential election, propelled the most comprehensive reorganization of intelligence since the creation of the Pearl Harbor system in 1947. The Commission had devised a strategy based on the looming election and the support of the Families to get their reforms enacted into law. They capitalized on the pent-up demand generated over years of previous studies recommending that the Intelligence Community needed more centralized leadership. The Commission's ability to dictate the congressional and executive agenda in the fall of 2004 and their considerable influence during the development of IRTPA ranks the 9/11 Commission as one of the most successful commissions in history. The fact that IRTPA even passed was a tremendous feat. Numerous commissions since 1947 had made similar recommendations that had gone nowhere. The extreme difficulty in forcing a reallocation of bureaucratic power was exhibited by IRTPA itself, which nearly collapsed on numerous occasions. But did the process yield the DNI a substantially greater package of authorities to succeed where the DCI was thought to have failed? Or did IRTPA create a "bureaucratic fifth wheel" as the 9/11 Commission's executive director worried? Has the DNI suffered, in the words of Lee Hamilton, because he is "off in center field someplace?"

The 9/11 Commission, President Bush, and Congress made affirmative decisions that they would only go so far in centralizing authority in a DNI. By leaving the largest intelligence agencies in the Defense Department, they considered and rejected a "Department of Intelligence" model in which all intelligence agencies would have been transferred under the explicit authority, direction, and control of the DNI. The Intelligence Community's sixteen entities, except for the CIA, were embedded and would remain in their homes in cabinet departments. Because the country was engaged in two wars, it was thought to be unwise to uproot the National Security Agency and the National Geospatial Agency from the Department of Defense where they supplied troops in the field real-time battlefield intelligence.

Even while preserving the "two masters'" system and rejecting wholesale change,[1] nonetheless, the 9/11 Commission was trying to flip the balance of power from the cabinet secretaries to the new DNI. But significantly augmenting the power of the DNI was especially tough. Most of the DNI's authority lies in the areas of building budgets. "The DNI will be required to manage the Community more by controlling resources than by command."[2] It is a hallmark of most legislative histories and democracy itself that original visions are compromised to accommodate the views of interest groups and bureaucracies. In this case, intense bureaucratic opposition from the Department of Defense and its congressional defenders limited the writ the DNI might have received. The final Congressional product contained less authority for the DNI than what the president had proposed and what passed the Senate. Despite the appeal of the 9/11 Commission and the 9/11 Families, the NSC and the legislative process jettisoned some of the features the Commission had recommended to give the DNI maximum authority. Specifically, the Commission's provision that the DNI be in the White House and that the heads of important intelligence agencies be dual-hatted as deputies to the DNI were both thrown out by the White House and even the Senate, the most aggressive advocates for a strong DNI. A third feature, that the top line be declassified to facilitate an appropriation of funds directly to the DNI, was adopted by the Senate but faltered under White House and House opposition and was abandoned early in conference negotiations.

The president, joined by the House, also insisted on a savings clause, a provision designed to ensure cabinet secretaries retained enough power to run their departments, a so-called chain-of-command provision. The provision arguably weakened the DNI's hand in forcing departments and agencies to submit to its direction.[3] Even though the ability of officers inferior to the secretary to refuse cooperation with the DNI by claiming abrogation of the chain of command was limited by President Bush's 2008 executive order, its inclusion in IRTPA, especially in the eyes of those favoring a decentralized intelligence system, signaled that the DNI was at least symbolically below the cabinet secretaries. Steve Cambone, Secretary Rumsfeld's USDI, saw it as a reaffirmation of the preexisting system of government whereby power flows from the president through the cabinet secretaries; nothing in IRTPA interposed the DNI in between the president and his cabinet secretaries.[4] The advocates of the clause believe that it preserved effective government and protected the unity of the chain of command that is essential to success in war. Advocates of a strong DNI feel otherwise.

Additionally, the 9/11 Commission's vision of a DNI as a quarterback directing the daily operations of the Intelligence Community did not make it into IRTPA. From his remarks on the position, President Bush also shut down the idea of the DNI being "operational," a decision that was not really challenged in Congress. In his confirmation hearing, Ambassador Negroponte saw the DNI as a strategic actor. "The legislation directs that the director of the CIA report to the office for which I have been nominated. So given the DNI's authority over the CIA specifically and the intelligence community generally, I would expect that the DNI would oversee all such activities at the strategic level."[5] As DNI, Negroponte affirmed this vision: "The ODNI has assumed responsibility for strategic leadership of the Intelligence Community," which he explained as "establishing priorities, standards, policies, and budgets."[6] A commentator reflected on the fifth anniversary of IRTPA that "the lack of operational control, however, has resulted in a de facto lack of visibility into intelligence operations and therefore the means for effective oversight."[7] While the merits of making a DNI in charge of operating the tactical capabilities on a daily basis is debatable, leaving the DNI's writ to strategic matters deprived him of a potential pool of authority. These decisions also affected the writ of the NCTC. Directing "operations" from the CSG did not raise chain-of-command concerns because the CSG was a White House–chaired enterprise. Generally, its directive was seen as the derivative of the commander in chief and had an impact. This was potentially lost in the migration of the CSG's implicit directive authority to the NCTC, unless the NCTC was seen as acting directly at the White House's behest. Again, like with the DNI, the ultimate authority was dependent upon personality and perception of White House backing rather than a command relationship.

The WMD Commission's recommendation for mission managers to push integration, and the Bush administration's embrace thereof, supplanted the

9/11 Commission's reliance on intelligence centers as a forcing mechanism for integration. Ambassador Negroponte explained that what "we've settled on for the time being is to not try to create too many of these. My feeling is that it would be disruptive to have a proliferation, if you will, of these intelligence centers."[8] "The 9/11 Commission's conception of a national intelligence center was that it would conduct strategic analysis in-house, while the Bush Administration's 'mission managers' would task out all other analysis to the preexisting intelligence entities."[9] Thus, opting for mission managers, and later national intelligence managers, was a different direction from centers as the intelligence analogue to the military's combatant commands.

Notable though less important, the DNI was expressly denied another source of power—proximity. Congressman Hamilton had worried about the DNI being off in "center field somewhere." As discussed previously, President Bush and Congress rejected outright the Commission's recommendation that the DNI be in the White House. The law went further and forbade the Office of the DNI from being housed at the CIA's Langley, Virginia, campus. Instead, the DNI would need to find new office space *not* located within the grounds of an established intelligence agency. The feeling was that the DNI might be "captured" by the CIA if housed at Langley. But its physical isolation contributes to a disconnection between the ODNI and the rest of the community and feeds the argument that the ODNI is a new layer of bureaucracy superimposed upon an existing structure. The real "proximity" that matters for a DNI to be effective is, of course, closeness to the president. If a president listens to and backs up a DNI, the DNI is "strong"; otherwise, the DNI is not. In reality, the "strength" of the DNI is up to each president; the same was true of the old DCI position.

The NSC and legislative process that yielded IRTPA is in many ways typical of the Washington policy process. Ideas go through a meat grinder of competing forces and no one person gets to dictate how something will work. Bloody battles yield compromises that elide differences and leave to the executive branch to settle in implementation. Steve Hadley noted that "this was the best we were going to do but this is how Washington works, you do things in increments."[10]

However, while imperfect, IRTPA created a structure that has the potential to positively benefit national security. First and foremost, the creation of a DNI ensures that it is someone's job to think of how to make the agencies in the Intelligence Community act more cohesively. The DNI can do what individual agencies are unable to do: think of anyone but themselves. Most intelligence experts conceded that serving as the principal intelligence advisor to the president and managing the Intelligence Community while being the director of the CIA was too big of a job.

While certain disadvantages spring from separation of the CIA from the community management function, there are numerous upsides. The creation of a DNI enabled impartiality in resource allocation. Whether or not the CIA acting as "player-coach" was a conflict of interest, the migration of budgetary functions to a DNI eliminated the perception as expressed by former DNI McConnell that "it was too much to ask CIA not to speak for itself."[11]

Indeed, the CIA director could be a beneficiary of the reorganization. Even before the attacks of 9/11, the duties of managing covert action and clandestine human collection worldwide were all-consuming. The CIA's responsibilities have grown exponentially since 2001, earning a new moniker for the CIA director: the combatant commander in the war on terrorism. "When I was the director of the CIA (the first occupant of that suite who was not also DCI), I would tell the CIA workforce that one of the advantages of the new DNI structure was that I could concentrate on being director. Indeed, hardly a day passed in that job when I did not wonder aloud how any of my predecessors could ever have given both tasks their due."[12]

Additionally, as many diagnoses of the problems on 9/11 included an inability to easily share and fuse intelligence obtained abroad with information collected within the United States, IRTPA constituted another effort to eliminate the formal distinction known as the "foreign-domestic" divide." The DNI and the NCTC were institutions expressly created to bridge the divide, and the DNI was further empowered via executive order to ensure artificial distinctions do not impede the ability to share information.[13] Indeed, the analytic fusion function of the NCTC has generally been considered a success (although the function of operational planning across the government, hobbled by the IRTPA's requirement that planning be restricted to "strategic" matters, has struggled).[14]

The creation of a DNI also enables better strategic management of the U.S. intelligence enterprise. It tipped the balance slightly to the center in the running debate on centralization and increased the "formal and informal aspects" of the DNI's authority.[15] Although the tools to manage the community were not *substantially* greater than the DCI's, since some considered the extant authorities to have gone unexercised under a DCI, arguably Congress was saying "we really mean it"[16] this time on managing the community. Critics of the DCI-led community management system faulted it for operating by consensus.[17] IRTPA can be interpreted as giving the DNI "more clear lines of authority and responsibility." General Hayden, as deputy DNI, believed the DNI's directive authority was stronger than the DCI, noting that DCI Tenet had to "negotiate." General Hayden testified to Congress in 2006 that "if you change the practice under the language, even though the language only changes a little bit, you may be making a big change. But DNI in the aggregate, does have strong budget authority. Tasking is strong, policy is strong."[18]

At a minimum, the DNI's job is ensuring that the community has the ability to operate optimally, sometimes called the "unsexy but critical" business of intelligence. A former senior CIA official even conceded that there were some important missions for the DNI, including being an enabler who tackles tough cross-agency problems like budgets and education and measures effectiveness against intelligence targets. Chairman Mike Rogers of the House Intelligence Committee said something similar in 2011: "The DNI should be an enabler. This means marshalling our forces against new threats, challenging fundamental assumptions and, at times, it could mean standing aside to allow the operators to find, fix and finish the target."[19] The DNI can focus on whether the community as a whole has the right policy and resource allocations to meet a changing threat picture. IRTPA also enabled a DNI to serve as an independent arbiter in the acquisition of intelligence systems. "This is not going to be a group answer; it is going to be the answer of the DNI."[20] The clearest grant of authority for the DNI was to improve information-sharing across the Intelligence Community. IRTPA explicitly empowered the DNI to ensure that information was created "in such a way that it is shareable, aggregating it in a way that is usable across the community."[21]

Furthermore, IRTPA created a structure that makes it more likely that the best intelligence, subjected to the rigor of competing views, is presented to policymakers. Making the DNI the principal intelligence advisor to the president potentially enables analysis from around the community to be at parity with the CIA's. To be sure, the CIA's Directorate of Intelligence remains the premier all-source analytic agency in the Intelligence Community and produces the great majority of the intelligence analysis for national policy-makers, including the president. But with a DNI separate from the CIA, the DNI may be in a better position to consider alternative views from other pockets of expertise in the Intelligence Community. Secretary Powell thought this could possibly have guaranteed better analysis on Iraq's WMD program. "What troubled me was that the sourcing was weak and the sourcing had not been vetted widely enough across the intelligence community. What also distressed me is that there were some in the intelligence community who had knowledge that the sourcing was suspect and that was not known to me. It did not all come together in a single way with a powerful individual and a powerful staff who could force these people to make sure that what one person knew, everyone else knew. . . . It seems to me that if you have a powerful, important, empowered national intelligence director, you are less likely to have those kinds of mistakes made."[22] A DNI can ensure that other agencies have access to relevant information and are heard.

• • • • • • • • • • • •

But did IRTPA give the DNI a substantially greater package of management tools to manage the IC with more authority than the DCI, especially enough to compensate for the loss of a base at the CIA? On the key authorities to be given to the DNI—budget and appointment—the DNI's authorities, even with the augmentations under President Bush's 2008 executive order, were only marginally improved over the DCI.[23] "While Congress increased the DNI's budgetary authority, the DNI still possesses less authority than the average department head and will likely have to continue to rely as much on interpersonal relationships and cooperation with department and agency heads as on budgetary authorities."[24] "With the exception of NCTC, the legislation did not fundamentally alter the structure of the IC."[25] Even if the statute had maximized the hire-fire and budget authority of the DNI within the existing dual masters' construct, would it have been determinative of overall success for the DNI?

The 9/11 Commission and its predecessors, commentators, and experts overemphasized the utility of budget and appointment authority. To be sure, money and hire-fire authority is critical to success, and under the two-masters system there are not many other potent tools to manage agencies that reside within other departments, but a host of factors degrade the utility of budget and appointment authority as a management tool when the agency resides in another department. The power to *determine* the budget was the greatest new grant of authority in IRTPA. It is also unique in that in building the intelligence budget, the DNI has a clear cut of authority over and above the other agencies. However, at the end of the day, it is the *president's* budget. The Office of the Management and Budget at the White House can overrule the DNI. Even though in practice, OMB gives the DNI great deference, it is just a *request* of Congress. Four Congressional committees also have a say in what actually gets funded in the national intelligence budget.

Additionally, because the budget cycle is as long as three years, the budget determination power is diffuse. A system whereby the DNI is determining a budget in one year that will be proposed the following and appropriated by Congress the next does not amount to much of a cudgel. Budgetary consequences for not cooperating with the DNI are too far in the future to be compelling, especially when it is not clear if the DNI can make good on his determinations given that there are other White House and congressional players in the process able to override the DNI and because the denial of funds for intelligence matters are unlikely to be withheld given national security exigencies. Moreover, denial or modification of a budget "basically was a nuclear bomb."[26] "While we do have the power of the purse, it often presents a Hobson's choice. Does one cut funds to compel compliance when the cut will probably degrade the very capability one is seeking to foster? More often than not, the answer is no."[27] If you have the DNI "pitted against the head of DIA or the head of NSA who is backed up by the secretary of defense, it is a battle you are not going to win, so you have this big bomb you could drop, but it was not even clear that it wouldn't be a dud."[28]

Of course, these vagaries of the budget process are true of other departments—but other departments have outright authority, direction, and control over their domain while budget and appointment authority are the tools, supposedly potent, given to the DNI to meet his responsibilities.

Second, the ability to affect the expenditure of funds in the year of execution is difficult to achieve and, at any rate, complicated by long-standing congressional prerogatives. IRTPA gave the DNI the sole authority to control the funds once appropriated, which at least in theory helped mitigate the threat of the defense secretary controlling the funds at they entered his department on the way to NSA, NRO, and NGA. However, again, the idea that the DNI would delay the funding is impractical given the national security imperative in intelligence programs. Moreover, OMB's role (defined in IRTPA as a partner with the DNI on budget execution matters) is to apportion dollars from Congress in batches to prevent a department from spending its entire appropriation at the beginning of the year. OMB is unlikely to micromanage the apportionment of money to help the DNI achieve a policy objective.

Third, IRTPA did give the DNI the authority to transfer already appropriated dollars for another purpose—the core of the 9/11 Commission's recommendation that the IC be flexible to move money to combat new threats—but subject to limits. Congress simply will not give unfettered ability to the executive to transfer funds for purposes for which Congress did not intend. Although there is an ability to "reprogram" funds that are unspent or should be dedicated to an emergent issue, the executive, as a matter of comity between the branches, must receive congressional approval. This process is unwieldy as the DNI must identify funds, consult the intelligence entity from whom the money is extracted, and get approval from OMB and concurrence from four congressional committees.

With regard to the DNI's appointments authority, the ability of the DNI to appoint the leaders of the intelligence agencies is complicated by the desire of the White House and the cabinet secretaries to retain authority of the selection of executive branch personnel. The DNI was only given sole authority over the appointment of a deputy DNI and the director of the CIA.[29] In practice, however, the White House ensures that actual appointments remain the province of the president. General Hayden recalled, "I can think of only one example where the DNI actually recommended the head of the CIA to the president of the United States and that was John Negroponte recommending me to be DCIA."[30] The CIA relationship to the White House is too intimate to leave the decision to the DNI. For intelligence agency heads residing in other departments, Congress and the White House decided that as a matter of bureaucratic necessity, the cabinet secretary must retain the ability to appoint inferior officers under his authority, direction, and control but only as far as to recommend to the president and with the concurrence of the DNI. Given these caveats, the DNI's authority is nowhere close to absolute, leaving the DNI in a position in which he must assiduously work the system to ensure personnel appointees come through the process feeling like they owe some fealty to the DNI.[31]

Thus within the boundaries set by the 9/11 Commission, Congress, and the president, and given the impediments to exercising decisive budgetary and appointments authority, the DNI appears to lack sufficient authorities to meet its responsibilities. Gates noted that "the DNI has huge responsibilities under the law and no line authority to carry them out."[32] The DNI can promulgate directives, but he cannot unilaterally implement any of them. "He remains the coordinator of U.S. intelligence, but unlike the DCIs, the DNI is not in charge of any major operational intelligence activity."[33] Even with the augmentation of the DNI's authorities in IRTPA and the revised executive order, it was only marginal; there is a mismatch between the responsibilities given to the DNI and the actual authorities in law. John McLaughlin called this a "fatal ambiguity."[34] As chief intelligence officer, you feel in charge, but have no real responsibility. "He's the senior intelligence advisor, but he does not touch any of the moving parts of the community on a daily basis."[35] "The DNI was given department-like responsibilities . . . but was not given department-like authorities as a 'Secretary of Intelligence' to carry out these responsibilities."[36] In remarkably frank testimony about the DNI's authorities, DNI McConnell spoke to four models for the intelligence community and where he saw the DNI along the spectrum,

> The first is overseer, probably the weakest form. Second would be a coordinator; third, an integrator; and fourth, a director, someone who actually directs all of the community's intelligence activities. I currently have the title of director, but the authorities created in statute and executive order put me more in the middle of that range of options—coordinator and integrator, rather than director with directive authority. This is because of the 16 agencies that make up this community, 15 of them work for a cabinet secretary in his or her department.[37]

The mismatch in responsibilities and authority contributes to a lack of consensus on the DNI's role: there is no meeting of the minds on precisely what role the new director of national intelligence should play as "head" of U.S. intelligence. The lack of a meeting of the minds is in part attributable to the expedited consideration of IRTPA. From the announcement of the 9/11 recommendations to enactment was a little over four and a half months. During this expedited consideration—historical analogues like the National Security Act of 1947 and the Goldwater-Nichols Defense Reorganization took much longer—many questions were unresolved and subject to future implementation. Whereas Goldwater-Nichols built slowly over several years, IRTPA was a lightning bolt.

The proponents of a DNI believed the congressional intent was clear: the DNI would be a leader of the Intelligence Community, empowered to determine budgets, move money and personnel to meet new threats, smash stovepipes, and lead joint intelligence centers as new means to centralize authority. "For the first time, we will have . . . an empowered quarterback for our intelligence team."[38] Jane Harman claimed its sponsors "envisioned a joint commander . . . across 16 intelligence agencies."[39] U.S. intelligence needed someone who was in charge across all intelligence disciplines. Senator Lieberman, the Commission's chief proponent, saw the DNI as someone "who would be in charge of marshaling all of the various resources of the various agencies to pursue and capture or kill Bin Laden."[40]

But other key players see the role of the DNI differently. Pointing to provisions in the law that preserved the chain of command within departments, defenders of defense primacy in intelligence see the DNI as a mere coordinator of bureaucratic positions limited by requirements to seek permission and with only indirect control over funding. As deputy DNI, Hayden rejected any notion of being operational as envisioned by the DNI's proponents in Congress.[41] When DNI Negroponte was asked who is in charge of the hunt for Usama bin Laden, he replied, "Not the NCTC" before explaining that it was a coordinated effort between the IC and DoD. When asked if it was his job to coordinate the two, Negroponte answered, "No, I do not have that operational responsibility."[42] Secretary Gates compared the DNI to a congressional committee chairman.[43] Former chairman Hoekstra saw him as chairman of the board of directors.[44] Hadley and Clapper see the DNI as a leader and a coordinator.[45] President Bush saw the DNI as akin to the chairman of the Joint Chiefs of Staff, which is a position that is prohibited by law from exercising any command authority. Others see the DNI as an "orchestra conductor."[46] General Hayden preferred a "coach" because quarterback was too operational.[47] Ambassador Negroponte agreed, likening the post to the manager of a baseball team: "He is not out there playing on the team but he is playing an important leadership role."[48] Negroponte also saw his role as "the overseer of the intelligence community."[49] David Ignatius likened it to a "holding company where you leave the managers of the operating divisions, the heads of the individual agencies, to do their jobs."[50]

Complicating the DNI's search for a mission was a tough bureaucratic rival in the CIA. Giving a DNI roles and responsibilities previously assigned to the CIA, in effect stripping the "Central" from the CIA, John McLaughlin admitted, "would take quite a bit of adjustment on the part of CIA employees."[51] The CIA had taken a beating from Congress. Its prestige and influence were extraordinarily low in the wake of intelligence failures in Iraq and September 11. Throughout most of the congressional consideration of the intelligence reform law, the directorship was vacant. Traditional congressional defenders were unwilling or unable to assist. Giving the CIA a new boss engendered profound bitterness. A DNI would complicate the CIA's direct relationship with the White House, exercised primarily through the director's delivery of the morning president's daily intelligence briefing. Its special relationship with the White House on the execution of covert action authorities, with a new actor in the mix, would seem to be threatened. In all, the process and the new system it produced were perceived to be a threat to the position the CIA had occupied as the world's premier intelligence agency.

Through the first years of IRTPA, however, the CIA has remained a central player. First, under President Bush and Obama, while the DNI leads the preparation and briefing of the president's daily intelligence briefing each morning, the CIA director has continued to play a prominent role at the White House, especially in National Security Council meetings. Despite Gates' admonition that "there can only be one," the CIA director *and* the DNI are at the table. In at least one case, according to Admiral Blair, it was he who was excluded from White House deliberations over the "administration's Afghanistan/Pakistan policy in the autumn of 2009."[52]

The continued prominence of the CIA is in part attributable to the forceful personalities leading the CIA in recent years. As one commentator put it, "If the DNI is supposed to be the intelligence czar, then he can't have such a high-profile political underling as the CIA director."[53] But the CIA's continued influence in the White House is also attributable to its sensitive missions. First, as discussed earlier, covert action is one of the primary tools exercised by the president to influence world events. As a result, even while conceding that perhaps the DNI could play a useful role in exercising some oversight over covert actions programs, the White House does not want anyone in between them and their covert operators. President Bush said as much in his first remarks on a DNI, insisting that the new system he was embracing would not complicate his control over the operators. And Vice President Biden, as the arbiter of the Blair-Panetta dispute on whether the DNI should be the White House's interlocutor on covert action, ruled that the CIA would submit its plans simultaneously to the White House and the DNI, leaving intact the CIA's direct relationship with the White House. Finally, even as signals intelligence becomes the greatest source of U.S. intelligence, the belief that human espionage is special persists. As a result, the CIA remains the preeminent espionage agency of the United States.

Clapper conceded in his confirmation hearing that "the true extent of the director's authority and the exact nature of the job he is supposed to do are still a matter of some debate."[54] Former acting DCI McLaughlin commented that "the relationship between the DNI level of intelligence governance and the CIA is not yet firmly established. The CIA is still, you know, figuring out how to not be the leader of the intelligence community, and the DNI operation is still a little uncomfortable when the CIA gets too much in the center of the spotlight."[55] Another commentator called the reorganization "still indigested."[56] Another observed that "we have tried now for 15 years to create the CEO of the Intelligence Community, and we keep failing. . . . I begin to wonder why we can't do it. Maybe it's not doable."[57] After stepping down as DNI, Admiral McConnell argued for the secretary of intelligence model. "So my view is that we need to revisit that law. We need to establish it on the principles of Goldwater-Nichols. And there are three important words in the English language that matter in a bureaucratic context. Those three words are authority, direction, and control."[58] Admiral Blair, after departing as DNI, called IRTPA "incomplete" and made similarly sweeping recommendations to augment the authorities of the DNI.[59]

Conclusion

Even with its disadvantages, the DNI has made progress on some important initiatives, including information-sharing. The DNI has been a leader on some issues; for example DNI McConnell initiated major efforts on cyber-security. Generally, the NCTC is deemed an "almost unalloyed success."[60] The DNI led the charge of the modernization of FISA and increased his authorities in the revision of the executive order governing the Intelligence Community. After a conference on the fifth anniversary of IRTPA, although Hamilton believed that "it is not clear . . . that the DNI is the driving force for intelligence community integration the Commission envisioned,"[61] Hamilton concluded that the Intelligence Community had accepted that the DNI is here to stay and a consensus that we need to make it work. Some veterans of the stand-up of the DNI thought some initial IC resistance to the

DNI for "fear of homogenization, of loss of mission, stature and capability" began to dissipate after the first few years after IRTPA.[62] While conceding that the new system is still dependent on a strong personality and willingness of other national security officials to cooperate, and that the "federated" intelligence system is "cumbersome,"[63] many experts, including Director Clapper[64] (despite his previous support for a Department of Intelligence), former senior intelligence officials like Mike Hayden, and some affiliated with the 9/11 Commission and the development of IRTPA, believe that the package of authorities is enough to make progress. Moreover, at least as of 2012, many plead "reorganization fatigue" when confronted with the question of whether to reopen IRTPA. At a minimum, the DNI's authorities need "maturation,"[65] and while perhaps there are some legislative fixes that could help, a Department of Intelligence model, as evidenced by the row over IRTPA, is politically impossible for the foreseeable future. To capitalize on the system enabled by IRTPA and to compensate for its weaknesses requires sustained presidential leadership, especially given that the law left some of the details to implementation by the executive. In 2011 congressional testimony, Lee Hamilton made a forceful plea for the president to step in and exercise leadership. "The repeated indication from the president that the DNI is the unequivocal leader of the intelligence community I think would be greatly helpful."[66] Admiral Blair noted that the president needs to define the lanes in the road and make explicit what he expects from a DNI to enable the DNI to push through initiatives. "This lack of White House support was the primary obstacle I faced in trying to integrate the intelligence community. From my experience, if the White House supports the authority of the DNI, he will be powerful. If it allows and even encourages the agencies to deal with it directly, bypassing the DNI, he will be much weakened."[67]

Given the bureaucratic impediments arrayed against the DNI, Hamilton sees presidential support as critical. "I think he cannot exercise [his authority], no matter what the statute says, without very strong presidential backing."[68]

The long view is that IRTPA set the outer boundary of what had to be accomplished, and like the evolution of the Department of Defense since its inception, the DNI will gradually define its role and augment its power over time. Clapper sees tight budgetary times as a "litmus test" for the office, a chance to realize the potency of budgetary power.[69] Increased focus on domestic intelligence, especially resulting from so-called "home-grown terrorists," may supply new areas for the DNI to exert influence.[70] More experience with the DNI, especially with vocal presidential support, would allow for a more definitive conclusion on the success of IRTPA. Director Clapper explained, "[There are] cultural things, sociological factors that can't be legislatively mandated." Gates hinted at this as well, believing that you can't change the mores of a sixty-year institution automatically and that it will take time. These large bureaucratic moves take time (decades usually) to play out, and it may differ from administration to administration.[71]

As chairman of the Senate Intelligence Committee, Pat Roberts noted that, "As I have said before, the Intelligence Reform Act is not the best possible bill, but rather the best bill possible under very difficult circumstances."[72] Steve Hadley underscored the iterative process of reform in Washington. "Do the 3 to 4 things we know are important and then see how it affects the system for a number of years, and then based on that decide what next level of changes we ought to make. That's how we ought to think about intelligence reform—not a big bang, you make some mistakes, you try and learn from mistakes, you make some structural changes, let it go for a while, draw lessons, and then go to the next level of reform."[73]

Notes

Preface

1. Allan Goodman et al., *In From the Cold: The Report of the Twentieth Century Fund Task Force on the Future of U.S. Intelligence* (Washington: Brookings Institution Press, 1996), 3.

2. Gordon Lederman, "Making Intelligence Reform Work," *The American Interest* 4, no. 4 (Spring 2009): 24.

3. Thomas H. Kean et al., *The 9/11 Commission Report: Final Report of the National Commission on Terrorist Attacks Upon the United States* (New York, W. W. Norton, 2004), 399.

4. Chris Ford, "The Bin Laden Raid: This Isn't your Father's CIA," New Paradigms Forum, August 4, 2011, http://newparadigmsforum/NPFtestsite/?=868.

5. Senate Homeland Security and Governmental Affairs Committee, *Hearing on Assessing America's Counterterrorism Capabilities*, 108th Congress, 2d session (2004).

6. "Whether the net effect of this reorganization is beneficial or detrimental, only history will reveal." Richard Falkenrath, "The 9/11 Commission Report," *International Security* 29, no. 3 (Winter 2004–2005): 187.

A Short History of the Intelligence Community

1. Douglas Stuart, *Creating the National Security State: A History of the Law That Transformed America* (Princeton, NJ: Princeton University Press, 2008), 137.

2. Ibid., 137.

3. Robert Wohlstetter, *Pearl Harbor, Warning and Decision* (Palo Alto, CA: Stanford University Press, 1962), 1.

4. Stuart, *Creating the National Security State*, 144.

5. James Taylor et al., *American Intelligence: A Framework for the Future* (Washington: internal classified CIA report approved for release February 2002). http://www.gwu.edu/~nsarchiv/NSAEBB/NSAEBB144/document%2010.pdf, 1975), 1.

6. Ibid., 35.

7. Amy Zegart, *Flawed by Design: The Evolution of the CIA, JCS, and NSC* (Palo Alto, CA: Stanford University Press, 2000), 163.

8. CIA History Staff, *Central Intelligence: Origin and Evolution*, ed. Michael Warner (Washington: Center for the Study of Intelligence, 2001), 1.

9. Taylor et al., *American Intelligence*, 38.

10. Zegart, *Flawed by Design*, 188.

11. Taylor et al., *American Intelligence*, 38.

12. Zegart, *Flawed by Design*, 188.

13. Ernest May, "Intelligence: Backing Into the Future," *Foreign Affairs* (Summer 1992): 66; "The community continued to be neglected. No one ran it from 1947 to 1955. . . . From 1947 to 1976 the DCI had no more real authority to manage the community than he did in 1947." Thomas F. Troy, "The Quaintness of the U.S. Intelligence Community: Its Origin, Theory, and Problems," *Journal of Intelligence and Counterintelligence* II, no. II (1988): 260.

14. James Schlesinger, *A Review of the Intelligence Community*, report for President Nixon, March 10, 1971.

15. Taylor et al., *American Intelligence*, 23.

16. John Bansemer, "Intelligence Reform: A Question of Balance," paper, Program on Information Resource Policy, Harvard University, May 2005, 28.

1. Blow Up

1. "There was a white-horse quality about the 9/11 Commission Report." Interview with Senator Lieberman, November 30, 2010, Washington, DC.

2. Paul Pillar, *Intelligence and U.S. Foreign Policy* (New York: Columbia University Press, 2011), 242.

3. "And we are told by both sides that there is an agreement in sight." Joe Johns, interview by Lou Dobbs, *Lou Dobbs Tonight*, November 19, 2004, describing that negotiators were "tantalizingly close to a deal." Philip Shenon, "Agreement May Be Near on 9/11 Bill," *New York Times*, November 19, 2004.

4. Interview with Joseph Lieberman, November 20, 2010, Washington, DC.

5. Philip Shenon, "Bush Says He'll Seek to Revive Intelligence Bill House Blocked," *New York Times*, November 22, 2004.

6. "We are now in a serious quandary and a quagmire [because the intelligence bill is being held up by] a few members of the House who wish to see the status quo maintained." Bob Graham, speaking on intelligence reform, on November 20, 2004, 108th Congress, 2d session, *Congressional Record* Volume 150, Number 135, S11736; "What these House Republican conferees have done is a slap in the face of the Senate, the bipartisan 9/11 Commission, and the 9/11 Families." Frank Lautenberg, speaking on intelligence reform, on November 20, 2004, 108th Congress, 2d session, *Congressional Record* Volume 150, Number 135, S11795.

7. Steny Hoyer, "House Republicans Scuttle Bipartisan Intelligence Reform," *Press Release*, November 20, 2004.

8. Joseph Lieberman, *Press Conference with Senator Collins, Senator Lieberman, Congresswoman Harman, and Congressman Hoekstra*, November 20, 2004.

9. John Lehman, *American Morning*, CNN, November 22, 2004.

10. Frank Gaffney and Peter Gadiel, *9/11 Families for a Secure America News Conference*, November 30, 2004.

11. Thomas Donnelly, "Intelligent Intelligence Reform," *AEI*, November 25, 2004, http://www.aei.org/article/foreign-and-defense-policy/intelligent-intelligence-reform/.

12. Philip Shenon and Carl Hulse, "House Leadership Blocks Vote on Intelligence Bill," *New York Times*, November 21, 2004.

13. "Well, this could be a sign that the congressional Republicans have been emboldened by the election results." John Yang, "9/11 Commission Recommendations Bill Fails to Pass," *World News Tonight*, November 21, 2004.

14. Ibid.

15. Ibid.

16. David Montgomery, "9-11 Victims' Families Assail Congress' Failure on Intelligence Reform," *Knight Ridder Newspapers*, November 22, 2004.

17. Beverly Eckert, *Representatives Chris Shays and Carolyn Maloney and Members of the 9/11 Family Steering Committee News Conference*, November 30, 2004.

18. Ibid.

19. Ibid.

2. The Making of a Juggernaut

1. Interview with Tim Roemer, February 13, 2012, Washington, DC.

2. Office of Management and Budget, "Statement of Administration Policy: H.R. 4628 - Intelligence Authorization Act for Fiscal Year 2003," July 24, 2002.

3. Ibid.

4. Carie Lemack, "The Journey to September 12th: A 9/11 Victim's Experiences with the Press, the President, and Congress," *Studies in Conflict and Terrorism* 30, no. 9 (September 2007): 12.

5. Ibid., 15.

6. Interview with Dennis Hastert, November 17, 2010, Washington, DC.

7. Alison Mitchell, "Traces of Terror: Congress; Daschle is Seeking a Special Inquiry on September 11 Attack," *New York Times*, May 22, 2002.

8. U.S. House of Representatives, *Final Vote Results for Roll Call 347*, July 25, 2002.

9. Interview with Slade Gorton, September 22, 2010, Washington, DC.

10. George Tenet, *At the Center of the Storm: My Years at the CIA* (New York: HarperCollins, 2007), 192.

11. Kean et al., *The 9/11 Commission Report*, 357.

12. U.S. Congress, *Joint Inquiry into Intelligence Community Activities Before and After the Terrorist Attacks of September 11* (Washington: GPO, 2004), 230.

13. Kean et al., *The 9/11 Commission Report*, 181.

14. Ibid.

15. Ibid.

16. Ibid., 267.

17. In George Tenet's book, he refers to the belief that FBI agents assigned to the CIA's Counterterrorism Center opened e-mails containing the information about al Hamzi and al Midhar. George Tenet, *At the Center of the Storm*, 194.

18. Kean et al., *The 9/11 Commission Report*, 269–71.

19. Joint Intelligence Committees, *Joint Inquiry into Intelligence Community Activities Before and After the Terrorist Attacks of September 11: Ninth Public Hearing*, 107th Congress, 2d session (2002).

20. U.S. Congress, *Joint Inquiry into Intelligence Community Activities Before and After the Terrorist Attacks of September 11*, 95.

21. Joint Intelligence Committees, *Joint Inquiry into Intelligence Community Activities Before and After the Terrorist Attacks of September 11: Ninth Public Hearing*, 107th Congress, 2d session (2002).

22. Kean et al., *The 9/11 Commission Report*, 273.

23. Ibid., 273–74.

24. Ibid., 274–75.

25. NSPD-5 was formally signed out on May 9, 2001. Members of the External Panel of NSPD-5 were Scowcroft, John S. Foster, Jamie Gorelick, David Jeremiah, Richard Kerr, Jeong Kim, Stapleton Roy, and William Schneider.

26. Interview with Condoleezza Rice, May 10, 2010, Palo Alto, CA.

27. Walter Pincus, "Military Espionage Cuts Eyed," *Washington Post*, March 17, 1995.

28. House Armed Services Committee, *Hearing on the Fiscal Year 1993 Budget*, 102d Congress, 2d session (1992).

29. Richard Cheney, letter to Les Aspin, March 17, 1992.

30. Phone interview with Richard Cheney, November 1, 2012.

31. See, for example, "Ensure that the elements of the Intelligence Community within the Department of Defense are responsive and timely with respect to satisfying the needs of operational military forces." Title 50, USC, Section 403-5(a)(4).

32. Taylor et al., *American Intelligence*, 21–22.

33. Les Aspin et al., "The Evolution of the U.S. Intelligence Community—An Historical Overview," in *Preparing for the 21st Century: An Appraisal of U.S. Intelligence* (Washington: Featured Commission, 1996), A23.

34. Senate Armed Services Committee, *Hearing on Implications of Defense and Military Operations of Proposals to Reorganize the United States Intelligence Community*, 108th Congress, 2d session (2004).

35. Dave McCurdy, "Glasnost for the CIA," *Foreign Affairs* 73, no. 1 (January/February 1994): 130.

36. Senate Armed Services Committee, *Hearing on the Conduct of the Gulf War*, 102d Congress, 1st session (1991).

37. Aspin et al., "The Evolution of the U.S. Intelligence Community—An Historical Overview," A23.

38. Ibid.

39. Michael Warner and J. Kenneth McDonald, *U.S. Intelligence Community Reform Studies Since 1947* (Washington: Center for the Study of Intelligence, 2005), 33.

40. Interview with Stephen Cambone, November 10, 2010, Tysons Corner, VA.

41. Phone interview with Kevin Scheid, August 27, 2012.

42. Ibid.

43. Interview with Brent Scowcroft, January 30, 2012, Washington, DC.

44. Interview with David Jeremiah, May 23, 2012, Vienna, VA.

45. Interview with Brent Scowcroft, January 30, 2012, Washington, DC.

46. Interview with Condoleezza Rice, May 10, 2010, Palo Alto, CA.

47. U.S. Congress, *Joint Inquiry into Intelligence Community Activities Before and After the Terrorist Attacks of September 11*, xv.

48. Ibid., xvi.

49. Ibid., 40.

50. Ibid., xvii.

51. U.S. Congress, *Joint Inquiry into Intelligence Community Activities Before and After the Terrorist Attacks of September 11: Errata Report*, 5.

52. Larry Kindsvater, "The Need to Reorganize the Intelligence Community," *Studies in Intelligence* 47, no. 1 (November 1, 2004), 33–37.

53. Senate Select Committee on Intelligence, *Hearing on the Nomination of Joan Dempsey to be Deputy Director of CIA for Community Management*, 105th Congress, 2d session (1998).

54. Interview with Condoleezza Rice, May 10, 2010, Palo Alto, CA.

55. Interview with Bryan Cunningham, June 2011, Washington, DC.

56. Interview with Richard Falkenrath, August 18, 2010, Washington, DC.

57. Interview with Bryan Cunningham, June 2011, Washington, DC.

58. Ibid.

59. Donald Rumsfeld to Stephen Cambone, memorandum on intelligence reform, October 5, 2002. http://library.rumsfeld.com/doclib/sp/1021/2002-10-05%20to%20Steve%20Cambone%20re%20Intel%20Reorganization.pdf#search="Donald Rumsfeld to Stephen Cambone October 2 2002".

60. Paul Wolfowitz, Memorandum Regarding Implementation Guidance on Restructuring Defense Intelligence—and Related Matters, May 8, 2003.

61. Senate Armed Services Committee, *Submission of Responses to Questions for the Record by Stephen Cambone*, 108th Congress, 1st session, February 24, 2003.

62. Interview with Stephen Cambone, November 15, 2010, McLean, VA.

63. David Ignatius, "The Book on Terror," *Washington Post*, August 1, 2004.

3. Tenet

1. Interview with Charlie Allen, March 2, 2012, Washington, DC.

2. Interview with Steve Slick, March 2012, Washington, DC.

3. Ibid.

4. Interview with Charlie Allen, March 2, 2012, Washington, DC.

5. Interview with Mark Lowenthal, November 10, 2010, Reston, VA.

6. Richard Shelby, *Press Conference with Nancy Pelosi, Bob Graham, and Porter Goss on the Joint Inquiry into Intelligence Community Activities Before and After the Terrorist Attacks of September 11*, December 11, 2002.

7. Senate Select Committee on Intelligence, *Annual Threat Assessment of the U.S. Intelligence Community*, 107th Congress, 2d session (2002).

8. Joint Intelligence Committees, *Joint Inquiry into Intelligence Community Activities Before and After the Terrorist Attacks of September 11: Second Public Hearing*, 107th Congress, 2d session (2002).

9. Kristen Breitweiser, *Wake-Up Call: The Political Education of a 9/11 Widow* (New York: Warner Books, 2006), 99.

10. U.S. Congress, *Joint Inquiry into Intelligence Community Activities Before and After the Terrorist Attacks of September 11*, vi.

11. See Philip Shenon, *The Commission: The Uncensored History of the 9/11 Investigation* (Washington: Twelve, 2008).

12. Interview with Mark Lowenthal, November 10, 2010, Reston, VA.

13. Interview with Philip Zelikow, November 1, 2010, Charlottesville, VA.

14. Ibid.

15. Ibid.

16. National Commission on Terrorist Attacks upon the United States, *Staff Statement #11: The Performance of the Intelligence Community*, 108th Congress, 2d session (2004), 9.

17. Ibid., 12.

18. National Commission on Terrorist Attacks upon the United States, *Part One of the Tenth Hearing: Law Enforcement and the Intelligence Community*, 108th Congress, 2d session (2004), 31.

19. Tenet, *At the Center of the Storm*, 502.

20. National Commission on Terrorist Attacks upon the United States, *Part One of the Tenth Hearing: Law Enforcement and the Intelligence Community*, 108th Congress, 2d session (2004).

21. CIA, "DCI Tenet Announces Appointment of David Kay as Special Advisor," June 11, 2003. https://www.cia.gov/news-information/press-releases-statements/press -release-archive-2003/pr06112003.htm.

22. Senate Select Committee on Intelligence, *Report on the U.S. Intelligence Community's Prewar Intelligence Assessments on Iraq*, 108th Congress, 2d session (2004), 1.

23. The White House was forced to make similar concessions later in July for its role in inserting the lines into the president's speech.

24. Senate Armed Services Committee, *Hearing on Iraqi Weapons of Mass Destruction and Related Programs*, 108th Congress, 1st session (2004).

25. George Tenet, DCI Remarks on Iraq's WMD Programs, February, 5, 2004, https://www.cia.gov/news-information/speeches-testimony/2004/tenet_georgetown speech_02052004.html.

26. Carl Levin, interview by George Stephanopoulos, *This Week with George Stephanopoulos*, ABC, November 21, 2004. (Subsequently, the Robb-Silberman Commission on the Intelligence Capabilities of the United States Regarding Weapons of Mass Destruction concluded after investigation that "the Intelligence Community did not make or change any analytical judgments in response to the political pressure to reach a particular conclusion.") Laurence H. Silberman et al., *Commission on the Intelligence Capabilities of the United States on Regarding Weapons of Mass Destruction* (Washington: Featured Commission Publications, 2005), 188.

27. Jane Harman, "Congresswoman Harman Urges President Bush to Take Immediate Action To Improve Intelligence, Introduces Legislative Package," *Press Release*, April 1, 2004.

28. See Intelligence Transformation Act of 2004, HR 4104, 108th Congress, 2d session (2004).

29. House Armed Services Committee, *Hearing on Future Worldwide Threats to U.S. National Security*, 108th Congress, 2d session (2004).

30. Senate Select Committee on Intelligence, *Hearing on Current and Projected Threats to U.S. National Security*, 108th Congress, 2d session (2004).

31. Ibid.

32. Ibid.

33. Bob Woodward, *Plan of Attack* (New York: Simon and Schuster, 2004), 249.

34. Tenet, *At the Center of the Storm*, 479.

35. Ibid., 480.

36. Ibid., 480–81.

37. See Siobhan Gorman, "Wanted: Spy Chief," *National Journal*, June 12, 2004.

38. Tenet, *At the Center of the Storm*, 478.

39. Ibid., 479.

40. National Commission on Terrorist Attacks upon the United States, *Part One of the Tenth Hearing: Law Enforcement and the Intelligence Community*, 108th Congress, 2d session (2004), 28.

41. Ibid., 33.

4. Revolution Is Coming

1. Senate Select Committee on Intelligence, *Report on the U.S. Intelligence Community's Prewar Intelligence Assessments on Iraq*, 108th Congress, 2d session (2004), 18.

2. Interview with John McLaughlin, May 11, 2010, Washington, DC.

3. National Commission on Terrorist Attacks upon the United States, *Hearing on Intelligence Oversight and the Joint Inquiry*, 108th Congress, 2d session (2004).

4. Trent Lott, interview by George Stephanopoulos, *This Week with George Stephanopoulos*, ABC, July 12, 2004.

5. Interview with Tom Corcoran, February 19, 2013.

6. John McLaughlin, *Remarks at Business Executives for National Security*, June 23, 2004, https://www.cia.gov/news-information/speeches-testimony/2004/ddci_speech_06242004 .html.

7. John McLaughlin, interview by Chris Wallace, *Fox News Sunday*, Fox, July 18, 2004, http://www.foxnews.com/story/0,2933,125998,00.html.

8. Tenet, *At the Center of the Storm*, 502.

9. See Stansfield Turner, "Intelligence for a New World Order," *Foreign Affairs* 70, no. 4 (Fall 1991): 150.

10. Senate Select Committee on Intelligence, *Hearing on the National Intelligence Reorganization and Reform Act of 1978*, 95th Congress, 2d session (1978).

11. Ibid.

12. Ibid.

13. Robert Gates, "Racing to Ruin the CIA," *New York Times*, June 8, 2004; see also Robert Gates, "How Not to Reform Intelligence," *Wall Street Journal*, September 3, 2004.

14. Joint Intelligence Committees, *Hearing on S. 2198 and S.421: To Reorganize the United States Intelligence Committee*, 102d Congress, 2d session (1992).

15. Joint Intelligence Committees, *Joint Inquiry into Intelligence Community Activities Before and After the Terrorist Attacks of September 11: Seventh Public Hearing*, 107th Congress, 2d session (2002).

16. House Permanent Select Committee on Intelligence, *IC21: The Intelligence Community in the 21st Century*, 104th Congress, 1st session (1995).

17. Senate Select Committee on Intelligence, *Hearing on S.2525: National Intelligence Reorganization and Reform Act of 1978*, 95th Congress, 2d session (1978).

18. Ibid.

19. Fritz Ermath, *Intelligence for a New Era in American Foreign Policy* (Charlottesville, VA: Center for the Study of Intelligence, September 2003), 207.

20. House Permanent Select Committee on Intelligence, *IC21: The Intelligence Community in the 21st Century*, 104th Congress, 1st session (1995).

21. McLaughlin, *Remarks at Business Executives for National Security*.

5. Grand Vision

1. Interview with Daniel Marcus, March 13, 2012, Washington, DC.

2. Interview with Tom Kean, July 20, 2010, Washington, DC.

3. Interview with Tim Roemer, February 13, 2012, Washington, DC.

4. Interview with Chris Kojm, January 3, 2012, Langley, VA.

5. Ernest May, "When Government Writes History," *History News Network*, June 24, 2005, http://hnn.us/articles/11972.html.

6. See Philip Shenon, "Sept. 11 Commission Plans a Lobbying Campaign to Push Its Recommendations," *New York Times*, July 19, 2004.

7. Phone interview with Kevin Scheid, August 27, 2012, Washington, DC.

8. "Retaking the Strategic Initiative on Transnational Terrorism, A Team 2 Interim Report: Intelligence Issues for Commission Discussion," Box 10, 1st file, Monograph, Presentation Slides, Slide 7, The 9/11 Commission Archives at the National Archives, Washington, DC. See also Slide 19.

9. E-mail from John Lehman to Jamie Gorelick, August 17, 2004.

10. United States Congress, *Joint Inquiry into Intelligence Community Activities Before and After the Terrorist Attacks of September 11*, 349.

11. Bob Kerrey, minutes of 9/11 Commission meeting, June 14, 2004, National Archives.

12. Interview with Slade Gorton, September 22, 2010, Washington, DC.

13. John Lehman, "USS *Cole*: An Act of War," *Washington Post*, October 15, 2000.

14. Interview with John Lehman, February 6, 2012, New York.

15. Phone interview with Kevin Scheid, August 27, 2012, Washington, DC.

16. E-mail from Philip Zelikow, March 29, 2010.

17. United States Congress, *Joint Inquiry into Intelligence Community Activities Before and After the Terrorist Attacks of September 11*, 347.

18. Ibid., 683.

19. Senate Select Committee on Intelligence, *Hearing the Nomination of Joan Dempsey to be Deputy Director of CIA for Community Management*, 105th Congress, 2d session (1998).

20. Philip Zelikow, "Integrating National Security Missions: Lessons from the National Counterterrorism Center," speech at Center for Strategic and International Studies, Washington, DC, March 26, 2010.

21. E-mail from Philip Zelikow, March 29, 2010.

22. Jamie Gorelick, minutes of 9/11 Commission meeting, June 14, 2004, National Archives.

23. E-mail from Jamie Gorelick, November 1, 2012.

24. Interview with John Lehman, February 6, 2012, New York, NY.

25. Interview with Tim Roemer, February 13, 2012, Washington, DC.

26. National Commission on Terrorist Attacks upon the United States, *Staff Statement #11: The Performance of the Intelligence Community*, April 14, 2004, 11; "But the facts of the 9/11 story—and our analysis of post–9/11 reforms—cried out for stronger leadership at the top of the Intelligence Community. It was unacceptable that a DCI could issue a directive in 1998 stating, 'We are at War' with AQ, with no discernible effect." Thomas H. Kean, *Without Precedent: The Inside Story of the 9/11 Commission* (New York: Knopf, 2006), 285.

27. Interview with Philip Zelikow, November 1, 2010, Charlottesville, VA.

28. Philip Zelikow, "Intelligence Reform, 2002–2004," *Studies in Intelligence* 56, no. 3 (September 2012): 1–20.

29. Ibid.

30. Lee Hamilton, Minutes of 9/11 Commission Meeting, June 14, 2004, The National Archives.

31. Senate Homeland Security and Governmental Affairs Committee, *Hearing on Making America Safer: Examining the Recommendations of the 9/11 Commission*, 108th Congress, 2d session (2004).

32. Senate Homeland Security and Governmental Affairs Committee, *Hearing on Assessing America's Counterterrorism Capabilities*, 108th Congress, 2d session, August 3, 2004.

33. Ibid.

34. Kean et al., *The 9/11 Commission Report*, 412.

35. Interview with Lee Hamilton, August, 4, 2010, Washington, DC.

36. Kean et al., *The 9/11 Commission Report*, 407.

37. Ibid., 400.

38. Ibid., 408.

39. Senate Homeland Security and Governmental Affairs Committee, *Hearing on Making America Safer: Examining the Recommendations of the 9/11 Commission*, 108th Congress, 2d session (2004).

40. Kean et al., *The 9/11 Commission Report*, 414.

41. Ibid., 409.

42. Senate Homeland Security and Governmental Affairs Committee, *Hearing on Making America Safer: Examining the Recommendations of the 9/11 Commission*, 108th Congress, 2d session (2004).

43. John Bansemer, "Intelligence Reform: A Question of Balance," paper, Program on Information Resource Policy, Harvard University, May 2005, 66.

44. Kean et al., *The 9/11 Commission Report*, 411.

45. Senate Homeland Security and Governmental Affairs Committee, *Hearing on Making America Safer: Examining the Recommendations of the 9/11 Commission*, 108th Congress, 2d session (2004).

46. "The DNI would have real authority. He will control . . . purse strings. . . . He will have real troops, as the NCTC and all of the joint mission centers would report to him." Ibid.

47. House Permanent Select Committee on Intelligence, *IC21: The Intelligence Community on the 21st Century*, 104th Congress, 1st session (1995).

48. Furthermore, for "the organization arrangements for the Intelligence Community," the DCI should concur in the appointments of NSA, NRO, and NIMA (now NGA)." Ibid.

49. Taylor et al., *American Intelligence*, 18.

50. Kean et al., *The 9/11 Commission Report*, 412.

51. See Taylor et al., *American Intelligence*, 73. The Taylor Report recommended that "the bulk of the intelligence budget now appropriated to Defense and CIA instead be appropriated to [a director general of intelligence] for further allocation to the various existing program managers in the community." See also James Schlesinger, *A Review of the Intelligence Community*, report for President Nixon, March 10, 1971. 32. The DCI "would also present a consolidated intelligence budget for review by the OMB. By this means the director would be able to guide resource allocation and influence community organization."

52. Kean et al., *The 9/11 Commission Report*, 416.

53. National Commission on Terrorist Attacks upon the United States, *Part One of the Tenth Hearing: Law Enforcement and the Intelligence Community*, 108th Congress, 2d session (2004), 30.

54. Kean et al., *The 9/11 Commission Report*, 410.

55. See House Permanent Select Committee on Intelligence, *IC21: The Intelligence Community on the 21st Century*, 104th Congress, 1st session (1995), 99: "Expand the authority of the DCI over personnel in all NFIP agencies" to "include the ability to detail personnel from one agency to another."

56. There is not a direct textual foundation for personnel authority in the 9/11 Commission Report, but it is instead implicit in the DNI's authority to create centers, as illustrated in the preceding recommendation for an NCTC, which was built upon TTIC, which relied on personnel from around the government.

57. Thomas H. Kean, *Without Precedent: The Inside Story of the 9/11 Commission* (New York: Knopf, 2006), 286.

58. House Committee on Homeland Security, *Towards a Paradigm for Homeland Security*, 108th Congress, 2d session (2004).

59. Ibid.

60. Interview with Philip Zelikow, August 29, 2012, Washington, DC.

61. Ibid.

62. House Committee on Homeland Security, *Towards a Paradigm for Homeland Security*, 108th Congress, 2d session (2004).

63. Kean et al., *The 9/11 Commission Report*, 404–5.

64. Philip Zelikow, "Integrating National Security Missions: Lessons from the National Counterterrorism Center," speech at Center for Strategic and International Studies, Washington, DC, March 26, 2010.

65. Interview with Gordon Lederman, June 2011, Washington, DC.

66. See James Schlesinger, *A Review of the Intelligence Community*, report for President Nixon, March 10, 1971, 33. The favored option "eliminates the present situation in which the DCI serves as both advocate for agency programs and judge in community-wide matters, a role which diminishes the community's willingness to accept his guidance as impartial."

67. Kean et al., *The 9/11 Commission Report*, 414–15.

68. Ibid., 415.

69. Ibid.

70. Phone interview with Kevin Scheid, August 27, 2012.

71. Kristin Childress et al., *Commission: Possible, Lessons Learned from the 9/11 and WMD Commissions* (College Station, TX: Bush School of Government and Public Service, 2010), 9.

72. Phone interview with Kevin Scheid, August 27, 2012.

73. Interview with Jamie Gorelick, February 27, 2012, Washington, DC.

74. Ibid.

75. Kean et al., *The 9/11 Commission Report*, 424.

76. Interview with Philip Zelikow, August 29, 2012, Washington, DC.

6. "The Fix Was In"

1. Ernest May, "When Government Writes History," *History News Network*, June 24, 2005, http://hnn.us/articles/11972.html.

2. Tom Kean, "September 11 Terrorist Attacks," speech at National Press Club, Washington, DC, September 11, 2006.

3. Interview with Tim Roemer, February 13, 2012, Washington, DC.

4. Ibid.

5. ABC News Transcripts, *Special Report Introduction*, July 22, 2004; CBS News Transcripts, Release of the Final 9-11 Commission Report, July 22, 2004.

6. Ibid.

7. John Lehman, quoted in *Wolf Blitzer Reports*, CNN, July 22, 2004.

8. Jamie Gorelick, "News Conference with Members of the National Commission on Terrorist Attacks upon the United States to Release Their Final Report," Federal News Service, July 22, 2004.

9. Ibid., Lee Hamilton.

10. Ibid., Tim Roemer.

11. Ibid., Jim Thompson.

12. "U.S. Senators Joseph Lieberman and John McCain Hold a News Conference with 9/11 Commission Chairman and Vice Chairman Kean and Hamilton," FDCH Political Transcripts, July 22, 2004.

13. Ibid., Joseph Lieberman.

14. Ibid.

15. Jane Harman, interview by Wolf Blitzer, *Wolf Blitzer Reports*, CNN, July 22, 2004.

16. Tim Roemer, quoted in, "Senate Leaders Calling for Intelligence Legislation," *Congressional Quarterly Today*, July 23, 2004.

17. Interview with Jamie Gorelick, Washington, DC, February 27, 2012.

18. John Kerry, "Statement on the 9/11 Commission Report, July 22, 2004, Detroit, MI.

19. See David S. Cloud and Scot J. Paltrow, "Tenet's CIA Exit Will Spur Debate on Spy Agencies: Chief's Departure Comes Ahead of Critical Reports on Intelligence Gathering," *Wall Street Journal*, June 4, 2004.

20. John Kerry, speech in Norfolk, VA, CNN, July 28, 2004, http://archives.cnn.com/TRANSCRIPTS/0407/28/se.03.html.

21. John Kerry, quoted on *Lou Dobbs Tonight*, CNN, July 22, 2004.

22. Interview with Eric Ueland, January 2010, Washington, DC.

23. Carl Hulse, "Democrats Press Strategy on 9/11 Report," *New York Times*, August 10, 2004.

24. Dennis Hastert, *Press Conference with Roy Blunt, Chris Cox, Deborah Pryce, Tom DeLay, Eric Cantor, Duncan Hunter, Porter Goss*, July 22, 2004.

25. Dan Bartlett, interview by Charlie Rose, *Charlie Rose Show*, PBS, July 22, 2004.

26. Interview with former Bush senior White House staffer.

27. Interview with Andrew Card, June 19, 2012, McLean, VA.

28. Richard Cheney, quoted in Steve Hadley's notes, July 24, 2004, George W. Bush Presidential Library, Dallas, TX.

29. George Bush, quoted in Steve Hadley's notes, July 24, 2004, George W. Bush Presidential Library, Dallas, TX.

30. Interview with Andy Card, June 19, 2012, McLean, VA.

31. Donald Rumsfeld to George Bush, Memorandum Regarding 9/11 Commission Report, George W. Bush Presidential Library, Dallas, TX, July 25, 2004.

32. Interview with Condoleezza Rice, May 10, 2010, Palo Alto, CA.

33. Interview with Steve Hadley, December 17, 2009, Washington, DC.

34. Interview with Fran Townsend, October 20, 2010, New York.

35. Interview with George W. Bush, May 21, 2010, Dallas, TX.

36. Andrew Card, *Press Briefing*, July 30, 2004.

37. Jordan Tama, *Terrorism and National Security Reform: How Commissions Can Drive Change in Moments of Crisis* (Cambridge: Cambridge University Press, 2011), 48.

38. John Updike, "The Great I Am," *New Yorker*, November 1, 2004.

39. David Ignatius, "The Book on Terror," *Washington Post*, August 1, 2004.

40. May, "When Government Writes History."

41. Adam Nagourney, "The 2004 Campaign: the Massachusetts Senator; Kerry Sees Hope of Gaining Edge on Terror Issue," *New York Times*, July 25, 2004.

42. Richard Stevenson and David Kirkpatrick, "Administration Moves to Regain Initiative on 9/11," *New York Times*, July 27, 2004.

43. Jodi Wilgoren and David Kirkpatrick, "Kerry Says Work of the 9/11 Panel Should Continue," *New York Times*, July 28, 2004.

44. Dan Eggen and Helen Dewar, "Leaders Pick Up Urgency of 9/11 Panel, Congress and Bush Vow to Speed Reforms," *Washington Post*, July 24, 2004.

45. Senate Homeland Security and Governmental Affairs Committee, *Hearing on Making America Safer: Examining the Recommendations of the 9/11 Commission*, 108th Congress, 2d session (2004).

46. Phone interview with Donald Rumsfeld, November 15, 2011.

47. Interview with Andrew Card, June 19, 2012, McLean, VA.

48. Interview with Fran Townsend, October 20, 2010, New York.

49. Interview with Condoleezza Rice, May 10, 2010, Palo Alto, CA.

50. Interview with Andrew Card, June 19, 2012, McLean, VA.

51. Ibid.

52. John McLaughlin, letter to President Bush, August 20, 2004.

53. Interview with John McLaughlin, May 11, 2010, Washington, DC.

54. Phone interview with Donald Rumsfeld, November 15, 2011.

55. Interview with Andrew Card, June 19, 2012, McLean, VA.

56. E-mail from John McLaughlin, October 19, 2012.

57. Interview with John McLaughlin, May 11, 2010, Washington, DC.

58. Interview with Ronald Burgess, October 29, 2010, Arlington, VA.

59. Interview with Condoleezza Rice, May 10, 2010, Palo Alto, CA.

60. Additionally, "I love the CIA and I understood that intelligence is inexact and I really don't hold the CIA responsible for the failure [in Iraq] because everyone else thought they had [WMD]." Bush did not feel betrayed. "I was disappointed, it was one of the real blows to my administration and undermined the Iraq War; if we had found weapons it would have been a different mindset." Interview with George W. Bush, May 21, 2010, Dallas, TX.

61. Interview with Andy Card, June 19, 2012, McLean, VA.

62. Interview with Fran Townsend, October 20, 2010, New York.

63. Ibid.

64. Interview with John McLaughlin, May 11, 2010, Washington, DC.

65. Interview with Fran Townsend, October 20, 2010, New York.

66. George W. Bush, "President's Remarks on Intelligence Reform," August 2, 2004.

67. E-mail from John McLaughlin, October 19, 2012.

68. Bush, "President's Remarks."

69. Fran Townsend, interview by Jim Lehrer, *PBS Newshour*, PBS, August 2, 2004.

70. Ibid.

71. Interview with Condoleezza Rice, May 10, 2010, Palo Alto, CA.

7. Congressional August

1. Martin Kady II, "Uproar Over Intelligence Bill Puts Hunter in the Bull's-Eye," *CQ Weekly*, November 27, 2004.

2. Ibid.

3. Interview with Robert Rangel, November 22, 2011, Arlington, VA.

4. House Armed Services Committee, *Hearing on the Implications of the Recommendations of the 9/11 Commission on the Department of Defense*, 108th Congress, 2d session (2004).

5. "Hunter has said that his son, Marine 1st Lieutenant Duncan Duane Hunter, an artillery officer who served in Fallujah, Iraq, told him not to do anything in overhauling the intelligence system that would endanger his brothers and sisters in arms. It was a message Hunter took to heart." John M. Donnelly, Martin Kady II, and Jonathan Allen, "Fate of Intelligence Overhaul Hangs on Troop Safety," *CQ Today*, November 24, 2004.

6. John Bansemer, "Intelligence Reform: A Question of Balance," paper, Program on Information Resource Policy, Harvard University, May 2005, 82.

7. House Armed Services Committee, *Hearing on United States Intelligence Reform*, 108th Congress, 2d session (2004).

8. Phone interview with Duncan Hunter, July 23, 2010.

9. Senate Homeland Security and Governmental Affairs Committee, *Hearing on Making America Safer: Examining the Recommendations of the 9/11 Commission*, 108th Congress, 2d session (2004).

10. Senate Select Committee on Intelligence, *Hearing on Reform of the United States Intelligence Community*, 108th Congress, 2d session (2004).

11. Ibid.

12. Senate Homeland Security and Governmental Affairs Committee, *Hearing on Assessing America's Counterterrorism Capabilities*, 108th Congress, 2d session (2004).

13. Senate Homeland Security and Governmental Affairs Committee, *Hearing on Reorganizing America's Intelligence Community: A View from the Inside*, 108th Congress, 2d session (2004).

14. Senate Armed Services Committee, *Hearing on Implications of Defense and Military Operations of Proposals to Reorganize the United States Intelligence Community*, 108th Congress, 2d session (2004).

15. Ibid.

16. Senate Select Committee on Intelligence, *Hearing on Reform of the United States Intelligence Community*, 108th Congress, 2d session (2004).

17. Senate Select Committee on Intelligence, *Hearing on Intelligence Community Reform*, 108th Congress, 2d session (2004).

18. Ibid.

19. Senate Select Committee on Intelligence, *Hearing on Nomination of the Honorable Porter Goss to be Director of Central Intelligence*, 108th Congress, 2d session (2004).

20. Senate Select Committee on Intelligence, *Hearing on Intelligence Community Reform*, 108th Congress, 2d session (2004).

21. Ibid.

22. Senate Select Committee on Intelligence, *Hearing on Reform of the United States Intelligence Community*, 108th Congress, 2d session (2004).

23. Michael O'Hanlon, "Can the C.I.A. Really Be That Bad?," *New York Times*, July 13, 2004.

24. Senate Homeland Security and Governmental Affairs Committee, *Hearing on Establishing Terrorist Threat Integration Center*, 108th Congress, 2d session (2003).

25. Senate Homeland Security and Governmental Affairs Committee, *Hearing on Reorganizing America's Intelligence Community: A View from the Inside*, 108th Congress, 2d session (2004).

26. Senate Homeland Security and Governmental Affairs Committee, *Hearing on Making America Safer: Examining the Recommendations of the 9/11 Commission*, 108th Congress, 2d session (2004).

27. See "The time for action is now." House Permanent Select Committee on Intelligence, *Hearing on 9/11 Commission Findings: Sufficiency of Time, Attention, and Legal Authority*, 108th Congress, 2d session (2004). See also "The time for change is now. And I'll repeat that: the time for change is now." House Armed Services Committee, *Hearing on the Implications of the Recommendations of the 9/11 Commission on the Department of Defense*, 108th Congress, 2d session (2004).

28. Senate Select Committee on Intelligence, *Hearing on Reform of the United States Intelligence Community*, 108th Congress, 2d session (2004).

29. Senate Armed Services Committee, *Hearing on Implications of Defense and Military Operations of Proposals to Reorganize the United States Intelligence Community*, 108th Congress, 2d session, (2004).

30. Senate Homeland Security and Governmental Affairs Committee, *Hearing on Intelligence Reorganization*, 108th Congress, 2d session (2004).

31. John Hamre, "A Better Way to Improve Intelligence; The National Director Should Oversee Only the Agencies That Gather Data," *Washington Post*, August 9, 2004; see also Senate Armed Services Committee, *Hearing on Implications of Defense and Military Operations of Proposals to Reorganize the United States Intelligence Community*, 108th Congress, 2d session (2004).

32. See Arlen Specter, speaking on S.421: National Intelligence Reorganization Act, on February 19, 1991, 102d Congress, 1st session, *Congressional Record*, S.1908. See

Richard Shelby, "Additional Views of Senator Richard C. Shelby," *September 11 and the Imperative of Reform in the U.S. Intelligence Community* (December 10, 2002), 16.

33. Pat Roberts, interview by Bob Schieffer, *Face the Nation*, CBS, August 22, 2004.

34. Pat Roberts et al., letter to Susan Collins and Joseph Lieberman, September 20, 2004.

35. Andrew Card, *White House Press Briefing*, August 2, 2004.

36. House Armed Services Committee, *Hearing on United States Intelligence Reform*, 108th Congress, 2d session (2004).

37. Senate Homeland Security and Governmental Affairs Committee, *Hearing on Assessing America's Counterterrorism Capabilities*, 108th Congress, 2d session (2004).

38. Senate Select Committee on Intelligence, *Hearing on Reform of the United States Intelligence Community*, 108th Congress, 2d session (2004).

39. Andrew Card, *White House Press Briefing*, August 2, 2004.

40. David Sanger, "Intelligence: Why a Fix Is So Elusive," *New York Times*, August 15, 2004.

8. The Devil in the Details

1. Daniel Eisenberg, "Bush's New Intelligence Czar," *Time*, February 21, 2005.

2. Michael Hayden, "The State of the Craft: Is Intelligence Reform Working?" *World Affairs* (September/October 2010), http://www.worldaffairsjournal.org/articles/2010 -SeptOct/full-Hayden-SO-2010.html.

3. James Clapper, "The Role of Defense in Shaping U.S. Intelligence Reform," in *The Oxford Handbook of National Security Intelligence*, ed. Loch Johnson (New York: Oxford University Press, 2010), 633. In written answers to the Senate Intelligence Committee during his confirmation process in 2010, Clapper couched it slightly differently, explaining that in 2004 he had argued for consideration of another "paradigm," and stating, "Moving the agencies whose first letter is *N* (as in *national*) out of the Department of Defense, and under the operational control of a DNI, might have merit." James Clapper, Senate Select Committee on Intelligence, Hearing on Confirmation of James Clapper as Director of National Intelligence Post Hearing Questions, 111th Congress, 2d session (July 23, 2010).

4. Interview with James Clapper, December 29, 2011, McLean, VA.

5. James Clapper, *A Proposed Restructuring of the Intelligence Community* (Cambridge, MA: Program on Information Resources Policy at Harvard University, January 1997).

6. Michael Hayden, "The State of the Craft: Is Intelligence Reform Working?" *World Affairs* (September/October 2010), http://www.worldaffairsjournal.org/articles/2010 -SeptOct/full-Hayden-SO-2010.html.

7. Interview with Fran Townsend, October 20, 2010, New York.

8. John McLaughlin, letter to George Bush, August 20, 2004.

9. Interview with John McLaughlin, May 11, 2010, Washington, DC.

10. John McLaughlin, letter to George Bush, August 20, 2004.

11. Interview with John McLaughlin, May 11, 2010, Washington, DC.

12. Interview with Mark Lowenthal, November 10, 2010, Reston, VA.

13. Interview with Michael Hayden, June 3, 2010, Washington, DC.

14. Hayden, "The State of the Craft: Is Intelligence Reform Working?"

15. Interview with Michael Hayden, June 3, 2010, Washington, DC.

16. Phone interview with Donald Rumsfeld, November 15, 2011.

17. Interview with Stephen Cambone, November 15, 2010, McLean, VA.

18. Phone interview with Donald Rumsfeld, November 15, 2011.

19. Hayden, "The State of the Craft: Is Intelligence Reform Working?"

20. Interview with Larry Kindsvater, April 15, 2010, Washington, DC.

21. Phone interview with Donald Rumsfeld, November 15, 2011.

22. George Bush, "Section Four," in *Legislative Submission to Congress*, September 16, 2004.

23. Executive Order 13355, *Strengthened Management of the Intelligence Community*, August 27, 2004.

24. Senior administration official, background briefing by telephone conference call on the president's executive orders, August 27, 2004, 4:05 p.m.

25. Ibid.

26. Ibid.

27. Ibid.

28. Both options stressed that execution functions would be left with the cabinet secretary.

29. National Security Council to George Bush, draft memorandum on national intelligence director organization options, August 19, 2004.

30. Ibid.

31. George Bush, "Section Five(a)," in *Legislative Submission to Congress*, September 16, 2004.

32. See National Security Council to National Security Principals, memorandum on draft intelligence reform legislation, September 13, 2004.

33. Interview with Stephen Cambone, November 15, 2010, McLean, VA.

34. Donald Rumsfeld to George Bush, memorandum on intelligence issue, September 8, 2004, http://library.rumsfeld.com/doclib/sp/1323/Re%20Intel%20Issue%20 09-08-2004.pdf#search="september 8 2004 rush to reform".

35. There were two options before the NSC around this time. The first option was essentially a perpetuation of the status quo, leaving the money in the control of the departments, but increasing the DNI's power to influence the manner in which the departments spent the money. A second option would give the appropriation directly to the DNI but give the defense secretary "sufficient legal and procedural safeguards to ensure consideration of other departmental views."

36. Ibid.

37. Ibid.

38. Donald Rumsfeld to George Bush, memorandum on "reform," September 11, 2004.

39. George Bush, "Section 4(a)," in *Legislative Submission to Congress*, September 16, 2004.

40. George Bush to National Security Principals, memorandum on draft intelligence reform legislation, September 13, 2004.

41. Donald Rumsfeld to George Bush, memorandum on intelligence reform bill—final thoughts, September 15, 2004.

9. Cabinet Room

1. Senate Homeland Security and Governmental Affairs Committee, *Hearing on Building an Agile Intelligence Community to Fight Terrorism and Emerging Threats*, 108th Congress, 2d session (2004).

2. Interview with Gordon Lederman, June 2011, Washington, DC.

3. Martin Kady II, "A Centrist Seeking the Middle on September 11 Overhaul," *Congressional Quarterly Today*, September 8, 2004.

4. Senate Homeland Security and Governmental Affairs Committee, *Hearing on Making America Safer: Examining the Recommendations of the 9/11 Commission*, 108th Congress, 2d session (2004).

5. Interview with Dennis Hastert, November 17, 2010, Washington, DC.

6. Interview with Brett Loper, July 2009, Washington, DC.

7. Interview with Dan Keniry, November 2, 2012, Washington, DC.

8. George W. Bush, "Remarks on Intelligence Reform," September 8, 2004, http://www.gpo.gov/fdsys/pkg/PPP-2004-book2/html/PPP-2004-book2-doc-pg1960-3.htm.

9. Senate Homeland Security and Governmental Affairs Committee, *Hearing on Assessing America's Counterterrorism Capabilities*, 108th Congress, 2d session (2004).

10. Deb Fiddelke, e-mail to Michael Allen, September 8, 2004, George W. Bush Presidential Library, Dallas, TX.

11. Rice explained that the "DNI would have enough effective authority to manage ... budget authority ... determine budgets ... separate account ... some authority over appointments ... other strong authorities to manage like Goldwater-Nichols ... collection and tasking, resolve conflicts, ensure info sharing." Michael Allen's notes, George W. Bush Presidential Library, Dallas, TX.

12. Ibid.

13. Ibid.

10. Attackers

1. U.S. Senate, "Senate Seal," http://www.senate.gov/artandhistory/history/common/briefing/Senate_Seal.htm.

2. Senate Armed Services Committee, *Hearing on Implications of Defense and Military Operations of Proposals to Reorganize the United States Intelligence Community*, 108th Congress, 2d session (2004).

3. Interview with Joseph Lieberman, November 20, 2010, Washington, DC.

4. Interview with Susan Collins, November 20, 2010, Washington, DC.

5. Senate Armed Services Committee, *Hearing on Implications of Defense and Military Operations of Proposals to Reorganize the United States Intelligence Community*, 108th Congress, 2d session (2004).

6. National Commission on Terrorist Attacks upon the United States, *Panel Four of the Eighth Public Hearing*, 108th Congress, 2d session (2004).

7. Interview with Dan Keniry, November 2, 2012.

8. Bryan Bender, "Rumsfeld Says He Backs Bush on Intelligence Overhaul," *Boston Globe*, November 24, 2004.

9. Senate Homeland Security and Governmental Affairs Committee, *National Intelligence Reform Act of 2004*, 108th Congress, 2d session, 2004, S. Rep. 108-359, 3.

10. Ibid., 2.

11. Ibid., 3.

12. Interview with Deborah Barger, June 11, 2004, McLean, VA.

13. Interview with Michael Bopp, December 3, 2010, Washington, DC.

14. Senate Homeland Security and Governmental Affairs Committee, *National Intelligence Reform Act of 2004*, 108th Congress, 2d session, 2004, S. Rep. 108-359, 4.

15. Pat Roberts, speaking on Ted Stevens, on November 20, 2008, 110th Congress, 2d session, *Congressional Record* Volume 154 Number 177 Cong. Record, S10687-S10703.

16. Lamar Alexander, speaking on Ted Stevens, on June 4, 2007, 110th Congress, 1st session, *Congressional Record* Volume 153 Number 88, S6996-7001.

17. Ibid.

18. Mitch McConnell, speaking on Ted Stevens, on April 12, 2007, 110th Congress, 1st session, *Congressional Record* Volume 153 Number 59, S4407-S4408.

19. U.S. Constitution, Article 1, Section 9.

20. Adam Clymer, "Ted Stevens, 86, Helped Shape Alaska in 40 Years in Senate," *New York Times*, August 11, 2010.

21. Mitch McConnell, speaking on Ted Stevens, on November 20, 2008, 110th Congress, 2d session, *Congressional Record* Volume 154 Number 177 Cong. Record, S10689-S10690.

22. Pat Roberts, speaking on Ted Stevens, on November 20, 2008, 110th Congress, 2d session, *Congressional Record* Volume 154 Number 177 Cong. Record, S10687-S10703.

23. Carl Hulse, "A Senator Whom Colleagues Are Hesitant to Cross," *New York Times*, October 25, 2003.

24. Sheryl Gay Stolberg, "Republicans Fight Off More Amendments to Spending Bill," *New York Times*, January 18, 2003.

25. Lisa Murkowski, speaking on Ted Stevens, on November 20, 2008, 110th Congress, 2d session, *Congressional Record* Volume 154 Number 177 Cong. Record, S10687-S10703.

26. Clymer, "Ted Stevens, 86, Helped Shape Alaska in 40 Years in Senate."

27. Interview with John Lehman, February 6, 2012, New York.

28. Senate Appropriations Committee, *Hearing on the Review of the 9/11 Commission's Intelligence Recommendations*, 108th Congress, 2d session (2004).

29. See Richard Posner, "The 9/11 Report: A Dissent," *New York Times*, August 29, 2004.

30. David Boren et al., letter on Guiding Principles for Intelligence Reform, on September 21, 2004, 108th Congress, 2d session, Congressional Record Volume 150, Issue 114, S9428-9429.

31. Senate Appropriations Committee, *Hearing on the Review of the 9/11 Commission's Intelligence Recommendations*, 108th Congress, 2d session (2004).

32. Senate Homeland Security and Governmental Affairs Committee, *Statement of Robert Gates: Hearing on Reorganizing America's Intelligence Community: A View from the Inside*, 108th Congress, 2d session (2004).

33. Ibid.

34. Christopher Bond, speaking on intelligence reform, on September 29, 2004, 108th Congress, 2d session, Congressional Record Volume 150, Issue 120, S9879-9881.

35. Letter from Senator Specter et al. to Senators Collins and Lieberman, September 20, 2004.

36. Michael DeWine, speaking on intelligence reform, on September 29, 2004, 108th Congress, 2d session, Congressional Record Volume 150, Issue 120, S98886-9888.

37. See Deborah G. Barger, "The Passage of the Intelligence Reform and Terrorism Prevention Act of 2004: An Intelligence Officer's Perspective," *Studies in Intelligence* 53, no. 3 (September 2009): 1 13.

38. See Warner-Levin amendments of September 20, 2004, that would have removed all military and DIA programs from the NIP; exempt military personnel from the DNI; and eliminate the DNI's ability to set collection requirements.

39. Senate Homeland Security and Governmental Affairs Committee, *Markup of the National Intelligence Reform Act*, 108th Congress, 2d session (2004).

40. Ibid.

41. Ibid.

42. John Warner, speaking on intelligence reform, on December 8, 2004, 108th Congress, 2d session, *Congressional Record*, Volume 150, Number 139, S12006.

43. "I think we struck the right balance." Senate Homeland Security and Governmental Affairs Committee, *Markup of the National Intelligence Reform Act*, 108th Congress, 2d session (2004).

44. Senate Homeland Security and Governmental Affairs Committee, *Markup of the National Intelligence Reform Act*, 108th Congress, 2d session (2004).

45. Ibid.

46. Interview with Michael Bopp, December 3, 2010, Washington, DC.

47. S. 2485: National Intelligence Reform Act, section 102 (d) (1)-(4).

48. Ibid., section 113(b).

49. Ibid., section 113(d)(1).

50. Ibid., Section 201 (a) and (b).

51. Ibid., section 143(d)(1)-(3).

52. Senate Homeland Security and Governmental Affairs Committee, *Collins Lieberman Intelligence Reform Legislation Bill Summary*, 108th Congress, 2d session (2004).

53. S. 2485: National Intelligence Reform Act, section 143(h)(3)(C).

54. Senate Homeland Security and Governmental Affairs Committee, *National Intelligence Reform Act of 2004*, 108th Congress, 2d session, 2004, S. Rep. 108-359, 5.

55. Senate Homeland Security and Governmental Affairs Committee, *Markup of the National Intelligence Reform Act*, 108th Congress, 2d session (2004).

56. S. 2485: National Intelligence Reform Act, Section 145.

57. Ibid., section 208.

58. Philip Zelikow, e-mail to 9/11 Public Discourse Project Board, "Views on Specter Amendment," September 20, 2004, Lee H. Hamilton 9/11 Commission Papers, MPP 7, Modern Political Papers Collection, Indiana University Libraries, Bloomington.

59. Barger, "The Passage of the Intelligence Reform and Terrorism Prevention Act of 2004."

60. Senate Homeland Security and Governmental Affairs Committee, *Markup of the National Intelligence Reform Act*, 108th Congress, 2d session (2004).

61. John Warner, speaking on intelligence reform, on December 8, 2004, 108th Congress, 2d session, *Congressional Record*, Volume 150, Number 139, S12005.

62. Paul Pillar, *Intelligence and U.S. Foreign Policy* (New York: Columbia University Press, 2011), 205.

63. John D. Rockefeller IV, letter to Susan Collins and Joseph Lieberman, August 27, 2004.

64. "Former CIA Chief Blasts Intelligence Reform Plan," CNN, August 24, 2004.

65. Philip Zelikow, e-mail to John Lehman and others on "Specter Amendment to C-L: they Need Help," September 20, 2004, Lee H. Hamilton 9/11 Commission Papers, MPP 7, Modern Political Papers Collection, Indiana University Libraries, Bloomington.

66. U.S. Senate, *Final Vote Results for Vote 192*, 108th Congress, 2d session (September 29, 2004).

67. S. 2845, amendment number 3845.

68. Robert Byrd, speaking on intelligence reform, on October 4, 2004, 108th Congress, 2d session, *Congressional Record* Volume 150 Number 123, S10298-S10299.

69. Philip Zelikow, e-mail to 9/11 Public Discourse Project Board on "Views on Pending Amendments to S. 2845," October 3, 2004, Lee H. Hamilton 9/11 Commission Papers, MPP 7, Modern Political Papers Collection, Indiana University Libraries, Bloomington.

70. S. 2845, amendment number 3903.

71. Philip Zelikow, e-mail to 9/11 Public Discourse Project Board on "Views on Pending Amendments to S. 2845," October 3, 2004, Lee H. Hamilton 9/11 Commission Papers, MPP 7, Modern Political Papers Collection, Indiana University Libraries, Bloomington.

72. Amy Klamper, "Angry Stevens Threatens to Tie Up 9/11 Overhaul Bill," *National Journal*, October 5, 2004.

73. James Thompson, e-mail to 9/11 Public Discourse Project Board on "Re: Comments of Angry Senator re Chair/Vice Chair," October 4, 2004, Lee H. Hamilton 9/11 Commission Papers, MPP 7, Modern Political Papers Collection, Indiana University Libraries, Bloomington.

74. Joseph Lieberman, speaking on intelligence reform, on October 4, 2004, 108th Congress, 2d session, *Congressional Record* Volume 150 Number 123, S10318-S10319.

75. Interview with Deborah Barger, June 11, 2004, McLean, VA.

76. Congress Daily, "October 5, 2004, Collins Stands Her Ground in 9/11 Fight," *National Journal*, October 5, 2004.

77. Ibid.

78. Mary Curtius, "Spy Reform Bill's Guiding Light is Up to the Task," *Los Angeles Times*, October 5, 2004.

11. High Ransom

1. Interview with Dennis Hastert, November 17, 2010, Washington, DC.

2. Ibid.

3. Interview with Brett Loper, July 2009, Arlington, VA.

4. Interview with Dan Keniry, November 1, 2012, Washington, DC.

5. Interview with Porter Goss, December 1, 2011, Washington, DC.

6. Interview with Mike Meermans, September 17, 2010, Washington, DC.

7. H.R. 10, Section 1011, sec. 101(b) (1)(2).

8. Ibid., sec. 101(c)(5)(B).

9. House Armed Services Committee, *Markup of H.R. 10: The National Security and Intelligence Improvement Act of 2004*, 108th Congress, 2d session (2004).

10. H.R. 10, Section 1011, (e) (3)(B).

11. Ibid., Section 1011, (e) (3)(A)(iv).

12. Ibid., Section 1021, sec. 119 (d) (2).

13. Office of Management and Budget, "Statement of Administration Policy: H.R. 10 -9/11 Recommendations Implementation Act," October 7, 2004.

14. Mary Curtius, "Senate to Wrestle Over New Intelligence Post's Powers," *Los Angeles Times*, September 28, 2004.

15. Tim Roemer, e-mail to 9/11 Commission Public Discourse Project Board on "House of Representatives and Limited Time to Act on Commission Recommendations,"

September 2, 2004, Lee H. Hamilton 9/11 Commission Papers, MPP 7, Modern Political Papers Collection, Indiana University Libraries, Bloomington.

16. Richard Ben-Veniste, e-mail to 9/11 Commission Public Discourse Project Board on "RE: Revised Analysis of Emerging Bills," September 28, 2004, Lee H. Hamilton 9/11 Commission Papers, MPP 7, Modern Political Papers Collection, Indiana University Libraries, Bloomington.

17. John Lehman, e-mail to 9/11 Commission Public Discourse Project Board on "RE: Draft Statement," September 29, 2004, Lee H. Hamilton 9/11 Commission Papers, MPP 7, Modern Political Papers Collection, Indiana University Libraries, Bloomington.

18. House Permanent Select Committee on Intelligence, *Markup of H.R. 10: The National Security and Intelligence Improvement Act of 2004*, 2d session (2004).

19. House Armed Services Committee, *Markup of H.R. 10: The National Security and Intelligence Improvement Act of 2004*, 108th Congress, 2d session (2004).

20. Chris Kojm, e-mail to 9/11 Commission Public Discourse Project Board on "RE: Today's Senate Action," October 8, 2004, Lee H. Hamilton 9/11 Commission Papers, MPP 7, Modern Political Papers Collection, Indiana University Libraries, Bloomington.

12. Touching Gloves

1. Interview with Carie Lemack, November 2, 2012, Washington, DC.

2. Michael Allen's notes, George Bush W. Presidential Library, Dallas, TX.

3. Martin Kady II, "House GOP Conferees Skeptical About Creating Powerful Intelligence Director," *CQ*, October 12, 2004.

4. Interview with Brett Shogren, March 11, 2010, Washington, DC.

5. Ibid.

6. Interview with Scott Palmer, April 22, 2010, Washington, DC.

7. George W. Bush, "Statement of Administration Policy: H.R. 10 -9/11 Recommendations Implementation Act," October 7, 2004.

8. Ibid.

9. Condoleezza Rice and Josh Bolten, letter to Peter Hoekstra and Senator Susan Collins, October 18, 2004.

10. Interview with Peter Hoesktra, November 20, 2010, Washington, DC.

11. Thomas Kean and Lee Hamilton, letter to Susan Collins, October 20, 2004.

12. Ibid.

13. House-Senate Conference Committee, *Intelligence Reform Implementation Conference*, 108th Congress, 2d session (2004).

14. Ibid.

15. Ibid.

16. Peter Hoekstra, *Press Conference with Senator Collins, Senator Lieberman, Congresswoman Harman, and Congressman Hoekstra*, November 20, 2004.

17. Interview with Peter Hoekstra, November 20, 2010, Washington, DC.

18. Tim Roemer, e-mail to 9/11 Public Discourse Project Board on "RE: Update on Conference Committee," October 21, 2004, Lee H. Hamilton 9/11 Commission Papers, MPP 7, Modern Political Papers Collection, Indiana University Libraries, Bloomington.

19. Interview with Scott Palmer, April 22, 2010, Washington, DC.

13. Dirty Bombs

1. Michael Hurley, e-mail to 9/11 Commission Public Discourse Project Board on "Conference Committee Afternoon Update," October 22, 2004, Lee H. Hamilton 9/11 Commission Papers, MPP 7, Modern Political Papers Collection, Indiana University Libraries, Bloomington.

2. Ibid.

3. Interview with Robert Rangel, November 22, 2011, Arlington, VA.

4. Phone interview with Duncan Hunter, July 23, 2010; see also interview with Duncan Hunter, Fox News, November 22, 2004; see also Duncan Hunter, *News Conference on Intelligence Reform Bill*, December 6, 2004.

5. Ibid.

6. Interview with Duncan Hunter, Fox News, November 22, 2004.

7. Ibid.

8. Recalling the episode, Myers wrote that Hunter's concern was that the Senate bill would "remove the secretary of defense from the budget process for all the Defense Department's intelligence agencies." Myers himself thought it would be a "management nightmare" resulting in a loss of control, and, given his obligation to Congress to give military advice, he was bound to defend the warfighters. Richard Myers, *Eyes on the Horizon: Serving on the Front Lines of National Security* (New York: Threshold Editions, 2009), 271.

9. Ibid., 271.

10. Myers, letter to Duncan Hunter, October 21, 2004.

11. See "But no one who is seriously engaged in the issue believed the president was doing more than paying lip service to it." Norman Ornstein, "Intel Reform Could Shed Light on Bush's Second-Term Approach," *Roll Call*, November 29, 2004.

12. Interview with Andrew Card, June 19, 2012, McLean, VA.

13. Ibid.

14. Ibid.

15. Myers, *Eyes on the Horizon*, 271.

16. Interview with Richard Myers, November 22, 2011, Arlington, VA.

17. Phone interview with Donald Rumsfeld, November 15, 2011. See also Donald Rumsfeld, *Known and Unknown: A Memoir* (New York: Sentinel Trade, 2012), 621.

18. Donald Rumsfeld to Andrew Card Jr., memorandum on possible talking points, October 22, 2004.

19. Interview with Susan Collins, November 20, 2010, Washington, DC.

20. Mary Curtius, "Intelligence Reform Bill Hits a Wall in Congress," *Los Angeles Times*, October 30, 2004.

21. Carolyn Maloney, *News Meeting on the First Meeting of the 9/11 Conferees*, October 20, 2004.

22. Jamie Gorelick, e-mail to Board of 9/11 Commission Public Discourse Project on "re: Hastert Comments on the Conferees Meeting on 9/11 Recommendations Implementation Act," October 18, 2004, Lee H. Hamilton 9/11 Commission Papers, MPP 7, Modern Political Papers Collection, Indiana University Libraries, Bloomington.

23. Philip Zelikow, e-mail to Board of 9/11 Commission Public Discourse Project on "Escalation Plan," October 21, 2004, Lee H. Hamilton 9/11 Commission Papers, MPP 7, Modern Political Papers Collection, Indiana University Libraries, Bloomington.

24. Interview with Philip Zelikow, November 1, 2010, Charlottesville, VA.

25. Interview with Chris Walker, December 17, 2009, Washington, DC.

26. Philip Zelikow, e-mail to Michael Bopp and Kevin Landy, October 23, 2004.

27. Ibid.

28. Philip Shenon, "Key Aide to 9/11 Panel Praises Offer By House," *New York Times*, October 27, 2004.

29. Interview with Joseph Lieberman, November 20, 2010, Washington, DC.

30. Interview with Susan Collins, November 20, 2010, Washington, DC.

31. Interview with Philip Zelikow, November 1, 2010, Charlottesville, VA.

32. Thomas Kean and Lee Hamilton, letter to House-Senate Conferees, October 20, 2004.

33. Philip Zelikow, e-mail to Bob Kerrey on "re: Latest House offer for the bill," October 24, 2004, Lee H. Hamilton 9/11 Commission Papers, MPP 7, Modern Political Papers Collection, Indiana University Libraries, Bloomington.

34. Having read the House bill, I "concluded that this is definately [*sic*] moving in the right direction." Bob Kerrey, e-mail to Public Discourse Project Board on "Conference," October 24, 2004, Lee H. Hamilton 9/11 Commission Papers, MPP 7, Modern Political Papers Collection, Indiana University Libraries, Bloomington.

35. "The core powers necessary for the success of the DNI are now in both draft bills." John Lehman, e-mail to Public Discourse Project Board on "RE: More Analysis of Latest House Proposal, and Thoughts on Next Steps," October 24, 2004, Lee H. Hamilton 9/11 Commission Papers, MPP 7, Modern Political Papers Collection, Indiana University Libraries, Bloomington.

36. Shenon, "Key Aide to 9/11 Panel Praises Offer By House."

37. Philip Shenon, "Negotiators See New Hope for Intelligence Bill," *New York Times*, November 8, 2004.

38. Curtius, "Intelligence Reform Bill Hits a Wall in Congress."

39. Philip Shenon, "Delays on 9/11 Bill Are Laid to Pentagon," *New York Times*, October 26, 2004. The General Myers letter stiffened the resolve of the House Republicans

to limit the powers of a director on military issues. A Senate Republican aide who supported the Senate bill said, "The letter has been very unhelpful."

40. See Congress Daily, "The Myers Letter," *National Journal*, October 28, 2004. The Myers letter "contradicting" the Bush position dropped like a "nuclear bomb" and the Zelikow e-mail was "the straw that broke the camel's back." "Advocates of the House position sought to portray the e-mail as a ringing endorsement from the Commission's top staffer."

41. Congress Daily, "Conferees Making Little Progress on Intelligence Overhaul," *National Journal*, October 27, 2004.

42. See Congress Daily, "Pre-Election Vote on Intel Overhaul Bill Increasingly Likely," *National Journal*, October 26, 2004. "'Intelligence reform isn't anywhere on our radar screen in our races,' a spokesman for the National Republican Congressional Committee said. Former Rep. Lee Hamilton . . . conceded media and voters are focusing on the looming election, which has not provided an impetus to pass intelligence changes."

43. Thomas Kean, *News Conference with Former Vice Chairman Lee Hamilton*, October 25, 2004.

44. Chris Kojm, e-mail to Lee Hamilton and Tom Kean on "FOR IMMEDIATE ATTENTION – conference committee in dire straits," October 27, 2004, Lee H. Hamilton 9/11 Commission Papers, MPP 7, Modern Political Papers Collection, Indiana University Libraries, Bloomington.

45. Interview with Dennis Hastert, November 17, 2010, Washington, DC.

46. Chris Kojm, e-mail to Lee Hamilton and Tom Kean on "Late afternoon update," October 26, 2004, Lee H. Hamilton 9/11 Commission Papers, MPP 7, Modern Political Papers Collection, Indiana University Libraries, Bloomington.

47. Interview with senior House congressional staffer.

48. Interview with Dennis Hastert, November 17, 2010, Washington, DC.

49. Ibid.

50. Interview with Chris Walker, December 17, 2009, Washington, DC.

51. Ibid.

52. Interview with Scott Palmer, April 22, 2010, Washington, DC.

53. Interview with Susan Collins, November 20, 2010, Washington, DC.

54. Interview with David Hobbs, May 26, 2010, Washington, DC.

55. Interview with Susan Collins, November 20, 2010, Washington, DC.

56. Interview with Jane Harman, November 20, 2010, Washington, DC.

57. Philip Shenon, "9/11 Families Group Rebukes Bush for Impasse on Overhaul," *New York Times*, October 28, 2004.

58. Breitweiser, *Wake-Up Call*, 217.

59. See Carie Lemack, "The Journey to September 12th." "Roughly half of the Family Steering Committee has decided to join the fray by endorsing John Kerry for President."

60. Joseph Lieberman, *News Teleconference on the House and Senate Intelligence Reform Bills Negotiations with Joseph Lieberman, Susan Collins, Jane Harman, and Pete Hoekstra*, October 29, 2004.

14. Time for a New Approach

1. Congress Daily, "House GOP Gains May Hurt Intel Overhaul Bill Prospects," *National Journal*, November 4, 2004.

2. Interview with Robert Rangel, November 22, 2011, Arlington, VA.

3. George W. Bush, *President Holds Press Conference*, November 4, 2004. http://georgewbush-whitehouse.archives.gov/news/releases/2004/11/20041104-5.html.

4. Phone interview with Duncan Hunter, July 7, 2012.

5. Ibid., July 24, 2012.

6. Regarding the NFIP—as in, the DNI is merely obligated to *coordinate* with the secretary of defense; secretary of defense *concurrence* should not be required.

7. Michael Allen's notes, George W. Bush Presidential Library, Dallas, TX.

8. Interview with Brett Shogren, March 11, 2010, Washington, DC.

9. Ibid.

10. Interview with Scott Palmer, April 22, 2010, Washington, DC.

11. Interview with Brett Shogren, March 11, 2010, Washington, DC.

12. Interview with Tom DeLay, June 7, 2012, Washington, DC.

13. Interview with congressional Republican staffer, 2012.

14. Interview with Brett Shogren, March 11, 2010, Washington, DC.

15. Chris Kojm, e-mail to Lee Hamilton and Tom Kean on "FW: Senate offer – Status of the conference," November 10, 2004, Lee H. Hamilton 9/11 Commission Papers, MPP 7, Modern Political Papers Collection, Indiana University Libraries, Bloomington.

16. Chris Kojm, e-mail to Lee Hamilton on "Kean Conversation with Collins," November 5, 2004, Lee H. Hamilton 9/11 Commission Papers, MPP 7, Modern Political Papers Collection, Indiana University Libraries, Bloomington.

17. Interview with Deborah Barger, June 11, 2012, McLean, VA.

18. Jonathan Allen, "No Mercy: Dead End in House for Certain Senators' Bills?," *CQ Today*, November 17, 2004.

19. Martin Kady II, "Intelligence Conferees Battle Clock, Each Other," *CQ Today*, November 16, 2004.

20. Interview with Susan Collins and Joseph Lieberman, November 20, 2010, Washington, DC.

21. See IRTPA, Sec 102(C)(5)(B).

22. See generally, Susan Collins, "I remember how difficult it was and that we did want the DNI to be responsible for determining the budget. But in order to get the bill through, I think we did create a compromise or some lack of clarity in order to get the

bill accomplished," Senate Homeland Security and Governmental Affairs Committee, *Ten Years After 9/11: Is Intelligence Reform Working?*, 108th Congress, 2d session (2011).

23. Interview with Joseph Lieberman, November 20, 2010, Washington, DC.

24. Philip Shenon, "Agreement May Be Near on 9/11 Bill."

25. Chris Kojm, e-mail to Tom Kean and Lee Hamilton on "Update—report on PZ's meeting with Scott Palmer," November 9, 2004, Lee H. Hamilton 9/11 Commission Papers, MPP 7, Modern Political Papers Collection, Indiana University Libraries, Bloomington.

26. Thomas Kean and Lee Hamilton, letter to Senator Collins, October 20, 2004.

27. Senate Homeland Security and Governmental Affairs Committee, *Principal Reasons Why the House Republican Offer Does Not Give the DNI or NCTC Director Sufficient Authorities and Powers to be Effective*, 108th Congress, 2d session (2004).

28. Ibid.

29. IRTPA, Section 1021

30. Interview with Philip Zelikow, August 29, 2012, Washington, DC.

31. How did it come to pass that the D/NCTC reported to the DNI for analytical matters and to the president for operational missions? Giving an intelligence officer, the head of the NCTC, an operational planning function seemed to run counter to the traditional practice of limiting intelligence to strictly collection and analysis rather than the development of policy or direction of action (with the notable exception of the CIA's covert action mission). Since the Commission envisioned a DNI in the White House, it considered the NCTC "indirectly reporting to the president." However, when President Bush and Congress emphatically rejected the placement of the DNI and the NCTC in the White House, proponents of a muscular, operational NCTC sought to preserve a direct connection to the president to facilitate the NCTC director's authority to conduct strategic operational planning and assign operational responsibilities to departments and agencies. Distinguishing between the NCTC's analytical and operational roles, the Senate inserted into the bill that the NCTC director would report directly to the president regarding operational matters and to the DNI on traditional intelligence functions. Although the White House supported the House NCTC approach and opposed a formal dual-reporting chain, the Senate provision prevailed.

32. Chris Kojm, e-mail to 9/11 Public Discourse Project Board on "Perils of Pauline," November 18, 2004, Lee H. Hamilton 9/11 Commission Papers, MPP 7, Modern Political Papers Collection, Indiana University Libraries, Bloomington.

33. Ibid.

34. Interview with Philip Kiko, October 2012, Washington, DC.

35. Chris Kojm, e-mail to 9/11 Public Discourse Project Board on "RE: Congress Daily PM," November 19, 2004, Lee H. Hamilton 9/11 Commission Papers, MPP 7, Modern Political Papers Collection, Indiana University Libraries, Bloomington.

36. Interview with David Hobbs, May 26, 2010, Washington, DC.

37. Philip Zelikow, e-mail to Tom Kean and Lee Hamilton on "Status Report – Confidential," November 11, 2004, Lee H. Hamilton 9/11 Commission Papers, MPP 7, Modern Political Papers Collection, Indiana University Libraries, Bloomington.

38. Ibid.

39. Ibid.

40. Mary Curtius, "White House Intervenes on Behalf of Intelligence Bill," *Los Angeles Times*, November 17, 2004.

41. Michael Allen's notes, George W. Bush Presidential Library, Dallas, TX.

15. Black Saturday

1. Shenon, "Bush Says He'll Seek to Revive Intelligence Bill House Blocked."

2. Ibid.

3. Ibid.

4. Interview with David Hobbs, May 26, 2010, Washington, DC.

5. Shenon, "Bush Says He'll Seek to Revive Intelligence Bill House Blocked."

6. Interview with Philip Kiko, October 2012, Washington, DC.

7. Senate Homeland Security and Governmental Affairs Committee, *Hearing on Intelligence Overhaul*, 112th Congress, 1st session (2011).

8. Interview with Scott Palmer, April 22, 2010, Washington, DC.

9. Bart Jansen, "Reform's Failure Is "Crushing" to Collins," *Portland Press Herald/ Maine Sunday Telegram*, November 21, 2004.

10. Interview with Robert Rangel, November 22, 2011, Arlington, VA.

11. Ibid.

12. Linda Douglass, interview by George Stephanopoulos, *This Week with George Stephanopoulos*, ABC, November 21, 2004.

13. Shenon and Hulse, "House Leadership Blocks Vote on Intelligence Bill."

14. Duncan Hunter, quoted in the *Los Angeles Times*, Mary Curtius, November 22, 2004.

15. Martin Kady II, "Intelligence Bill Falls Short Again, Put Off Until December," *CQ Quarterly Today*, November 21, 2004. Mike Pence quoted as saying, "It's a war," of the split in the Republican ranks.

16. Interview with Dennis Hastert, November 17, 2010, Washington, DC.

17. Susan Collins, *Speech to Oxford Hills Chamber of Commerce*, February 4, 2005.

18. Kady II, "Intelligence Bill Falls Short Again, Put Off Until December."

19. Chris Kojm, e-mail to 9/11 Public Discourse Project Board on "Statement by Tom and Lee," November 20, 2004, Lee H. Hamilton 9/11 Commission Papers, MPP 7, Modern Political Papers Collection, Indiana University Libraries, Bloomington.

20. Fred Fielding, e-mail to Board of 9/11 Public Discourse Project, November 20, 2004, Lee H. Hamilton 9/11 Commission Papers, MPP 7, Modern Political Papers Collection, Indiana University Libraries, Bloomington.

21. Philip Zelikow, e-mail to 9/11 Public Discourse Project Board on "Important Update on Status of the Bill," November 20, 2004, Lee H. Hamilton 9/11 Commission Papers, MPP 7, Modern Political Papers Collection, Indiana University Libraries, Bloomington.

22. Interview with Brett Loper, June 2010, Arlington, VA.

23. Interview with Tom DeLay, June 7, 2012, Washington, DC.

24. Interview with Brett Shogren, March 11, 2010, Washington, DC.

25. Interview with Scott Palmer, April 22, 2010, Washington, DC.

26. Interview with Jim Sensenbrenner, November 18, 2010, Washington, DC.

27. Senator Collins called it "Black Saturday." "It was the blackest moment in the arduous battle to get this bill passed." Susan Collins, *Speech to Oxford Hills Chamber of Commerce*, February 4, 2005.

28. Ron Hutcheson and James Kuhnhenn, "Intel Showdown Will Be Key Test for Bush," *Knight Ridder Newspapers*, December 2, 2004.

29. Shenon and Hulse, "House Leadership Blocks Vote on Intelligence Bill."

30. Interview with David Hobbs, May 26, 2010, Washington, DC.

31. Ibid.

32. Interview with Dennis Hastert, November 17, 2010, Washington, DC.

33. Ibid.

34. Interview with Tom DeLay, June 7, 2012, Washington, DC.

35. Interview with Scott Palmer, April 22, 2010, Washington, DC.

36. Interview with Robert Rangel, November 22, 2011, Arlington, VA.

37. George W. Bush, *Media Availability with President Ricardo Lagos of Chile*, November 21, 2004.

38. Interview with Susan Collins, November 20, 2010, Washington, DC.

39. Jamie Gorelick, e-mail to Board of 9/11 Commission Public Discourse Project on "re: Statement by Tom and Lee," November 20, 2004, Lee H. Hamilton 9/11 Commission Papers, MPP 7, Modern Political Papers Collection, Indiana University Libraries, Bloomington.

40. Philip Zelikow, e-mail to Board of 9/11 Commission Public Discourse Project on "Update on Bill – Still Alive," November 20, 2004, Lee H. Hamilton 9/11 Commission Papers, MPP 7, Modern Political Papers Collection, Indiana University Libraries, Bloomington.

41. John McCain, interview by Tim Russert, *Meet the Press*, NBC, November 21, 2004.

42. Kristen Breitweiser, interview by Chris Matthews, *Hardball with Chris Matthews*, MSNBC, December 1, 2004.

43. Shenon and Hulse, "House Leadership Blocks Vote on Intelligence Bill."

44. See generally, Claire Buchan, *Press Gaggle*, Crawford, Texas, November 23, 2010.

45. Duncan Hunter, interview with Duncan Hunter, *Fox News*, November 22, 2004.

46. John Warner, *News Conference on Intelligence Reform Bill*, December 6, 2004.

47. Juan Williams, interview by Brit Hume, *Special Report with Brit Hume*, Fox News, November 23, 2004.

48. Tim Russert, interviewing Tom Kean and Lee Hamilton, *Meet the Press*, NBC, November 28, 2004.

49. Chris Wallace, interviewing Jane Harman, *Fox News Sunday*, Fox News, November 21, 2004.

50. Jane Harman, interview by Chris Wallace, *Fox News Sunday*, Fox News, November 21, 2004.

51. Martin Kady and Jonathan Allen, "Hunter Placated as Bush Renews Plea for Intelligence Bill Vote," *Congressional Quarterly Today*, December 6, 2004.

52. Tom Kean, Interview by Tom Brokaw, *NBC Nightly News*, NBC, November 28, 2004.

53. Duncan Hunter, interview with Duncan Hunter, *Fox News*, November 22, 2004.

54. Duncan Hunter, *Christian Science Monitor Breakfast*, December 2, 2004.

55. Congress Daily, "Intelligence Bill Supporters Seek Options, Gauge Support," *National Journal*, November 22, 2004.

56. Jay Rockefeller, interview by George Stephanopoulos, *This Week with George Stephanopoulos*, ABC, November 21, 2004.

57. "Yeah, because we know there's another attack coming." Tom Kean, interview by Tim Russert, *Meet the Press*, NBC, November 28, 2004.

58. Walter Pincus, "Intelligence Deal Remains Elusive," *Washington Post*, November 23, 2004.

59. Jim Sensenbrenner, interview by George Stephanopoulos, *This Week with George Stephanopoulos*, ABC, November 28, 2004.

60. Lemack, "The Journey to September 12th."

61. Tom Kean, interview by Tim Russert, *Meet the Press*, NBC, November 28, 2004.

62. "A Truly Lame Duck," *New York Times*, November 23, 2004.

63. Ron Hutcheson and James Kuhnhenn, "Intel Showdown Will be Key Test for Bush," *Knight Ridder Newspapers*, December 2, 2004.

16. Win at All Costs

1. Phone interview with David Hobbs, September 25, 2012, Washington, DC.

2. Interview with David Hobbs, May 26, 2010, Washington, DC.

3. Interview with Brett Shogren, March 11, 2010, Washington, DC.

4. Ibid.

5. Janet Hook, "Bush on Notice Despite Win in Congress," *Los Angeles Times*, December 9, 2004.

6. Ibid.

7. Interview with Brett Loper, June 2010, Arlington, VA.

8. Duncan Hunter, letter to Dennis Hastert on "Bottom Line Requirements," December 2, 2004.

9. Interview with Robert Rangel, November 22, 2011, Arlington, VA.

10. Michael Allen's notes, George W. Bush Presidential Library, Dallas, TX.

11. Richard Myers, *Christian Science Monitor Breakfast*, December 2, 2004.

12. United Press International, "Intel Reform Remains Stalled in Congress," December 2, 2004.

13. Walter Pincus and Thomas E. Ricks, "Intelligence Bill Gets Fresh Bush Support," *Washington Post*, December 3, 2004.

14. Michael Allen's notes, George W. Bush Presidential Library, Dallas, TX.

15. John Lehman and Bob Kerrey, "Safety in Intelligence," *Wall Street Journal*, November 30, 2004.

16. Thomas Kean, *News Conference with Lee Hamilton*, November 30, 2004.

17. George W. Bush, *Joint News Conference with Prime Minister Martin of Canada*, November 30, 2004.

18. "Well, we've asked for the meeting, and we hope to coordinate with the vice president and coordinate with the administration. The president cannot meet with us today because he's out of the country, so we're meeting with the vice president." Lee Hamilton and Thomas Kean, *Press Conference*, November 30, 2004.

19. Interview with Dennis Hastert, November 17, 2010, Washington, DC.

20. Ibid.

21. Interview with Thomas Kean, July 20, 2010, Washington, DC.

22. Interview with former senior White House official.

23. Interview with Robert Rangel, November 22, 2011, Arlington, VA.

24. Ibid.

25. Ibid.

26. Susan Collins, *Speech to Oxford Hills Chamber of Commerce*, February 4, 2005.

27. Duncan Hunter, *News Conference on the Intelligence Reform Bill*, December 6, 2004.

28. Phone interview with Duncan Hunter, July 24, 2012.

29. Interview with Robert Rangel, November 22, 2011, Arlington, VA.

30. Ibid.

31. James Sensenbrenner, "Statement on 9/11 Bill," December 6, 2004, Lee H. Hamilton 9/11 Commission Papers, MPP 7, Modern Political Papers Collection, Indiana University Libraries, Bloomington.

32. Michael Allen's notes, George W. Bush Presidential Library, Dallas, TX.

33. Ibid.

34. Congress Daily, "Compromise Clears Way for Intel Vote," *National Journal*, December 7, 2004.

35. Duncan Hunter, *News Conference on Intelligence Reform Bill*, December 6, 2004.

36. See Trent Duffy, *White House News Briefing Aboard Air Force One En Route to California*, December 7, 2004.

37. Susan Collins, *Press Conference*, December 7, 2004.

38. White House Pool Report, *#4*, filed by Mark Silva, released by the White House, December 7, 2004.

39. U.S. Congress, on December 7, 2004, 108th Congress, 2d session, *Congressional Record*, Volume 150, Number 138, H11028.

40. White House Pool Report, *#4*, filed by Mark Silva, released by the White House, December 7, 2004.

41. Interview with Jane Harman, November 20, 2010, Washington, DC.

42. Interview with Joseph Lieberman, November 20, 2010, Washington, DC.

43. Interview with Peter Hoekstra, November 20, 2010, Washington, DC.

44. Martin Kady II and John M. Donnelly, "Bush, GOP Leaders Quell Rebellion on Intelligence," *CQ Today*, December 6, 2004.

45. Thomas Ferraro, "Bush Reasserts Himself as Force for Second Term," *Reuters*, December 9, 2004.

46. Interview with Tim Roemer, February 13, 2012, Washington, DC.

47. Tim Roemer, e-mail to Board of 9/11 Public Discourse Project, December 7, 2004, Lee H. Hamilton 9/11 Commission Papers, MPP 7, Modern Political Papers Collection, Indiana University Libraries, Bloomington.

48. Senator Susan Collins, *Congressional Record*, December 8, 2004, Page S11939, at S11940.

49. E-mail from Michael Warner, October 17, 2012.

50. Senator Susan Collins, *Congressional Record*, December 8, 2004, Page SII939, at SII940.

51. The Speaker "has designated his top aide, Scott Palmer, to work on this bill, and Scott Palmer has done that diligently." (Hamilton) "Scott Palmer was very, very, helpful to the 9/11 Commission, and so was the speaker." (Tim Roemer). National Commission on Terrorist Attacks upon the United States, *Press Conference*, November 30, 2004.

52. Philip Zelikow, Speech at Center for Strategic & International Studies, "Integrating National Security Missions: Lessons from the National Counterterrorism Center," March 26, 2010.

53. Susan Collins, *Press Conference*, December 8, 2004.

54. White House Pool Report, *#1*, filed by Julie Mason, December 17, 2004.

55. Ibid.

17. Bureaucratic Black Arts

1. Chris Kojm, e-mail to 9/11 Commission Public Discourse Project Board, December 6, 2004, Lee H. Hamilton 9/11 Commission Papers, MPP 7, Modern Political Papers Collection, Indiana University Libraries, Bloomington.

2. Susan Collins, speaking on the necessity of a national intelligence director, on December 8, 2004, 108th Congress, 2d session, *Congressional Record* Volume 150 Number 139, S11939, S11968-9. (See also "The department heads may not interpose themselves between the DNI and the heads of agencies and organizations within the intelligence community." See also, with regard to personnel transfer, "those department heads will no longer have the right to object to such transfers.")

3. Ibid., S11970.

4. Ibid., S11971.

5. Ibid.

6. Ibid., S11972.

7. Ibid.

8. Ibid., S11972.

9. Ibid.

10. Ibid.

11. Peter Hoekstra, speaking on the conference report on S. 2845, on December 20, 2004, 108th Congress, 2d session, *Congressional Record - Extension of Remarks*, E2209-E2210.

12. Ibid.

13. Ibid.

14. Ibid.

15. Ibid.

16. Robert Gates, e-mail to Andy Card, January, 11, 2005.

17. Handwritten note from Robert Gates, January 20, 2005.

18. Ibid.

19. Interview with Robert Gates, April 19, 2012, Washington, DC.

20. Robert Gates, e-mail to Andy Card, January, 11, 2005.

21. Handwritten note from Robert Gates, January 20, 2005.

22. Robert Gates, e-mail to Andy Card, January, 11, 2005.

23. Interview with Robert Gates, April 19, 2012, Washington, DC.

24. Ibid.

25. Ibid.

26. Ibid.

27. Interview with Steve Hadley, July 5, 2012, Washington, DC.

28. Interview with John Negroponte, June 11, 2012, Washington, DC.

29. George W. Bush, *Bush Announces New Intel Chief*, February 17, 2005, http://www.washingtonpost.com/wp-dyn/articles/A32210-2005Feb17.html.

30. Laurence H. Silberman et al., *Commission on the Intelligence Capabilities of the United States on Regarding Weapons of Mass Destruction* (Washington: Featured Commission Publications, 2005).

31. Interview with Stewart Baker, April 11, 2012, Washington, DC.

32. Silberman et al., *Commission on the Intelligence Capabilities of the United States on Regarding Weapons of Mass Destruction*, 314.

33. Interview with Stewart Baker, April 11, 2012, Washington, DC.

34. Ibid.

35. Silberman et al., *Commission on the Intelligence Capabilities of the United States on Regarding Weapons of Mass Destruction*, 314.

36. Ibid.

37. Ibid., 317.

38. Interview with Stewart Baker, April 11, 2012, Washington, DC.

39. Silberman et al., *Commission on the Intelligence Capabilities of the United States on Regarding Weapons of Mass Destruction*, 318.

40. Ibid.

41. Ibid., 471.

42. Ibid., 457.

43. Ibid., 461.

44. George W. Bush, "Administration's Response to Recommendations of the Commission in the Intelligence Capabilities of the United States Regarding Weapons of Mass Destruction," June 25, 2005.

45. Interview with John Negroponte, June 11, 2012, Washington, DC.

46. Senate Select Committee on Intelligence, *Hearing on Nomination of Ambassador John Negroponte to be Director of National Intelligence*, 109th Congress, 1st session (2005).

47. Ibid.

48. John Brennan, "Is This Intelligence, We Added Players, but Lost Control of the Ball," *Washington Post*, November 20, 2005.

49. Douglas Jehl, "The Spymaster Question," *New York Times*, December 8, 2004.

50. John Negroponte, *Remarks at CIA University Leadership Day*, June 28, 2006.

51. David Kaplan and Kevin Whitelaw, "Remaking U.S. Intelligence—Part III: The Spies," *U.S. News and World Report*, November 3, 2006.

52. Peter Hoekstra, letter to George W. Bush, May 18, 2006.

53. See, for example, House Permanent Select Committee on Intelligence, *Hearing on Status of Director of National Intelligence*, 109th Congress, 1st session (2005).

54. Mary Louise Kelly, "Fearing Bloating, House Cuts Some Spy Funds," NPR, April 5, 2006.

55. John Lehman, "Getting Spy Reform Wrong," *Washington Post*, November 16, 2005.

56. John Lehman, 9/11 Public Discourse Project Forum, Challenges for the Director of National Intelligence, June 13, 2005.

57. Senate Select Committee on Intelligence, *Hearing on Intelligence Reform*, 110th Congress, 1st session (January 23, 2007).

58. Interview with James Clapper, December 29, 2011, McLean, VA.

59. Brennan, "Is This Intelligence, We Added Players, but Lost Control of the Ball."

60. Interview with Porter Goss, December 1, 2011, Washington, DC.

61. Joseph Lieberman, speaking on intelligence reform, on December 8, 2004, 108th Congress, 2d session, *Congressional Record*, Volume 150, Number 139, S11969.

62. Senate Homeland Security and Governmental Affairs Committee, *Hearing on Intelligence Overhaul*, 112th Congress, 1st session (2011).

63. See, for example, NPR Weekend Edition, "Negroponte's Departure shows Pressure of the Post," January 7, 2007 (quoting Professor Amy Zegart, "I think that his departure is a very public indicator that the DNI's office is not working well").

64. Memorandum of agreement between the secretary of defense and the director of national intelligence, May 2007.

65. House Permanent Select Committee on Intelligence, *Hearing on the Director of National Intelligence's 500 Day Plan*, 110th Congress, 1st session (2007).

66. Mike McConnell, *Intelligence Community Directive Number 501: Discovery and Dissemination or Retrieval of Information within the Intelligence Community*, January 21, 2009.

67. Jack Devine, "An Intelligence Reform Reality Check," *Washington Post*, February 18, 2008.

68. Tim Starks, "Lost in the Reshuffle," *CQ Weekly*, May 5, 2008.

69. Ibid.

70. Ibid.

71. Senate Select Committee on Intelligence, *Hearing on DNI Authorities and Personnel Issues*, 110th Congress, 2d session (2008).

72. Amy Zegart, "Built to Fail: Our Clueless Intelligence System," *Washington Post*, July 8, 2007.

73. House Permanent Select Committee on Intelligence, *Hearing on the Director of National Intelligence's 500 Day Plan*, 110th Congress, 1st session (2007).

74. Tim Roemer, speaking at Bipartisan Policy Center, *Ten Years After: The Status on National Security and Implementation of the 9/11 Commission's Recommendations*, August 31, 2011.

75. Dennis Blair, *Remarks and Q&A at a National Security Task Force*, U.S. Chamber of Commerce, Washington, DC, July 22, 2009.

76. "Q&A: General Michael Hayden," *U.S. News and World Report*, November 3, 2006, http://www.usnews.com/usnews/news/articles/061103/3qahayden_3.htm.

77. Interview with Robert Gates, April 19, 2012, Washington, DC.

78. Gordon Lederman, "Making Intelligence Reform Work," *The American Interest* (Spring 2009): 26.

79. Executive Order 12333, United States Intelligence Activities, December 4, 1981 (as amended by Executive Orders 13284 (2003), 13355 (2004) and 13470 (2008)), Part 1.3 (e)(1).

80. Ibid, Part 1.3.

81. Ibid, Part 1.3 (c). See also, Background Briefing by Senior Administration Officials on the Revision of Executive Order 12333, via conference call, July 31, 2008.

82. Senate Homeland Security and Governmental Affairs Committee, *Ten Years after 9/11: Is Intelligence Reform Working? Part II*, 112th Congress, 1st session (2011).

83. Interview with senior intelligence official, 2012.

84. Senate Select Committee on Intelligence, *Nomination of Leon Panetta to be Director of the Central Intelligence Agency: Part One*, 111th Congress, 1st session (2009) ("But before I get to those, I wasn't clear in your answer to Senator Levin. Is the DNI your boss or not? Mr. Panetta: The DNI is my boss. He's a person I respond to.").

85. Senate Select Committee on Intelligence, *Hearing on the Nomination of Leon Panetta to be the Director of the Central Intelligence Agency: Part Two*, 111th Congress, 1st session (2009).

86. Melissa Kronfeld, "New Intelligence Chief Celebrates Five Years," *GSN*, April 22, 2010.

87. Dennis Blair, *Remarks and Q&A at a National Security Task Force*, U.S. Chamber of Commerce, Washington, DC, July 22, 2009.

88. E-mail from Dennis Blair, November 20, 2012.

89. Mark Mazzetti, "Turf Battles on Intelligence Pose Test for Spy Chiefs," *New York Times*, June 9, 2009.

90. Ibid.

91. Dennis Blair, "Intelligence Reform," 2011 (unpublished).

92. Senate Homeland Security and Governmental Affairs Committee, *Hearing on Intelligence Overhaul*, 112th Congress, 1st session (2011).

93. Karen DeYoung, "Obama to Get Report on Intelligence Breakdown: Agencies Didn't Share or Flag Information on Man Accused in Attempted Plane Bombing," *Washington Post*, December 31, 2009.

94. David Ignatius, "Dennis Blair Erred—But He Had an Impossible Job," *Washington Post*, May 20, 2010.

95. John Negroponte, interview by Deborah Amos, *Morning Edition*, NPR, January 13, 2010.

96. Blair, "Intelligence Reform."

97. E-mail from Dennis Blair, November 20, 2012.

98. David Ignatius, "Duel of the Spy Chiefs," *Washington Post*, June 11, 2009.

99. Senate Homeland Security and Governmental Affairs Committee, *Hearing on Implementation of 9/11 Commission Recommendations*, 111th Congress, 2d session (2010).

Epilogue

1. See discussion at Senate Homeland Security and Governmental Affairs Committee, *Hearing on Assessing America's Counterterrorism Capabilities*, 108th Congress, 2d session (2004).

2. Silberman et al., *Commission on the Intelligence Capabilities of the United States on Regarding Weapons of Mass Destruction*, 314.

3. Patrick C. Neary, "The Post 9/11 Intelligence Community, Intelligence Reform, 2001–2009: Requiescat in Pace?," *Center for the Studies in Intelligence* 54, no. 1 (March 2010): 1–16.

4. Interview with Steve Cambone, October 5, 2012, Washington, DC.

5. Senate Select Committee on Intelligence, *Hearing on Nomination of Ambassador John Negroponte to be Director of National Intelligence*, 109th Congress, 1st session (2005).

6. John Negroponte, speaking at DNI Headquarters, "Intelligence Reform Progress Report," January 19, 2007.

7. Bipartisan Policy Center, "State of Intelligence Reform Conference: Summary of Proceedings," April 6, 2010, http://bipartisanpolicy.org/sites/default/files/Summary%20 of%20Intel%20Conference%20for%20Release%20051910.pdf.

8. John Negroponte, Joint Military Intelligence College Conference, "A Vision for Intelligence in a Time of Change," September 29, 2005.

9. Gordon Lederman, "Making Intelligence Reform Work," *The American Interest* 4 no. 4 (Spring 2009): 27.

10. Interview with Steve Hadley, July 5, 2012, Washington, DC.

11. Interview with Michael McConnell, 2010, Washington, DC.

12. Michael Hayden, "The State of the Craft: Is Intelligence Reform Working?," *World Affairs* (September/October 2010), http://www.worldaffairsjournal.org/articles/2010 -SeptOct/full-Hayden-SO-2010.html.

13. See Executive Order 12333, United States Intelligence Activities, December 4, 1981 (as amended by Executive Orders 13284 [2003], 13355 [2004] and 13470 [2008]), Part 1.3 (b)(1).

14. "The value added of [NCTC] to its customers is not universally understood … overlapping authorities in the counterterrorism system—real and perceived—have inhibited planning and operations." Robert Kravinsky et al., *Toward Integrating Complex National Missions: Lessons from the National Counterterrorism Center's Directorate of Intelligence* (Washington: Project on National Security Reform, 2010), xv; "Departments and agencies interpret their counterterrorism responsibilities largely based on their individual statues, histories, bureaucratic cultures, and current leadership. Those departments and agencies are not accountable to [NCTC] and there is insufficient incentive for departments and agencies to participate in and fully support the interagency integration processes at [NCTC]." Ibid., 113; and Senate Homeland Security and Governmental Affairs Committee, *Statement of Rick Nelson on the Lessons and Implications of the Christmas Day Attacks: Intelligence Reform and Interagency Integration*, 111th Congress, 2d session (2010).

15. John Bansemer, "Intelligence Reform: A Question of Balance," paper, Program on Information Resource Policy, Harvard University, May 2005, 71.

16. Senate Select Committee on Intelligence, *Hearing on Reform of the United States Intelligence Community*, 108th Congress, 2d session (2004).

17. House Permanent Select Committee on Intelligence, *Hearing on DNI Status*, 109th Congress, 1st session (2005).

18. Senate Armed Services Committee, *Hearing on Security Threats to the United States*, 109th Congress, 2d session (2006).

19. Joint Hearing of the House (Select) Intelligence Committee and Senate (Select) Intelligence Committee Subject: *"The State of Intelligence Reform 10 Years After 9/11"* Chairs: Representative Mike Rogers (R-MI) and Senator Dianne Feinstein (D-CA); Witnesses: Director of National Intelligence James Clapper; Central Intelligence Agency Director David Petraeus, September 13, 2011.

20. House Permanent Select Committee on Intelligence, *Hearing on DNI Status*, 109th Congress, 1st session (2005).

21. Ibid.

22. Senate Homeland Security and Governmental Affairs Committee, *Hearing on Ensuring the U.S. Intelligence Community Supports Homeland Defense and Departmental Needs*, 108th Congress, 2d session (2004).

23. See generally, Larry Kindsvater, *Intelligence Integration: Impossible Under the Present System, Building Strategic Concepts for the Intelligence Enterprise* (Washington: ODNI, 2009).

24. Bansemer, "Intelligence Reform: A Question of Balance," 75.

25. Ibid.

26. Interview with Robert Gates, April 19, 2012, Washington, DC.

27. National Commission on Terrorist Attacks upon the United States, *Statement of Richard Shelby*, 108th Congress, 1st session (2003).

28. Interview with Robert Gates, April 19, 2012, Washington, DC.

29. IRTPA, Section 1014.

30. Senate Homeland Security and Governmental Affairs Committee, *Hearing on Intelligence Overhaul*, 112th Congress, 1st session (2011).

31. See generally David Shedd, speaking at Bipartisan Policy Center, "State of Intelligence Reform Conference," April 6, 2012.

32. Robert M. Gates, "Problem and Fixes," 2005 (unpublished).

33. Kindsvater, *Intelligence Integration*.

34. John McLaughlin, interview by Charlie Rose, *Charlie Rose Show*, PBS, January 9, 2009.

35. Mark Lowenthal, interview by Charlie Rose, *Charlie Rose Show*, PBS, January 9, 2009.

36. Bipartisan Policy Center, "State of Intelligence Reform Conference: Summary of Proceedings," April 6, 2010, http://bipartisanpolicy.org/sites/default/files/Summary%20of%20Intel%20Conference%20for%20Release%20051910.pdf.

37. Senate Select Committee on Intelligence, *Hearing on DNI Authorities and Personnel Issues*, 110th Congress, 2d session (2008).

38. Susan Collins, speaking on the necessity of a national intelligence director, on December 8, 2004, 108th Congress, 2d session, *Congressional Record* Volume 150 Number 139, S11939, 11941.

39. Senate Homeland Security and Governmental Affairs Committee, *Hearing on Intelligence Overhaul*, 112th Congress, 1st session (2011).

40. Senate Homeland Security and Governmental Affairs Committee, *Hearing on Making America Safer: Examining the Recommendations of the 9/11 Commission*, 108th Congress, 2d session (2004).

41. House Permanent Select Committee on Intelligence, *Hearing on DNI Status*, 109th Congress, 1st session (2005).

42. "Q&A: John Negroponte."

43. John Banusiewicz, "Gates Calls Clapper Right Choice for Top Intel Post," *American Forces Press*, June 6, 2010.

44. Interview with Peter Hoekstra, November 20, 2010, Washington, DC.

45. Senate Select Committee on Intelligence, *Nomination of Lieutenant General James Clapper, Jr., USAF, Ret., to Be Director of National Intelligence*, 111th Congress, 2d session (2010); interview with Steve Hadley, December 17, 2009, Washington, DC.

46. Jane Harman, speaking at Bipartisan Policy Center, "State of Intelligence Reform Conference," April 6, 2012.

47. Senate Homeland Security and Governmental Affairs Committee, *Hearing on Intelligence Overhaul*, 112th Congress, 1st session (2011).

48. Interview with John Negroponte, June 11, 2012, Washington, DC.

49. John Negroponte, interview by Neal Conan, *Talk of the Nation*, NPR, June 15, 2010.

50. David Ignatius, interview by Charlie Rose, *Charlie Rose Show*, PBS, January 9, 2009.

51. Senate Armed Services Committee, *Hearing on Implications of Defense and Military Operations of Proposals to Reorganize the United States Intelligence Community*, 108th Congress, 2d session (2004).

52. Blair, "Intelligence Reform."

53. Ignatius, "Dennis Blair Erred—But He Had an Impossible Job."

54. Senate Select Committee on Intelligence, *Nomination of Lieutenant General James Clapper, Jr., USAF, Ret., to Be Director of National Intelligence*, 111th Congress, 2d session (2010).

55. John McLaughlin, interview by Charlie Rose, *Charlie Rose Show*, PBS, January 9, 2009.

56. David Ignatius, interview by Charlie Rose, *Charlie Rose Show*, PBS, January 9, 2009.

57. Mark Lowenthal, interview by Charlie Rose, *Charlie Rose Show*, PBS, January 9, 2009.

58. Michael McConnell, speaking at Bipartisan Policy Center, "State of Intelligence Reform Conference," April 6, 2012.

59. Dennis Blair, "Intelligence Reform," 2011 (unpublished).

60. Michael Hayden, speaking at Bipartisan Policy Center, "State of Intelligence Reform Conference," April 6, 2012.

61. Senate Homeland Security and Governmental Affairs Committee, *Hearing on Ten Year Review of 9/11 Counterterrorism Reforms*, 112th Congress, 1st session (2011).

62. Thomas Fingar, remarks at Intelligence and National Security Alliance Conference, September 4, 2008.

63. Bipartisan Policy Center, "State of Intelligence Reform Conference: Summary of Proceedings," April 6, 2010, http://bipartisanpolicy.org/sites/default/files/Summary%20of%20Intel%20Conference%20for%20Release%20051910.pdf.

64. James Clapper, *Remarks and Q&A at GEOINT*, November 2, 2010, New Orleans, LA.

65. Bipartisan Policy Center, "State of Intelligence Reform Conference: Summary of Proceedings," April 6, 2010.

66. Senate Homeland Security and Governmental Affairs Committee, *Hearing on Ten Year Review of 9/11 Counterterrorism Reforms*, 112th Congress, 1st session (2011).

67. E-mail from Dennis Blair, November 20, 2012.

68. Senate Homeland Security and Governmental Affairs Committee, *Hearing on the Lessons and Implications of the Christmas Day Attacks: Focusing on the Attempted Bombing Incident on Flight 253 to Detroit (Part Two)*, 111th Congress, 2d session (2010).

69. House Permanent Select Committee on Intelligence, *Hearing on the State of Intelligence Reform 10 Years after 9/11*, 112th Congress, 1st session (2011).

70. Ibid.

71. Interview with Robert Gates, April 19, 2012, Washington, DC.

72. Senate Select Committee on Intelligence, *Hearing on Nomination of Ambassador John Negroponte to be Director of National Intelligence*, 109th Congress, 1st session (2005).

73. Interview with Steve Hadley, July 5, 2012, Washington, DC.

Bibliography

ABC News Transcripts. *Special Report Introduction*. July 22, 2004.

Alexander, Lamar. Speaking on Ted Stevens, on June 4, 2007. 110th Congress, 1st session. *Congressional Record* Volume 153 Number 88, S6996-7001.

Allen, Jonathan. "No Mercy: Dead End in House for Certain Senators' Bills?" *CQ Today*, November 17, 2004.

Aspin, Les, et al. "The Evolution of the U.S. Intelligence Community—An Historical Overview." In *Preparing for the 21st Century: An Appraisal of U.S. Intelligence*. Washington: Featured Commission, 1996.

Bansemer, John. "Intelligence Reform: A Question of Balance." Paper, Program on Information Resource Policy, Harvard University. May 2005.

Banusiewicz, John. "Gates Calls Clapper Right Choice for Top Intel Post." *American Forces Press*, June 6, 2010.

Barger, Deborah G. "The Passage of the Intelligence Reform and Terrorism Prevention Act of 2004: An Intelligence Officer's Perspective." *Studies in Intelligence* 53, no. 3 (September 2009), 1–13.

Bartlett, Dan. Interview by Charlie Rose. *Charlie Rose Show*. PBS. July 22, 2004.

Beach Jr., Chester Paul. Letter to Les Aspin. March 17, 1992.

Bellinger, John, to Michael Bopp. E-mail to Michael Allen on "Revised Comments on Bopp Analysis of House Offer." October 25, 2004.

———. Memorandum on the construct of the NCTC. August 12, 2004.

Ben-Veniste, Richard. E-mail to 9/11 Commission Public Discourse Project Board on "RE: Revised Analysis of Emerging Bills." September 28, 2004. Lee Hamilton's Papers, Indiana University, Bloomington, IN.

Bipartisan Policy Center. National Security Preparedness Group. *Has Intelligence Reform Made the Country Safer?*, April 7, 2010, Washington, DC.

Blair, Dennis. "Intelligence Reform." 2011 (unpublished).

———. Speaking at Bipartisan Policy Center. "State of Intelligence Reform Conference." April 6, 2012.

Bond, Christopher. Speaking on intelligence reform, on September 29, 2004. 108th Congress, 2d session. *Congressional Record* Volume 150, Issue 120, S9879-9881.

Boren, David, et al. Letter on guiding principles for intelligence reform, on September 21, 2004. 108th Congress, 2d session. *Congressional Record* Volume 150, Issue 114, S9428-9429.

Breitweiser, Kristen. Interview by Chris Matthews. *Hardball with Chris Matthews.* December 1, 2004.

———. *Wake-Up Call: The Political Education of a 9/11 Widow.* New York: Warner Books, 2006.

Brennan, John. "Is This Intelligence, We Added Players, but Lost Control of the Ball." *Washington Post*, November 20, 2005.

Bruemmer, Russell. "Intelligence Community Reorganization: Declining the Invitation to Struggle." *Yale Law Journal* 101 (1992): 853–65.

Bush, George W. *Bush Announces New Intel Chief.* February 17, 2005. http://www.washington post.com/wp-dyn/articles/A32210-2005Feb17.html.

———. *Joint News Conference with Prime Minister Martin of Canada.* November 30, 2004.

———. *Media Availability with President Ricardo Lagos of Chile.* November 21, 2004.

———. Memorandum to National Security Principals. Memorandum on draft intelligence reform legislation. September 13, 2004.

———. *President Holds Press Conference.* November 4, 2004. http://georgewbush-whitehouse .archives.gov/news/releases/2004/11/20041104-5.html.

———. *President's Weekly Radio Address.* July 24, 2004.

———. *Press Conference.* April 13, 2004.

———. Quoted in Stephen Hadley's notes. July 24, 2004. Bush Presidential Library, Dallas, TX.

———. "Section Four," in *Legislative Submission to Congress.* September 16, 2004.

———. "Statement of Administration Policy: H.R. 10 - 9/11 Recommendations Implementation Act." October 7, 2004.

———. "Statement of Administration Policy: H.R. 4628 - Intelligence Authorization Act for Fiscal Year 2003." July 24, 2002.

Byrd, Robert. Speaking on intelligence reform, on October 4, 2004. 108th Congress, 2d session. *Congressional Record* Volume 150 Number 123, S10298-S10299.

Card, Andrew. *Press Briefing.* July 30, 2004.

———. *White House Press Briefing.* August 2, 2004.

CBS News Transcripts. Release of the Final 9-11 Commission Report. July 22, 2004.

Cheney, Richard. Letter to Les Aspin. March 17, 1992.

Childress, Kristin, et al. *Commission: Possible, Lessons Learned from the 9/11 and WMD Commissions.* College Station, TX: Bush School of Government and Public Service.

CIA. "DCI Tenet Announces Appointment of David Kay as Special Advisor." June 11, 2003. https://www.cia.gov/news-information/press-releases-statements/press-release -archive-2003/pr06112003.htm.

CIA History Staff. *Central Intelligence: Origin and Evolution*. Edited by Michael Warner. Washington: Center for the Study of Intelligence, 2001.

Clapper Jr., James R. *A Proposed Restructuring of the Intelligence Community*. Cambridge, MA: Program on Information Resources Policy at Harvard University, January 1997.

———. *Remarks and Q&A at GEOINT*. November 2, 2010. New Orleans, LA.

———. "The Role of Defense in Shaping U.S. Intelligence Reform." In *The Oxford Handbook of National Security Intelligence*, ed. Loch Johnson, 629–40. New York: Oxford University Press, 2010.

Cloud, David S., and Scot J. Paltrow. "Tenet's CIA Exit Will Spur Debate on Spy Agencies: Chief's Departure Comes Ahead of Critical Reports on Intelligence Gathering." *Wall Street Journal*, June 4, 2004.

Clymer, Adam. "Ted Stevens, 86, Helped Shape Alaska in 40 Years in Senate." *New York Times*, August 11, 2010.

Cohen, William. Interview by Chris Matthews. *Hardball with Chris Matthews*. MSNBC. March 25, 2004.

Collins, Susan. "Compromise Clears Way for Intel Vote." *National Journal*, December 7, 2004.

———. "Conferees Making Little Progress on Intelligence Overhaul." *National Journal*, October 27, 2004.

———. "House GOP Gains May Hurt Intel Overhaul Bill Prospects." *National Journal*, November 4, 2004.

———. "Intelligence Bill Supporters Seek Options, Gauge Support." *National Journal*, November 22, 2004.

———. Interview by Lawrence Kudlow and Jim Cramer. *Kudlow and Cramer*. CNBC. July 22, 2004.

———. "The Myers Letter." *National Journal*, October 28, 2004.

———. *News Teleconference on the House and Senate Intelligence Reform Bills Negotiations with Joseph Lieberman, Susan Collins, Jane Harman, and Pete Hoekstra*, October 29, 2004.

———. "Pre-Election Vote on Intel Overhaul Bill Increasingly Likely." *National Journal*, October 26, 2004.

———. *Press Conference*. December 7, 2004.

———. Speaking on the necessity of a national intelligence director, on December 8, 2004. 108th Congress, 2d session. *Congressional Record* Volume 150 Number 139, S11941.

———. Speech to Oxford Hills Chamber of Commerce. February 4, 2005. Congress Daily. "Collins Stands Her Ground in 9/11 Fight." *National Journal*, October 5, 2004.

Curtius, Mary. "Intelligence Bill Struck an Armed Services Reef." *Los Angeles Times*, November 22, 2004.

———. "Intelligence Reform Bill Hits a Wall in Congress." *Los Angeles Times*, October 30, 2004.

———. "Senate to Wrestle Over New Intelligence Post's Powers." *Los Angeles Times*, September 28, 2004.

———. "Spy Reform Bill's Guiding Light is Up to the Task." *Los Angeles Times*, October 5, 2004.

———. "White House Intervenes on Behalf of Intelligence Bill." *Los Angeles Times*, November 17, 2004.

Devine, Jack. "An Intelligence Reform Reality Check." *Washington Post*, February 18, 2008.

DeWine, Michael. Speaking on intelligence reform, on September 29, 2004. 108th Congress, 2d session. *Congressional Record* Volume 150, Issue 120, S9879-9881.

DeYoung, Karen. "Obama to Get Report on Intelligence Breakdown: Agencies Didn't Share or Flag Information on Man Accused in Attempted Plane Bombing." *Washington Post*, December 31, 2009.

Donnelly, John M., Martin Kady II, and Jonathan Allen. "Fate of Intelligence Overhaul Hinges on Troop Safety." *CQ Today*, November 24, 2004.

Donnelly, Thomas. "Intelligent Intelligence Reform." *AEI*, November 25, 2004. http://www.aei.org/article/foreign-and-defense-policy/intelligent-intelligence-reform/.

Douglass, Linda. Interview by George Stephanopoulos. *This Week with George Stephanopoulos*. ABC. November 21, 2004.

Duffy, Trent. *White House News Briefing Aboard Air Force One En Route to California*. December 7, 2004.

Eckert, Beverly. *Representatives Chris Shays and Carolyn Maloney and Members of the 9/11 Family Steering Committee News Conference*. November 30, 2004.

Eggen, Dan, and Helen Dewar. "Leaders Pick Up Urgency of 9/11 Panel, Congress and Bush Vow to Speed Reforms." *Washington Post*, July 24, 2004.

Eisenberg, Daniel. "Bush's New Intelligence Czar." *Time*, February 21, 2005.

Ermath, Fritz. *Intelligence for a New Era in American Foreign Policy*. Charlottesville, VA: Center for the Study of Intelligence, September 2003.

Falkenrath, Richard. "The 9/11 Commission Report." *International Security* (Winter 2004/05): 170–90.

Felzenberg, Al. *Governor Tom Kean: From the New Jersey Statehouse to the 9/11 Commission*. Piscataway: University of Rutgers Press, 2006.

Ferraro, Thomas. "Bush Reasserts Himself as Force for Second Term." *Reuters*, December 9, 2004.

Fielding, Fred. E-mail to Board of 9/11 Discourse Project. November 20, 2004. Lee Hamilton's Papers, Indiana University, Bloomington, IN.

Ford, Chris. "The Bin Laden Raid: This Isn't your Father's CIA." August 4, 2011, http://newparadigmsforum/NPFtestsite/?_868.

Franks, Trent. *Press Conference with Duncan Hunter*. December 6, 2004.

Gaffney, Frank, and Peter Gadiel. *9/11 Families for a Secure America News Conference*. November 30, 2004.

Garthoff, Douglas. *Directors of Central Intelligence as Leaders of the U.S. Intelligence Community 1946–2005*. Washington: GPO, 2005.

Gates, Robert. E-mail to Andy Card. January 11, 2005.

———. "Problem and Fixes." 2005 (unpublished).

———. "Racing to Ruin the CIA." *New York Times*, June 8, 2004.

Goodman, Allan, et al. *In From the Cold: The Report of the Twentieth Century Fund Task Force on the Future of U.S. Intelligence*. Washington: Brookings Institution Press, 1996.

Gorelick, Jamie. E-mail to Board of 9/11 Commission Public Discourse Project on "re: Hastert Comments on the Conferees Meeting on 9/11 Recommendations Implementation Act." October 18, 2004. Lee Hamilton's Papers, Indiana University, Bloomington, IN.

———. E-mail to Board of 9/11 Commission Public Discourse Project on "re: Statement by Tom and Lee." November 20, 2004. Lee Hamilton's Papers, Indiana University, Bloomington, IN.

———. Minutes of 9/11 Commission Meeting. June 14, 2004. National Archives.

———. News Conference with Members of the National Commission on Terrorist Attacks upon the United States to Release Their Final Report. *Federal News Service*. July 22, 2004.

Gorman, Siobhan. "Wanted: Spy Chief." *National Journal*, June 12, 2004.

Graham, Bob. Speaking on intelligence lessons, on February 3, 2004. 108th Congress, 2d session. *Congressional Record* Volume 150, Number 11, S385.

———. Speaking on intelligence reform, on November 20, 2004. 108th Congress, 2d session. *Congressional Record* Volume 150, Number 135, S11736.

Hamilton, Lee. Minutes of 9/11 Commission meeting. June 14, 2004. National Archives.

———. News Conference with Members of the National Commission on Terrorist Attacks upon the United States to Release Their Final Report. Federal News Service. July 22, 2004.

Hamilton, Lee, and Thomas Kean. *Press Conference*. November 30, 2004.

Hamilton, William. "Bush Began to Plan War Three Months after 9/11." *Washington Post*, April 17, 2004.

Hamre, John. "A Better Way to Improve Intelligence; The National Director Should Oversee Only the Agencies That Gather Data." *Washington Post*, August 9, 2004.

Harman, Jane. "Congresswoman Harman Urges President Bush to Take Immediate Action to Improve Intelligence, Introduces Legislative Package." *Press Release*, April 1, 2004.

———. "Five-Point Plan for Intelligence Community Reform." Speech at the American Enterprise Institute, Washington, DC, March 5, 2004. http://www.fas.org/irp/congress/2004_cr/harman030504.html.

———. Interview by Chris Wallace. *Fox News Sunday*. Fox News. November 21, 2004.

———. Interview by Wolf Blitzer. *Wolf Blitzer Reports*. CNN. July 22, 2004.

———. *Press Conference with Senators Lieberman and Collins, and Congressman Hoekstra*. November 20, 2004.

———. Speaking at the Bipartisan Policy Center. "State of Intelligence Reform Conference." April 6, 2012.

Hastert, Dennis. *Press Conference with Roy Blunt, Chris Cox, Deborah Pryce, Tom Delay, Eric Cantor, Duncan Hunter, Porter Goss*. July 22, 2004.

Hayden, Michael. Speaking at the Bipartisan Policy Center. "State of Intelligence Reform Conference." April 6, 2012.

———. "The State of the Craft: Is Intelligence Reform Working?" *World Affairs* (September/October 2010). http://www.worldaffairsjournal.org/articles/2010-SeptOct/full-Hayden-SO-2010.html.

Hedley, John. "A Colloquium: The IC - Is it Broken, How to Fix It." Winter 1994/1995. https://www.cia.gov/library/center-for-the-study-of-intelligence/csi-publications/csi-studies/studies/96unclass/hedley.htm#author1.

Hoekstra, Peter. Letter to George W. Bush. May 18, 2006.

———. *Press Conference with Senator Collins, Senator Lieberman, Congresswoman Harman, and Congressman Hoekstra*. November 20, 2004.

———. Speaking on the conference report on S. 2845, on December 20, 2004. 108th Congress, 2d session. *Congressional Record - Extension of Remarks*, E2209-E2210.

Hook, Janet. "Bush on Notice Despite Win in Congress." *Los Angeles Times*, December 9, 2004.

Hoyer, Steny. "House Republicans Scuttle Bipartisan Intelligence Reform." *Press Release*, November 20, 2004.

Hulse, Carl. "Democrats Press Strategy on 9/11 Report." *New York Times*, August 10, 2004.

———. "A Senator Whom Colleagues Are Hesitant to Cross." *New York Times*, October 25, 2003.

Hunter, Duncan. *Christian Science Monitor Breakfast*. December 2, 2004.

———. Interview with Duncan Hunter. *Fox News*. November 22, 2004.

———. Letter to Dennis Hastert on "Bottom Line Requirements." December 2, 2004.

———. *News Conference on Intelligence Reform Bill*. December 6, 2004.

Hurley, Michael. E-mail to 9/11 Commission Public Discourse Project Board on "Conference Committee Afternoon Update." October 22, 2004. Lee Hamilton's Papers, Indiana University, Bloomington, IN.

Ignatius, David. "The Book on Terror." *Washington Post*, August 1, 2004.

———. "Dennis Blair Erred—But He Had an Impossible Job." *Washington Post*, May 20, 2010.

———. "Duel of the Spy Chiefs." *Washington Post*, June 11, 2009.

———. Interview by Charlie Rose. *Charlie Rose Show*. PBS. January 9, 2009.

Jansen, Bart. "Reform's Failure is 'Crushing' to Collins." *Portland Press/Herald Marine Sunday Telegram*, November 21, 2004.

Jehl, Douglas. "The Spymaster Question." *New York Times*, December 8, 2004.

Johns, Joe. Interview by Lou Dobbs. *Lou Dobbs Tonight*. November 19, 2004.

Kady II, Martin. "Bush, GOP Leaders Quell Rebellion on Intelligence." *CQ Today*, December 6, 2004.

———. "A Centrist Seeking the Middle on September 11 Overhaul." *CQ Today*, September 8, 2004.

———. "House GOP Conferees Skeptical About Creating Powerful Intelligence Director." *CQ Today*, October 12, 2004.

———. "Intelligence Bill Falls Short Again, Put Off Until December." *CQ Today*, November 21, 2004.

———. "Intelligence Conferees Battle Clock, Each Other." *CQ Today*, November 16, 2004.

———. "Uproar Over Intelligence Bill Puts Hunter in the Bull's-Eye." *CQ Weekly*, November 27, 2004.

Kady II, Martin, and Jonathan Allen. "Hunter Placated as Bush Renews Plea for Intelligence Bill Vote." *CQ Today*, December 6, 2004.

Kaplan, Robert. "Five Days in Fallujah." *Atlantic*, July/August 2004.

Kean, Thomas. Interview by Tim Russert. *Meet the Press*. NBC. November 28, 2004.

———. Interview by Tom Brokaw. *NBC Nightly News*. NBC. November 28, 2004.

———. *News Conference with Lee Hamilton*. November 30, 2004.

———. *Without Precedent: The Inside Story of the 9/11 Commission*. New York: Knopf, 2006.

Kean, Thomas, and Lee Hamilton. Letter to Susan Collins. October 20, 2004.

Kean, Thomas, and Lee Hamilton to 9/11 Commissioners. Memorandum on agenda for the December 8th Commission meeting. December 3, 2003.

Kean, Thomas, et al. *The 9/11 Commission Report: Final Report of the National Commission on Terrorist Attacks upon the United States*. New York: W. W. Norton & Company, 2004.

Kelly, Mary Louise. "Fearing Bloating, House Cuts Some Spy Funds." NPR, April 5, 2006.

Kerrey, Bob. E-mail to Public Discourse Project Board on "Conference." October 24, 2004. Lee Hamilton's Papers, Indiana University, Bloomington, IN.

———. Minutes of 9/11 Commission meeting. June 14, 2004. National Archives. Kerry, John. Quoted on Lou Dobbs Tonight. CNN. July 22, 2004.

———. Speech in Norfolk, VA, CNN, July 28, 2004. http://archives.cnn.com/TRANSCRIPTS/0407/28/se.03.html.

———. "Statement on the 9/11 Commission Report. July 22, 2004. Detroit, MI.

Kindsvater, Larry. *Intelligence Integration: Impossible under the Present System, Building Strategic Concepts for the Intelligence Enterprise*. Washington: ODNI, 2009.

Klamper, Amy. "Angry Stevens Threatens to Tie Up 9/11 Overhaul Bill." *National Journal*, October 5, 2004.

Kojm, Chris. E-mail to 9/11 Public Discourse Project Board on "RE: Today's Senate Action." October 8, 2004. Lee Hamilton's Papers, Indiana University, Bloomington, IN.

———. E-mail to 9/11 Public Discourse Project Board on "Perils of Pauline." November 18, 2004. Lee Hamilton's Papers, Indiana University, Bloomington, IN.

———. E-mail to 9/11 Public Discourse Project Board on "RE: Congress Daily PM." November 19, 2004. Lee Hamilton's Paper, Indiana University, Bloomington, IN.

———. E-mail to 9/11 Public Discourse Project Board on "Statement by Tom and Lee." November 20, 2004. Lee Hamilton's Papers, Indiana University, Bloomington, IN.

———. E-mail to 9/11 Public Discourse Project Board. December 6, 2004. Lee Hamilton's Papers, Indiana University, Bloomington, IN.

———. E-mail to Lee Hamilton and Tom Kean on "Late afternoon update." October 26, 2004. Lee Hamilton's Papers, University of Indiana.

———. E-mail to Lee Hamilton and Tom Kean on "FOR IMMEDIATE ATTENTION—conference committee in dire straits." October 27, 2004. Lee Hamilton's Papers, Indiana University.

———. E-mail to Lee Hamilton on "Kean Conversation with Collins." November 5, 2004. Lee Hamilton's Papers, Indiana University, Bloomington, IN.

———. E-mail to Lee Hamilton and Tom Kean on "FW: Senate offer – Status of the conference." November 10, 2004. Lee Hamilton's Papers, University of Indiana.

———. E-mail to Tom Kean and Lee Hamilton on "Update—report on PZ's meeting with Scott Palmer." November 9, 2004. Lee Hamilton's Papers, Indiana University, Bloomington, IN.

Lautenberg, Frank. Speaking on intelligence reform, on November 20, 2004. 108th Congress, 2d session. *Congressional Record* Volume 150, Number 135, S11795.

Lederman, Gordon. "Making Intelligence Reform Work." *The American Interest* 4, no. 4 (Spring 2009): 23–31.

Lehman, John. *American Morning*. CNN, November 22, 2004.

———. E-mail to 9/11 Commission Public Discourse Project Board on "RE: Draft Statement." September 29, 2004. Lee Hamilton's Papers, Indiana University, Bloomington, IN.

———. E-mail to 9/11 Commission Public Discourse Project Board on "RE: More Analysis of Latest House Proposal." October 24, 2004. Lee Hamilton's Papers, Indiana University, Bloomington, IN.

———. "Getting Spy Reform Wrong" *Washington Post*, November 15, 2006.

———. Interview by Brit Hume. *Special Report with Brit Hume*. Fox. July 23, 2004.

———. Quoted in Wolf Blitzer Reports. CNN. July 22, 2004.

———. Speaking at Bipartisan Policy Center. "Ten Years After: The Status on National Security and Implementation of the 9/11 Commission's Recommendations." August 31, 2012.

———. "USS *Cole*: An Act of War." *Washington Post*, October 15, 2000.

Lehman, John, and Bob Kerrey. "Safety in Intelligence." *Wall Street Journal*, November 30, 2004.

Lemack, Carie. "The Journey to September 12th: A 9/11 Victim's Experiences with the Press, the President, and Congress." *Studies in Conflict and Terrorism* 30 no. 9 (2007): 739–66.

Levin, Carl. Interview by George Stephanopoulos. *This Week with George Stephanopoulos*. ABC. November 21, 2004.

Lieberman, Joseph. News Conference with Members of the National Commission on Terrorist Attacks upon the United States to Release Their Final Report. *Federal News Service*. July 22, 2004.

———. *News Teleconference on the House and Senate Intelligence Reform Bills Negotiations with Joseph Lieberman, Susan Collins, Jane Harman, and Pete Hoekstra*. October 29, 2004.

———. *Press Conference with Senator Collins, Senator Lieberman, Congresswoman Harman, and Congressman Hoekstra*. November 20, 2004.

———. Speaking on intelligence reform, on December 8, 2004. 108th Congress, 2d session. *Congressional Record*, Volume 150, Number 139, S11969.

———. Speaking on the necessity of a national intelligence director, on October 4, 2004. 108th Congress, 2d session. *Congressional Record* Volume 150 Number 123, S10318-S10319.

———. Speaking on the necessity of a national intelligence director, on December 8, 2004. 108th Congress, 2d session. *Congressional Record* Volume 150 Number 139, S11941.

Lott, Trent. Interview by George Stephanopoulos. *This Week with George Stephanopoulos*. ABC. July 12, 2004.

Lowenthal, Mark. Interview by Charlie Rose. *Charlie Rose Show*. PBS. January 9, 2009.

Maloney, Carolyn. *Representatives Chris Shays and Carolyn Maloney and Members of the 9/11 Family Steering Committee News Conference*. November 30, 2004.

May, Ernest. "Intelligence: Backing Into the Future." *Foreign Affairs* (Summer 1992): 63–72.

———. "When Government Writes History" *History News Network*, June 24, 2005. http://hnn.us/articles/11972.html.

Mazzetti, Mark. "Turf Battles on Intelligence Post Test for Spy Chiefs." *New York Times*, July 9, 2009.

McCain, John. Interview by Tim Russert. *Meet the Press*. November 21, 2004.

———. News Conference with Members of the National Commission on Terrorist Attacks upon the United States to Release Their Final Report. *Federal News Service*. July 22, 2004.

McConnell, Michael. Speaking at the Bipartisan Policy Center. "State of Intelligence Reform Conference." April 6, 2012.

McConnell, Mitch. Speaking on Ted Stevens, on November 20, 2008. 110th Congress, 2d session. *Congressional Record* Volume 154 Number 177 Cong. Record, S10689-S10703.

McCurdy, Dave. "Glasnost for the CIA." *Foreign Affairs* (January/February 1994): 125–40.

McLaughlin, John. "The CIA is No 'Rogue' Agency." *Washington Post*, November 24, 2004.

———. Interview by Charlie Rose. *Charlie Rose Show*. PBS. January 9, 2009.

———. Interview by Chris Wallace, *Fox News Sunday*. Fox. July 18, 2004. http://www.foxnews.com/story/0,2933,125998,00.html.

———. Letter to President Bush. August 20, 2004.

———. *Remarks at Business Executives for National Security*. June 23, 2004. https://www.cia.gov/news-information/speeches-testimony/2004/ddci_speech_06242004.html.

Mitchell, Alison. "Traces of Terror: Congress; Daschle is Seeking a Special Inquiry on September 11 Attack." *New York Times*, May 22, 2002.

Montgomery, David. "9-11 Victims' Families Assail Congress' Failure on Intelligence Reform." *Knight Ridder Newspapers*, November 22, 2004.

Murkowski, Lisa. Speaking on Ted Stevens, on November 20, 2008. 110th Congress, 2d session. *Congressional Record* Volume 154 Number 177 Cong. Record, S10687-S10703.

Myers, Richard. *Christian Science Monitor Breakfast*. December 2, 2004.

———. *Eyes on the Horizon: Serving on the Front Lines of National Security*. Threshold Editions, 2009.

———. Letter to Duncan Hunter. October 21, 2004.

———. *Press Conference with Secretary Rumsfeld*. November 23, 2004. http://www.fas.org/irp/news/2004/11/dod112304.html.

Nagourney, Adam. "The 2004 Campaign: The Massachusetts Senator; Kerry Sees Hope of Gaining Edge on Terror Issue." *New York Times*, July 25, 2004.

National Security Council to George W. Bush. Draft Memorandum on National Intelligence Director Organization Options. August 19, 2004.

National Security Council to National Security Principals. Memorandum on the Construct of the NCTC. August 14, 2004.

———. Memorandum on Draft Intelligence Reform Legislation. September 13, 2004.

Neary, Patrick C. "The Post 9/11 Intelligence Community, Intelligence Reform, 2001–2009: Requiescat in Pace?" *Center for the Studies in Intelligence* 54, no. 1 (2010): 1–16.

Negroponte, John. Interview by Deborah Amos. *Morning Edition*. NPR. January 13, 2010.

———. Interview by Neal Conan. *Talk of the Nation*. NPR. June 15, 2010.

———. Joint Military Intelligence College Conference. "A Vision for Intelligence in a Time of Change." September 29, 2005.

———. Speaking at DNI Headquarters. "Intelligence Reform Progress Report." January 19, 2007.

New York Times. "A Truly Lame Duck." November 23, 2004.

O'Hanlon, Michael. "Can the C.I.A. Really Be That Bad?" *New York Times*, July 13, 2004.

Ornstein, Norman. "Intel Reform Could Shed Light on Bush's Second-Term Approach." *Roll Call*, November 29, 2004.

Pillar, Paul. "Good Literature and Bad History: The 9/11 Commission's Tale of Strategic Intelligence." *Intelligence and National Security* 21, no. 6 (December 2006): 1022–44.

———. *Intelligence and U.S. Foreign Policy*. New York: Columbia University Press, 2011.

Pincus, Walter. "Intelligence Deal Remains Elusive." *Washington Post*, November 23, 2004.

——— . "Military Espionage Cuts Eyed." *Washington Post*, March 17, 1995.

Pincus, Walter, and Thomas E. Ricks. "Intelligence Bill Gets Fresh Bush Support." *Washington Post*, December 3, 2004.

Posner, Richard. "The 9/11 Report: A Dissent." *New York Times*, August 29, 2004.

Push, Stephen. *Alliance of Families of 9/11 Victims Holds News Conference*. September 9, 2002.

Ratnesar, Romesh. "Richard Clarke, at War with Himself." *Time*, March 25, 2004. http://www.time.com/time/nation/article/0,8599,604598,00.html.

Retaking the Strategic Initiative on Transnational Terrorism, A Team 2 Interim Report: Intelligence Issues for Commission Discussion, The 9/11 Commission Archives at the National Archives, Washington, DC.

Rice, Condoleezza, and Josh Bolten. Letter to Peter Hoekstra and Senator Susan Collins. October 18, 2004.

Ridge, Thomas, et al. Letter to Susan Collins and Carl Levin. April 13, 2004.

Roberts, Pat. Interview by Bob Schieffer. *Face the Nation*. CBS. August 22, 2004.

———. Speaking on Ted Stevens, on November 20, 2008. 110th Congress, 2d session. *Congressional Record* Volume 154 Number 177 Cong. Record, S10687-S10703.

———, et al. Letter to Susan Collins and Joseph Lieberman. September 20, 2004.

Rockefeller, John. Interview by George Stephanopoulos, *This Week with George Stephanopoulos*, ABC, November 21, 2004.

Roemer, Tim. "Additional Views of Congressman Tim Roemer." In *September 11 and the Imperative of Reform in the U.S. Intelligence Community*. December 10, 2002.

———. CBS News Transcripts, Release of the Final 9-11 Commission Report, July 22, 2004.

———. E-mail to 9/11 Commission Public Discourse Project Board on "House of Representatives and Limited Time to Act on Commission Recommendations." September 2, 2004. Lee Hamilton's Papers, Indiana University, Bloomington, IN.

———. E-mail to 9/11 Commission Public Discourse Project Board on "RE: Update on Conference Committee." October 21, 2004. Lee Hamilton's Papers, Indiana University, Bloomington, IN.

———. E-mail to 9/11 Commission Public Discourse Project Board. December 7, 2004. Lee Hamilton's Papers, Indiana University, Bloomington, IN.

———. Interview by Lou Dobbs. *Lou Dobbs Tonight*. CNN. April 14, 2004.

———. News Conference with Members of the National Commission on Terrorist Attacks upon the United States to Release Their Final Report. *Federal News Service.* July 22, 2004.

———. Speaking at Bipartisan Policy Center. "Ten Years After: The Status on National Security and Implementation of the 9/11 Commission's Recommendations." August 31, 2012.

Rumsfeld, Donald. *Press Conference.* November 23, 2004.

———, et al. *Report of the Commission to Assess the Ballistic Missile Threat to the United States.* Washington: GPO, 1998.

Rumsfeld, Donald, to Andrew Card Jr. Memorandum on Possible Talking Points. October 22, 2004.

Rumsfeld, Donald, to George W. Bush. Memorandum on Intelligence Issue. September 8, 2004.

———. Memorandum on Intelligence Reform Bill – Final Thoughts. September 15, 2004.

———. Memorandum on "Reform." September 11, 2004.

———. Memorandum Regarding 9/11 Commission Report. Bush Presidential Library. July 25, 2004.

Rumsfeld, Donald, to Steve Cambone. Memorandum on Intelligence Reform. October 2, 2002.

Russert, Tim. Interviewing Tom Kean and Lee Hamilton. *Meet the Press.* NBC. November 28, 2004.

Sanger, David. "August '01 Brief is Said to Warn of Attack Plans." *New York Times,* April 10, 2004.

———. "Intelligence: Why a Fix Is So Elusive." *New York Times,* August 15, 2004.

Schlesinger, James. *A Review of the Intelligence Community.* Report for President Nixon. March 10, 1971.

Sensenbrenner, Jim. Interview by George Stephanopoulos. *This Week with George Stephanopoulos.* ABC. November 28, 2004.

———. "Statement on 9/11 Bill." December 6, 2004. Lee Hamilton's Papers, Indiana University, Bloomington, IN.

Shelby, Richard. "Additional Views of Senator Richard C. Shelby." In *September 11 and the Imperative of Reform in the U.S. Intelligence Community.* December 10, 2002.

———. *Press Conference with Nancy Pelosi, Bob Graham, and Porter Goss on the Joint Inquiry into Intelligence Community Activities Before and After the Terrorist Attacks of September 11.* December 11, 2002.

Shenon, Philip. "9/11 Families Group Rebukes Bush for Impasse on Overhaul." *New York Times,* October 28, 2004.

———. "9/11 Family Members Put Backing Behind Senate Bill." *New York Times,* October 21, 2004.

———. "Agreement May Be Near on 9/11 Bill." *New York Times*, November 19, 2004.

———. "Bush Says He'll Seek to Revive Intelligence Bill House Blocked." *New York Times*, November 22, 2004.

———. *The Commission: The Uncensored History of the 9/11 Investigation*. New York: Twelve, 2008.

———. "Delays on 9/11 Bill Are Laid to Pentagon." *New York Times*, October 26, 2004.

———. "Key Aide to 9/11 Panel Praises Offer By House." *New York Times*, October 27, 2004.

———. "Negotiators See New Hope for Intelligence Bill." *New York Times*, November 8, 2004.

——— "Sept. 11 Commission Plans a Lobbying Campaign to Push Its Recommendations." *New York Times*, July 19, 2004.

Shenon, Philip, and Carl Hulse. "House Leadership Blocks Vote on Intelligence Bill." *New York Times*, November 21, 2004.

Silberman, Lawrence H., et al. *Commission on the Intelligence Capabilities of the United States on Regarding Weapons of Mass Destruction*. Washington, DC: Featured Commission Publications, 2005.

Starks, Tim. "Lost in the Reshuffle." *CQ Weekly*, May 5, 2008.

Stevens, Ted. Speaking on Susan Collins, on October 6, 2004. 108th Congress, 2d session. *Congressional Record*, Volume 150, Number 125, S10519.

Stevenson, Richard, and David Kirkpatrick. "Administration Moves to Regain Initiative on 9/11." *New York Times*, July 27, 2004.

Stolberg, Sheryl Gay. "Republicans Fight Off More Amendments to Spending Bill." *New York Times*, January 18, 2003.

Stuart, Douglas. *Creating the National Security State: A History of the Law That Transformed America*. Princeton, NJ: Princeton University Press, 2008.

Tama, Jordan. *Terrorism and National Security Reform: How Commissions Can Drive Change in Moments of Crisis*. Cambridge: Cambridge University Press, 2011.

Taylor, James, et al. *American Intelligence: A Framework for the Future*. Washington: CIA, 1975.

Tenet, George. *At the Center of the Storm: My Years at the CIA*. New York: HarperCollins, 2007.

———. DCI Remarks on Iraq's WMD Programs. February, 5, 2004. https://www.cia.gov/news-information/speeches-testimony/2004/tenet_georgetownspeech_02052004.html.

———. Letter to Porter J. Goss in response to the Intelligence Authorization Act for FY 2005. June 24, 2004.

Thompson, James. CBS News Transcripts, Release of the Final 9-11 Commission Report, July 22, 2004.

————. E-mail to 911 Public Discourse Project Board on "Re: Comments of Angry Senator re Chair/Vice Chair." October 4, 2004. Lee Hamilton's Papers, Indiana University, Bloomington, IN.

————. News Conference with Members of the National Commission on Terrorist Attacks upon the United States to Release Their Final Report. *Federal News Service.* July 22, 2004.

Tower, John, et al. *Report of the President's Special Review Board.* Washington: GPO, 1987.

Townsend, Fran. Interview by Jim Lehrer. *PBS Newshour.* PBS. August 2, 2004.

Troy, Thomas F. "The Quaintness of the U.S. Intelligence Community: Its Origin, Theory, and Problems." *Journal of Intelligence and Counterintelligence* II, no. II (1988): 245–66.

Truman, Harry. "Address on the Occasion of the Signing of the North Atlantic Treaty," April 4, 1949. http://www.trumanlibrary.org/calendar/viewpapers.php?pid=1062.

Turner, Stansfield. "Intelligence for a New World Order." *Foreign Affairs* (Fall 1991): 150–66.

United Press International. "Intel Reform Remains Stalled in Congress." December 2, 2004.

Updike, John. "The Great I Am." *New Yorker*, November 1, 2004.

U.S. Congress, on December 7, 2004, 108th Congress, 2d session, *Congressional Record*, Volume 150, Number 138, H11028.

————. Armed Services Committee. *Hearing on Future Worldwide Threats to U.S. National Security.* 108th Congress, 2d session (March 9, 2004).

————. Armed Services Committee. *Hearing on the Implications of the Recommendations of the 9/11 Commission on the Department of Defense.* 108th Congress, 2d session (August 11, 2004).

————. Armed Services Committee. *Hearing on United States Intelligence Reform.* 108th Congress, 2d session (August 10, 2004).

————. Armed Services Committee. *Mark-Up of H.R. 10: The National Security and Intelligence improvement Act of 2004.* 108th Congress, 2d session (September 29, 2004).

————. House-Senate Conference Committee. *Intelligence Reform Implementation Conference.* 108th Congress, 2d session (October 20, 2004).

————. *Joint Inquiry into Intelligence Community Activities Before and After the Terrorist Attacks of September 11.* GPO, 2004.

————. Joint Intelligence Committees. *Hearing on S. 2198 and S.421: To Reorganize the United States Intelligence Committee.* 102d Congress, 2d session (April 1, 1992).

————. Joint Intelligence Committees. *Joint Inquiry into Intelligence Community Activities Before and After the Terrorist Attacks of September 11: Seventh Public Hearing.* 107th Congress, 2d session (October 3, 2002).

————. Joint Intelligence Committees. *Joint Inquiry into Intelligence Community Activities Before and After the Terrorist Attacks of September 11: Ninth Public Hearing.* 107th Congress, 2d session (October 17, 2002).

————. Joint Intelligence Committees. *Joint Inquiry into Intelligence Community Activities Before and After the Terrorist Attacks of September 11: Second Public Hearing.* 107th Congress, 2d session (September 19, 2002).

————. National Commission on Terrorist Attacks upon the United States. *Eight Public Hearing: Regarding the Formulation and Conduct of U.S Counterterrorism Policy.* 108th Congress, 2d session (March 24, 2004).

————. National Commission on Terrorist Attacks upon the United States. *George Tenet: Written Statement for the Record before the National Commission on Terrorist Attacks upon the United States.* 108th Congress, 2d session (March 24, 2004).

————. National Commission on Terrorist Attacks upon the United States. *Hearing on Intelligence Oversight and the Joint Inquiry.* 108th Congress, 2d session (April 14, 2004).

————. National Commission on Terrorist Attacks upon the United States. *Hearing Regarding the Formulation and Conduct of U.S. Counterterrorism Policy.* 108th Congress, 2d session (April 8, 2004).

————. National Commission on Terrorist Attacks upon the United States. *Panel Four of the Eighth Public Hearing.* 108th Congress, 2d session (March 23, 2004).

————. National Commission on Terrorist Attacks upon the United States. *Part One of the Tenth Hearing: Law Enforcement and the Intelligence Community.* 108th Congress, 2d session (April 13, 2004).

————. National Commission on Terrorist Attacks upon the United States. *Press Conference.* November 30, 2004.

————. National Commission on Terrorist Attacks upon the United States. *Staff Statement #11: The Performance of the Intelligence Community.* 108th Congress, 2d session (April 14, 2004).

————. National Commission on Terrorist Attacks upon the United States. *Statement of Richard Shelby.* 108th Congress, 1st session (May 22, 2003).

U.S. House of Representatives. Armed Services Committee. *Hearing on the Fiscal Year 1993 Budget.* 102d Congress, 2d session (February 6, 1992).

————. *Final Vote Results for Roll Call 347,* 107th Congress, 2d session (July 25, 2002).

————. Homeland Security Committee. *Hearing on the President's Fiscal Year 2010 Budget Request for the Department of Homeland Security.* 111th Congress, 1st session (May 13, 2009).

————. Homeland Security Committee. *Towards a Paradigm for Homeland Security.* 108th Congress, 2d session (August 17, 2004).

————. National Security Committee. *Hearing on H.R. 3237: The Intelligence Community Act.* 104th Congress, 2d session (July 11, 1996).

————. Permanent Select Committee on Intelligence. *Hearing on 9/11 Commission Findings: Sufficiency of Time, Attention, and Legal Authority.* 108th Congress, 2d session (August 11, 2004).

———. Permanent Select Committee on Intelligence. *Hearing on the Director of National Intelligence's 500 Day Plan*. 110th Congress, 1st session (December 6, 2007).

———. Permanent Select Committee on Intelligence. *Hearing on DNI Status*. 109th Congress, 1st session (July 28, 2005).

———. Permanent Select Committee on Intelligence. *Hearing on the State of Intelligence Reform 10 Years after 9/11*. 112th Congress, 1st session (September 13, 2011).

———. Permanent Select Committee on Intelligence. *IC21: The Intelligence Community in the 21st Century*. 104th Congress, 1st session (May 22, 1995)

———. Permanent Select Committee on Intelligence. *Intelligence Authorization Act for Fiscal Year 2005 Report*. 108th Congress, 2d session (June 21, 2004), Report 108-558.

———. Permanent Select Committee on Intelligence. *Markup of H.R. 10: The National Security and Intelligence Improvement Act of 2004*. 108th Congress, 2d session (September 29, 2004).

U.S. Senate. Appropriations Committee. *Hearing on the Review of the 9/11 Commission's Intelligence Recommendations*. 108th Congress, 2d session (September 22, 2004).

———. Armed Services Committee. *Hearing on the Conduct of the Gulf War*. 102d Congress, 1st session (July 12, 1991).

———. Armed Services Committee. *Hearing on Implications of Defense and Military Operations of Proposals to Reorganize the United States Intelligence Community*. 108th Congress, 2d session (August 16, 2004).

———. Armed Services Committee. *Hearing on Implications of Defense and Military Operations of Proposals to Reorganize the United States Intelligence Community*. 108th Congress, 2d session (August 17, 2004).

———. Armed Services Committee. *Hearing on Security Threats to the United States*. 109th Congress, 2d session (February 28, 2006).

———. Armed Services Committee. *Nomination of Donald Rumsfeld to be Secretary of Defense*. 107th Congress, 1st session (January 11, 2001).

———. Armed Services Committee. *Stephen Cambone: Answers to Advance Questions for Nominee for the Position of Under Secretary of Defense for Intelligence before the Senate Armed Services Committee*. 108th Congress, 1st session (February 27, 2003), http://www.fas.org/irp/congress/2003_hr/022703cambone.pdf.

———. *Final Vote Results for Vote 192*. 108th Congress, 2d session (September 29, 2004.)

———. Homeland Security and Governmental Affairs Committee. *Collins Lieberman Intelligence Reform Legislation Bill Summary*. 108th Congress, 2d session (September 15, 2004).

———. Homeland Security and Governmental Affairs Committee. *Hearing on 9/11 Commission Recommendations and Findings*. 108th Congress, 2d session (July 30, 2004).

———. Homeland Security and Governmental Affairs Committee. *Hearing on Assessing America's Counterterrorism Capabilities*. 108th Congress, 2d session (August 3, 2004).

———. Homeland Security and Governmental Affairs Committee. *Hearing on Building an Agile Intelligence Community to Fight Terrorism and Emerging Threats: Susan Collins's Opening Statement.* 108th Congress, 2d session (September 8, 2004).

———. Homeland Security and Governmental Affairs Committee. *Hearing on Building an Agile Intelligence Community to Fight Terrorism and Emerging Threats: Joseph Lieberman's Opening Statement.* 108th Congress, 2d session (September 8, 2004).

———. Homeland Security and Governmental Affairs Committee. *Hearing on Ensuring the U.S. Intelligence Community Supports Homeland Defense and Departmental Needs.* 108th Congress, 2d session (September 13, 2004).

———. Homeland Security and Governmental Affairs Committee. *Hearing on Establishing Terrorist Threat Integration Center.* 108th Congress, 2d session (February 14, 2003).

———. Homeland Security and Governmental Affairs Committee, *Hearing on Implementation of 9/11 Commission Recommendations*, 111th Congress, 2d session (January 26, 2010).

———. Homeland Security and Governmental Affairs Committee. *Hearing on Intelligence Overhaul.* 112th Congress, 1st session (May 12, 2011).

———. Homeland Security and Governmental Affairs Committee. *Hearing on Intelligence Reorganization.* 108th Congress, 2d session (August 16, 2004).

———. Homeland Security and Governmental Affairs Committee. *Hearing on the Lessons and Implications of the Christmas Day Attacks: Focusing on the Attempted Bombing Incident on Flight 253 to Detroit (Part Two).* 111th Congress, 2d session (January 26, 2010).

———. Homeland Security and Governmental Affairs Committee. *Hearing on Making America Safer: Examining the Recommendations of the 9/11 Commission.* 108th Congress, 2d session (July 30, 2004).

———. Homeland Security and Governmental Affairs Committee. *Hearing on Reorganizing America's Intelligence Community: A View from the Inside.* 108th Congress, 2d session (August 16, 2004).

———. Homeland Security and Governmental Affairs Committee. *Hearing on Ten-Year Review of 9/11 Counterterrorism Reforms.* 112th Congress, 1st session (March 30, 2011).

———. Homeland Security and Governmental Affairs Committee. *Markup of the National Intelligence Reform Act.* 108th Congress, 2d session, (September 21, 2004).

———. Homeland Security and Governmental Affairs Committee. *Principal Reasons Why the House Republican Offer Does Not Give the DNI or NCTC Director Sufficient Authorities and Powers to be Effective.* 108th Congress, 2d session (Fall 2004).

———. Homeland Security and Governmental Affairs Committee. *Report on the National Intelligence Reform Act of 2004.* 108th Congress, 2d session, 2004. S. Rep. 108-359.

———. Homeland Security and Governmental Affairs Committee. *Report to Accompany S.2840: National Intelligence Reform Act of 2004.* 108th Congress, 2d session (September 27, 2004), 108-359.

————. Homeland Security and Governmental Affairs Committee. *Ten Years after 9/11: Is Intelligence Reform Working? Part II.* 112th Congress, 1st session (May 19, 2011).

————. Select Committee on Intelligence. *Annual Threat Assessment of the U.S. Intelligence Community,* 107th Congress, 2d session (February 6, 2002).

————. Select Committee on Intelligence. *Hearing on Current and Projected Threats to U.S. National Security.* 108th Congress, 2d session (February 22, 2004).

————. Select Committee on Intelligence. *Hearing on DNI Authorities and Personnel Issues.* 110th Congress, 2d session (February 14, 2008).

————. Select Committee on Intelligence. *Hearing on Intelligence Community Reform.* 108th Congress, 2d session (July 20, 2004).

————. Select Committee on Intelligence. *Hearing on the National Intelligence Reorganization and Reform Act of 1978.* 95th Congress, 2d session, (April 5, 1978).

————. Select Committee on Intelligence. *Hearing on Nomination of Ambassador John Negroponte to be Director of National Intelligence.* 109th Congress, 1st session (April 12, 2005).

————. Select Committee on Intelligence. *Hearing on Nomination of the Honorable Porter Goss to be Director of Central Intelligence.* 108th Congress, 2d session (September 14, 2004).

————. Select Committee on Intelligence. *Hearing on Nomination of the Honorable Porter Goss to be Director of Central Intelligence.* 108th Congress, 2d session (September 20, 2004).

————. Select Committee on Intelligence. *Hearing on the Nomination of Leon Panetta to be the Director of the Central Intelligence Agency: Part Two.* 111th Congress, 1st session (February 5, 2009).

————. Select Committee on Intelligence. *Hearing on Reform of the United States Intelligence Community.* 108th Congress, 2d session (August 18, 2004).

————. Select Committee on Intelligence. *Hearing on Reform of the United States Intelligence Community.* 108th Congress, 2d session (September 7, 2004).

————. Select Committee on Intelligence. *Nomination of Lieutenant General James Clapper, Jr., USAF, Ret., to Be Director of National Intelligence.* 111th Congress, 2d session (July 20, 2010).

————. Select Committee on Intelligence. *Report on the U.S. Intelligence Community's Prewar Intelligence Assessments on Iraq.* 108th Congress. 2d Session (July 7, 2004).

————. Select Committee on Intelligence. *Report to Accompany Authorizing Appropriations for Fiscal Year 1992.* 102d Congress, 1st session (July 24, 1991).

————. Select Committee on Intelligence. *Statutory Authorities of the Director of National Intelligence.* 110th Congress, 2d session (February 14, 2008).

Wallace, Chris. Interviewing Jane Harman. *Fox News Sunday.* Fox News. November 21, 2004.

Warner, John. News Conference on Intelligence Reform Bill, December 6, 2004.

———. Speaking on intelligence reform, on December 8, 2004. 108th Congress, 2d session. *Congressional Record*, Volume 150, Number 139, S12004.

Warner, Michael, and J. Kenneth McDonald. *U.S. Intelligence Community Reform Studies Since 1947*. Washington: Center for the Study of Intelligence, 2005.

White House Pool Report. *#1*. Filed by Julie Mason. December 17, 2004.

———. *#4*. Filed by Mark Silva. Released by the White House. December 7, 2004.

Wilgoren, Jodi, and David Kirkpatrick. "Kerry Says Work of the 9/11 Panel Should Continue." *New York Times*, July 28, 2004.

Williams, Juan. Interview by Brit Hume. *Special Report with Brit Hume*. Fox News. November 23, 2004.

Wohlstetter, Robert. *Pearl Harbor, Warning and Decision*. Palo Alto, CA: Stanford University Press, 1962.

Wolfowitz, Paul. Memorandum Regarding Implementation Guidance on Restructuring Defense Intelligence—and Related Matters. May 8, 2003.

Yang, John. "9/11 Commission Recommendations Bill Fails to Pass." *World News Tonight*, November 21, 2004.

Zegart, Amy. "Built to Fail: Our Clueless Intelligence System." *Washington Post*, July 8, 2007.

———. *Flawed by Design: The Evolution of the CIA, JCS, and NCS*. Palo Alto, CA: Stanford University Press, 2000.

Zelikow, Philip. E-mail to 9/11 Public Discourse Project Board on "Important Update on Status of the Bill." November 20, 2004. Lee Hamilton's Papers, Indiana University, Bloomington, IN.

———. E-mail to 9/11 Public Discourse Project Board on "Views on Pending Amendments to S. 2845." October 3, 2004. Lee Hamilton's Papers, Indiana University, Bloomington, IN.

———. E-mail to Board of 9/11 Commission Public Discourse Project on "Escalation Plan." October 21, 2004. Lee Hamilton's Papers, Indiana University, Bloomington, IN.

———. E-mail to Board of 9/11 Commission Public Discourse Project on "Update on Bill—Still Alive." November 20, 2004. Lee Hamilton's Papers, Indiana University, Bloomington, IN.

———. E-mail to Bob Kerrey on "re: Latest House offer for the bill." October 24, 2004. Lee Hamilton's Papers, Indiana University, Bloomington, IN.

———. E-mail to John Lehman and others on "Specter Amendment to C-L: they Need Help." September 20, 2004.

———. E-mail to Michael Bopp and Kevin Landy. October 23, 2004.

———. E-mail to Tom Kean and Lee Hamilton on "Status Report—Confidential." November 11, 2004. Lee Hamilton's Papers, Indiana University, Bloomington, IN.

———. "Integrating National Security Missions: Lessons from the National Counterterrorism Center." Speech at Center for Strategic and International Studies. Washington, DC. March 26, 2010.

———. "Intelligence Reform, 2002–2004." *Studies in Intelligence* 56, no. 3 (September 2012).

———. Speech at Center for Strategic & International Studies. "Integrating National Security Missions: Lessons from the National Counterterrorism Center." March 26, 2010.

Zelikow, Philip, et al. "Catastrophic Terrorism: Tackling the New Danger." *Foreign Affairs* (November/December 1998).

Index

Panetta, Leon, 162–63
"pulling the bill," 1–5, 133–40

Rangel, Robert, 134, 137, 144–47
Rice, Condoleezza, 51, 80
    Commission's recommendations,
      53–57
    intelligence reform, 12, 17, 74
    Scowcroft Report, 16–17
Ridge, Tom, 18
Robb-Silberman Commission. *See*
  Iraq
Roberts, Pat, 63–64, 86, 89, 158, 179
Roemer, Tim, 7, 104, 138–39, 161
    citing the need for a DNI, 36
    Commission's recommendations,
      48–49
    domestic intelligence service, 44
    9/11 Families, 47, 150
    Roemer amendment and the 9/11
      Commission, 8–9
Rogers, Mike, 170
Rove, Karl, 141, 143
Rumsfeld, Donald, 14
    Commission's recommendations,
      52, 54–56, 82
    DNI's budgetary authority, 74–75,
      107–10
    increased centralization of the IC,
      14, 55–56, 68–70, 82
    retaining command authority,
      58–59, 68–70
    strategy for intelligence reform,
      19–20, 74–75, 138
    Congress, views on, 54, 70
    DCI, views on, 16
    Scowcroft Report, views on, 15–17

Schwarzkopf, Norman, 15

Scowcroft, Brent, 12
    Cheney's views on Scowcroft
      Report, 15
    NCTC, 13
    recommendations of Scowcroft
      Report, 12–17
    Rumsfeld's views on Scowcroft
      Report, 15–17
    Scowcroft Report (External
      Review Board Report), 12, 20
    separation between the head of
      the IC and CIA, 32
Senate and House Democrats' legisla-
  tive proposal and strategy, 101–2,
  123
Senate Armed Services Committee
  (SASC), 63–64, 86–87, 89
Senate Homeland Security and
  Governmental Affairs Committee
  (SHSGAC), 46, 50, 83.
    See also Lieberman, Joseph; Col-
    lins, Susan
Senate Select Committee on Intel-
  ligence (SSCI), 64, 86, 89
Sensenbrenner, Jim, 2–3, 78, 96–98,
  103, 105, 115, 126, 130, 135–36, 139,
  148–49
Shelby, Richard, 23, 86
"specials," 6
Stevens, Ted, 83–85, 90, 141
support to warfighter, xi, xxi, 5, 13–16,
  108–9
    Cheney's views on, 14–15
    Hunter's views on, 61, 103
    SASC's views on, 63–64, 82

Tenet, George, 21–28, 158
    criticism of, 23–28
    "declaration of war," x, 31, 36

About the Author

Michael Allen joined the House Permanent Select Committee on Intelligence (HPSCI) as the majority staff director in January 2011. Prior to joining the HPSCI, he was director for the Bipartisan Policy Center's successor to the 9/11 Commission, the National Security Preparedness Group, cochaired by former U.S. representative Lee Hamilton and former governor Tom Kean. Previously, he served in the White House for seven years in a variety of national security policy and legislative roles. At the National Security Council (NSC), Allen served as special assistant to the president and senior director for counterproliferation strategy from June 2007 to January 2009 under National Security Advisor Steve Hadley. From February 2005 to June 2007, he was the special assistant to the president and senior director for legislative affairs at the NSC. From December 2001 to February 2005, Allen worked in the legislative affairs office of the White House's Homeland Security Council. At the beginning of the Bush administration, he worked in the Bureau of Legislative Affairs at the Department of State. He received his LLM with distinction in International Law from the Georgetown University Law Center, his JD from the University of Alabama, and his BA from Vanderbilt University.